Collins

Caribbean
Social Studies

3

**Naam Thomas, Nicole Philip-Dowe, Lisa Greenstein,
Bruce Nicholson & Daphne Paizee**

Collins

William Collins' dream of knowledge for all began with the publication of his first book in 1819. A self-educated mill worker, he not only enriched millions of lives, but also founded a flourishing publishing house. Today, staying true to this spirit, Collins books are packed with inspiration, innovation and practical expertise. They place you at the centre of a world of possibility and give you exactly what you need to explore it.

Collins. Freedom to teach.

Published by Collins
An imprint of HarperCollins*Publishers*
The News Building
1 London Bridge Street
London
SE1 9GF

Browse the complete Collins Caribbean catalogue at
www.collins.co.uk/caribbeanschools

10 9 8 7 6 5 4 3 2 1

ISBN 978-0-00-825648-7

British Library Cataloguing in Publication Data
A catalogue record for this publication is available from the British Library.

Authors: Naam Thomas, Nicole Philip-Dowe, Lisa Greenstein, Bruce Nicholson & Daphne Paizee
Publisher: Dr Elaine Higgleton
Development editor: Bruce Nicholson
In-house senior editor: Julianna Dunn
Project manager: Alissa McWhinnie, QBS Learning
Copyeditor: Karen Williams
Proofreader: Helen Bleck
Indexer, Illustrator, Photo researcher: QBS Learning
Cover designer: Gordon MacGilp
Cover photo: Darryl Brooks/Shutterstock
Series designer: Kevin Robbins
Typesetter: QBS Learning
Production controller: Tina Paul
Printed and bound by: Grafica Veneta SpA in Italy

See also page 290 for photograph acknowledgements

The publishers gratefully acknowledge the permission granted to reproduce the copyright material in this book. Every effort has been made to trace copyright holders and to obtain their permission for the use of copyright material. The publishers will gladly receive any information enabling them to rectify any error or omission at the first opportunity.

Contents

How to use this book

These learning objectives tell you what you will be learning about in the lesson.

Each topic has colourful photographs and illustrations to add context and meaning.

Each topic is divided into headings.

Discussion features allow you to work in pairs, in a group or as a class to explore the topic further.

Try these questions to check your understanding of each topic.

Regional integration

We are learning to:
- define relevant terms and concepts: regional integration, bilateral agreement, cooperation, dependence, economy, interdependence, region.

Regional integration is when countries in a region cooperate and work together towards common goals. This has been a priority since the 1950s, when the first attempts were made by Caribbean states to work cooperatively towards common goals. This came about because states wanted to be less dependent on former colonial powers.

Carnival is an event where people from different cultural backgrounds can come together.

Integration

To **integrate** means to bring together ideas and people so that they work together or become part of the same group. The aim of integration is to give members equal status in a group and to share the advantages and strengths that the group brings. There are several types of integration:

- **Social integration** happens when people of different cultural backgrounds learn tolerance and respect for each other.
- **Racial integration** is when people of different races are treated equally so they can live and work together.
- **Economic integration** is achieved when two or more states in a geographic area set common economic goals and reduce the barriers to trade between them. This complements a country's own economy, which is made up of businesses that provide goods and services to meet people's needs.

Discussion

Work in groups and discuss how interdependence can help the states in the Caribbean to develop.

Project

Do your own research in groups. Take one of the terms explained on these pages, and find out more about the term. Then look in newspapers and find examples of events that illustrate what it means. For example, a community event could illustrate integration in an area. Some news about trade between different Caribbean states could illustrate interdependence in the Caribbean region.

Cooperation

Cooperation means working together and helping each other to achieve common goals. For example, we need to cooperate with our neighbours and other members of our community. If there is a problem in a community and everyone cooperates fully, the problem can be solved.

Exercise

1. In your own words, define regional integration.
2. How many different types of integration are there? Write your own definition of each.
3. Why do you think social integration is important in Caribbean countries?

In 1989, the CARICOM heads of government agreed to advance the process of economic integration and to increase their ability to respond as a group to the challenges and opportunities of globalisation. This led to the creation of the CARICOM Single Market and Economy (**CSME**).

Globalisation is a process of making the world more connected, with goods, services and people moving and communicating easily and quickly all around the world.

The main economic objectives of the CSME are:

The CARICOM flag.

- improved standards of living and work
- full employment of labour and other factors of production
- coordinated and sustained economic development and convergence
- expansion of trade and economic relations with other states
- increased levels of international competitiveness
- increased production and productivity
- greater economic leverage in dealing with other states
- coordination of members' economic policies
- increased cooperation of common services and activities.

The CSME also allows for the free movement of money and skilled labour between member states, the right to set up a business in another member state, free movement of goods and a common trade policy.

Several other states have associate member states, including the British Virgin Islands, Turks and Caicos, Anguilla, the Cayman Islands and Bermuda.

Exercise

1. What are the main objectives of CARICOM?

2. Why was the CSME agreement signed?

3. If they want to set up a new business, what advantages do businesspeople from CARICOM member states have?

4. Compile a timeline of the key dates in both CARICOM and the CSME's history.

Activity

Work in pairs and look online and in newspapers for interesting reports about CARICOM activities. Select a report, then describe what you have discovered to the class.

Activity features allow you to do practical activities related to the topic.

Key vocabulary

CARICOM

CSME

These are the most important new social studies words in the topic. You can check their meanings in the Glossary at the end of the book.

This page gives a summary of the exciting new ideas you will be learning about in the unit.

These lists at the end of a unit act as a checklist of the key ideas of the unit.

This is the topic covered in the unit, which links to the syllabus.

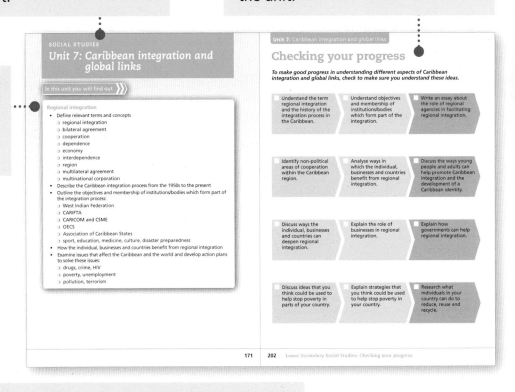

These end-of-unit questions allow you and your teacher to check that you have understood the ideas in each unit and can explain social studies using the skills and knowledge you have gained.

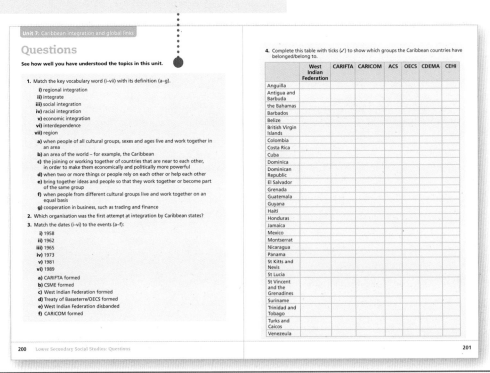

Unit 1: Our heritage

In this unit you will find out

People and our heritage

- The people in the history of the Eastern Caribbean who have made a significant contribution to our heritage
  - our political icons
  - our arts and culture icons
  - our track and field sporting icons
  - our sports icons
  - our labour, environment and science icons
  - our icons in social work
  - our literary icons
- Explain the different subcultures of the Eastern Caribbean:
  - calypso
  - steel band
  - chutney
  - soca
  - bouyon
  - big drum

Our heritage: conservation and preservation

- The value of conservation and preservation for sustainability and social living
  - threats to our heritage
  - illegal poaching
  - economic development
  - infusion of external cultures
- Legacy for future generations
  - sustainability
  - employment
  - cultural transmission
  - standard of living
- The role of the individual and state in conserving and preserving our national heritage
  - survival of the species
  - global cooperation
  - interdependence
  - state initiatives
  - legislation

People and our heritage

We are learning to:

- identify Eastern Caribbean people who have made a significant contribution to national and regional heritage: politics, arts and culture, sports
- describe how the people identified above have made their contributions.

National heroes/icons are individuals who have contributed significantly to the development of a country. They are usually individuals whose life's work has been dedicated to a particular area such as sports, politics, science, art or culture. Through their work they have demonstrated patriotism and a love for their country.

Political icons

A political icon is an individual who has significantly improved the way a country handles its administration and affairs. Some of our political heroes/icons in the Eastern Caribbean include:

- Sir Errol Barrow (1920–87) founded the Democratic Labour Party (DLP) in 1955 and as its leader became the Premier of Barbados in 1961. Following independence in 1966 he became Prime Minister. He expanded free education, set up National Health Insurance and is credited with enacting policy that rapidly increased industry and tourism in the island. He was a major supporter of regional integration and trade and co-founded CARIFTA (Caribbean Free Trade Association).
- Sir John Compton (1925–2007) was the first Prime Minister of St Lucia and 'father of independence'; he co-founded the United Workers' Party (UWP) in 1964. He led the country through colonialism, independence and returned to politics after retirement to lead the UWP to election victory in 2006.
- Sir Lester Bird (1938–) was Prime Minister of Antigua and Barbuda from 1994 to 2004; he led the Antiguan Labour Party to victory in 1994 and 1999. He is credited with the development of Antigua's service industry through tourism, offshore banking and financial services, and creating education and economic policy that raised the standard of living of Antiguans. He served as both Organisation of Eastern Caribbean States (OECS) and CARICOM chairman.

Statue of Errol Barrow in Heroes Square, Barbados.

Research

Research a national political figure from your country and write a biography of about 200 words on their life and legacy. Also discuss, in 50 words, how you think their achievements have affected you as a citizen.

Arts and culture icons ▶▶▶

Some people, through their creative self-expression in areas such as drama, dance and music, have made an impact on their countries.

- Jeff Joseph (1953–2011) was a Dominican musician credited with bringing the Dominican musical style called kadans to international popularity.
- Toriano 'King Onyan' Edwards is an Antiguan musician and soca singer who, as part of the band Burning Flames and as a solo act, brought Antiguan soca to the international scene.
- Dr John Hunte is an accomplished Barbadian performer, whose cultural contributions include work as National Dance Officer, co-founder of the Barbados Dance Project, CARIFESTA XIII Artistic Coordinator and cultural studies and performing arts lecturer.

Kim Collins after winning the 400 m at the 2003 IAAF World Championship.

Track and field sporting icons ▶▶▶

Track and field athletes inspire Eastern Caribbean people to evaluate their talents through competition on the world stage.

- Kim Collins (1976–) is the 2003 World 100 m sprint champion, St Kitts and Nevis.
- Kirani James (1992–) is the 2011 World 400 m sprint champion and won Grenada's first Olympic gold medal in the 400 m sprint.
- Levern Spencer (1984–) is a St Lucian high jumper who has won six Central American and Caribbean (CAC) Championship titles.

Activity

Create a timeline of all the individuals on these two pages, adding their achievements.

Exercise

1. In your own words, define a national hero.

2. Explain how a national hero can also be a regional hero.

3. What economic contributions did Sir Lester Bird make to development in Antigua?

4. What social contributions did Errol Barrow make to Barbados?

5. Jeff Joseph increased the popularity of what musical style?

6. What distinctions do each of the following athletes hold?

   a) Kim Collins
   b) Kirani James
   c) Levern Spencer

Key vocabulary

national hero/icon

National heroes and icons

We are learning to:

- identify Eastern Caribbean people who have made a significant contribution to national and regional heritage: sports, trade union movement, science and the environment
- describe how the people identified have made their contributions.

Sporting icons 》

Sporting heroes from the Eastern Caribbean have made significant contributions on the international stage. Examples of individuals recognised in these sports include:

- **Cricket** – Sir Viv Richards (1952–) is an Antiguan batsman, considered one of the five greatest cricketers of the twentieth century. As team captain from 1984–99, he was the only West Indies captain never to lose a Test series. Nadine George MBE (1968–) is a St Lucian cricketer holding the distinction of being the first female West Indian cricketer to score 100 in a Test match and she has captained the West Indies women's team.
- **Swimming** – Leah Martindale (1978–) represented Barbados twice in the Olympic Games (1996, 2000) becoming the first black female swimmer to reach a final, in the 50 m freestyle.
- **Basketball** – Adonal Foyle (1975–) is a Vincentian-born basketballer who has achieved significant success in the North American National Basketball Association, playing for the Orlando Magic, Memphis Grizzlies and for ten seasons with the Golden State Warriors.
- **Tennis** – Vernon Lewis (1965–) is St Lucia's most decorated tennis player; he is a former St Lucia Sportsman of the Year and has received the International Tennis Federation Davis Cup Commitment Award (2013).

Sir Viv Richards batting for the West Indies at The Oval, London, 11 August 1991.

Did you know...?

Along with Sir Viv Richards, Sir Garfield Sobers of Barbados is also included among the five greatest cricket players of the twentieth century.

Exercise

1. Which athlete is among the five greatest cricketers of the twentieth century?

2. Which athlete holds a Davis Cup Commitment Award and in which sport?

3. Adonal Foyle has played for which three North American basketball teams?

Activity

Create a timeline of all the sporting achievements listed on this page.

Labour icons »»

- Hubert Nathaniel Critchlow OBE (1884–1958) is known as the father of the **trade union** movement in Guyana, establishing the British Guiana Labour Union in 1919.
- Sir Joseph Nathaniel France (1907–97) was the first General Secretary of the St Kitts and Nevis Trades and Labour Union, and held the post for 57 years until his death. He is noted for his negotiations for the recognition of workers' rights in the sugar industry.

Environment icons »»»

- Andrew Simmons is a Vincentian **environmentalist** who specialises in community-based conservation and natural resource preservation through education. He founded the JEMS Progressive Community Organisation and the Caribbean Youth Environment Network, and received the prestigious Goldman Environmental Prize in 1994 for his work and experience.

Science icons »

- Professor Kathleen Coard is a Grenadian **pathologist** who was the first female professor of pathology in the Caribbean. Her work has led to advances in cancer research and cardiovascular disease. Of particular note is her work on risk factors for prostate cancer in men of African descent.
- Professor Leonard O'Garro is a Vincentian plant pathologist whose research has led to the implementation of crop disease control programmes across the Caribbean. He specialises in **biotechnology** and plant biosafety and is currently a coordinator of the United Nations Global Biosafety Programme.

Adonal Foyle played for the Orlando Magic 2007–09.

Project

Choose an icon from your country and use the internet to research their life, achievements and legacy. Collect photographs, draw pictures or create a poster. Then, as a group, create your presentation on a computer and present it to the class.

Exercise

4. In what year and by whom was the British Guiana Labour Union established?

5. What prestigious international prize does Andrew Simmons hold?

6. Who was the first female professor of pathology in the Caribbean?

7. What UN programme does Professor Leonard O'Garro currently coordinate?

Key vocabulary

trade union
environmentalist
pathologist
biotechnology

Icons in social work and literature

We are learning to:

- identify Eastern Caribbean people who have made a significant contribution to national and regional heritage: social work, literature
- describe how the people identified above have made their contributions.

Icons in social work 》》

Profiles

Oscar Allen (1942–2017)

Oscar Allen was a Vincentian Methodist preacher and social activist known for his community work in Diamond Village, St Vincent, and for his criticism of the politics that disadvantaged the citizens of St Vincent. He promoted **pan-Africanist** views and access to education for all, with a strong focus on adult literacy and the importance of community-based discussion and decision-making on matters that affect citizens.

His achievements included involvement in the community group ARWE and chairman of the social pressure group People's Movement for Change (PMC).

Ganesh Singh (1980–)

Ganesh Singh is a Guyanese disability rights activist who works to increase access for those with disabilities to opportunities in all fields in Guyana, especially sports, higher education and government.

Included in his list of important roles, Ganesh is a Commissioner on the National Commission of Disability, CXC Coordinator and executive board member of the Guyana Society for the Blind, the Public Relations Officer for the Guyana Council of Organisation for Persons with Disabilities, Coordinator of the Regional Youth Network for the Disabled Peoples' International North America and the Caribbean, an executive board member of the Guyana Blind Cricket Association and a director of the West Indies Blind Cricket Council.

> **Did you know...?**
>
> Oscar Allen was a teacher and would invite villagers to his home to sharpen their academic skills, and annually on July 31st he would recite African poems for the villagers in Earlene Horne Square, Diamond Village.

> **Research**
>
> Describe some of the ways Eastern Caribbean icons and heroes have been recognised, for example, by the naming of monuments, streets and buildings or national awards and prizes in their honour. Choose five icons, three from your country and two from another, collect photographs of some examples and create a poster to present to the class.

Exercise

1. Why do you think Oscar Allen's work critiquing politics and promoting community decision-making were important to St Vincent?
2. What benefits do you think Ganesh Singh's social activism will have on Guyanese society?

Profiles

Garth St Omer (1931–)

Garth St Omer is a St Lucian novelist who is known for writing in St Lucian settings and paying particular attention to the use of St Lucian **patois**. St Omer has been awarded the St Lucian Medal of Merit for his literary achievement.

St Omer's works include *Syrop* (1964), *A Room on the Hill* (1968), *Shades of Grey* (1968), *Nor Any Country* (1969) and *J–, Black Bam and the Masqueraders* (1972). His novels are known for a writing style which conveys the uneasiness of the main character as they try to explain circumstances that they do not understand and to cope with the anguish of personal failure. He is known for conveying the experiences of St Lucians from all backgrounds, from poor to middle class, and those who have migrated to different countries.

Caryl Phillips (1958–)

Caryl Phillips is a St Kitts-born writer who is known for his plays, essays, novels and historical fiction. He studied English at Queen's College, Oxford University, in the UK and after teaching at prestigious universities all over the world, is currently a professor of English at Yale University.

Much of his writing focuses on the effects of displacement caused by the African slave trade on the African **diaspora**. His novels include *The Final Passage* (1985), *A State of Independence* (1986), *Crossing the River* (1993), *A Distant Shore* (2003), and essay collections such as *The European Tribe* (1987) and *The Atlantic Sound* (2000).

He has won many prizes for his work, including the Martin Luther King Memorial Prize for *The European Tribe*, and is a fellow of the Royal Society of Literature and the Royal Society of Arts.

Caryl Phillips, iconic Kittitian novelist, essayist and playwright.

Project

In groups, research an author who either comes from your country or from the Eastern Caribbean. Write a biography of their life and details of their best known works. Then, produce a timeline of their life.

Exercise

3. Garth St Omer's writing style was effective in conveying what about the main characters?

4. What theme does much of Caryl Phillips' writing focus on?

5. Compile a timeline of the life and works of Garth St Omer and of Caryl Phillips, as mentioned in this topic.

Key vocabulary

pan-Africanist

patois

diaspora

Subcultures of the Eastern Caribbean

We are learning to:

- explain the origins of musical subcultures in the Eastern Caribbean.

Calypso

Calypso music has roots in West African tribal songs of the eighteenth century and became popular in the early twentieth century, originating in Trinidad and spreading to the rest of the Caribbean. Calypso originally was sung in a French creole, led by a **griot** (a storyteller). As English replaced French creole, calypso began to be sung in English. This drew the attention of the British colonial powers, because calypso song lyrics were often politically critical of the British.

Calypso became popular in the Eastern Caribbean because the use of African beats and rhythms united people of African descent across the region. It was a musical form that was unique to the Caribbean and provided a sense of identity. Use of the musical form to express critical views of the ruling class also boosted its popularity. Today, most Eastern Caribbean countries have their own form of annual calypso competitions, usually held in association with carnival.

Barbadian Alison Hinds is known worldwide as the first lady of soca.

Soca

Soca is another Trinidadian import, a **fusion** of the typical calypso sound with funk, soul, reggae and other musical styles that became popular during the 1970s. The fusion was intended to bring new life to calypso since these new musical styles appealed to younger people at the time.

Therefore, soca has a more complex, up-tempo sound with less focus on social commentary and more use of lyrics relating to scandal, gossip, partying and revelry. Each island has added their musical influence to the genre. For example, bashment soca developed in Barbados as a mix of Jamaican dancehall and soca.

Artists such as Scrilla, Stabby and Marzville are popular in this genre. High-energy performance and use of Barbadian creole is characteristic of bashment soca.

Exercise

1. Why did calypso music become popular in the Eastern Caribbean?
2. How did soca music bring new life to calypso?
3. Describe two differences between calypso and soca, and one similarity.

Project

Divide the class into groups so that each group can research the national calypso competition in one country of the Eastern Caribbean. Use photographs to create a poster to show the development of the competition throughout the years including: when it started, changes in venue, performers, winners and other interesting information. Display the posters in your class.

Steel band ⟫⟫⟫

Trinidad and Tobago is known as the place where steel band originated. In 1880, stick fighting and percussion music were banned in Trinidad and Tobago as a result of the Canboulay riots. The replacements, bamboo sticks, were also banned. In 1937, an orchestra of frying pans, dustbin lids and oil drums emerged in Laventille. As with calypso and soca, steel band became popular throughout the Eastern Caribbean as a unique part of regional heritage and a source of regional pride.

Chutney ⟫

A dholak is one of the traditional instruments used in chutney music.

Chutney music developed in the southern Caribbean territories, such as Trinidad and Guyana, among those of Indo-Caribbean descent. It was first traditionally heard at weddings, religious celebrations and in the sugarcane fields. Chutney is a fusion of Indian and local music styles. The main instruments are the dholak (a hand drum), dhantal (a steel rod) and harmonium. Modern chutney has a strong soca influence which has increased its popularity among the islands of the Eastern Caribbean.

Bouyon ⟫⟫

Bouyon is a musical form developed by Dominican singers and which found mass appeal across the French Antilles. It is characterised by use of Antillean creole (French and English), and strong keyboard rhythmic patterns, accordion and acoustic percussion. It fuses two earlier traditional Dominican musical styles called jing ping and kadans, and draws influence from zouk.

> **Did you know...?**
>
> Windward Caribbean Kulture are credited with being the first band to develop and popularise the bouyon musical style. Songs such as *Follow the Leader* (1991) are still popular today.

Big drum ⟫⟫⟫

This is a musical style most strongly associated with St Vincent and the Grenadines, where drums made from tree-trunks and rum kegs were used to create strong African percussive beats coupled with socially conscious lyrics or satire. This style is accompanied by traditional colourful headdresses and skirts. It is a significant part of celebrating creole culture in the Windward islands and is heard at ceremonies and festivals of national importance, especially those to respect and remember African ancestors. Variations of big drum are found in St Kitts and Nevis and Grenada. A female singer called a **chantwell** usually sings the lyrics.

Exercise

4. Chutney and bouyon are fusions of which musical genres?
5. During what occasions are you likely to hear big drum music in the Windward Islands?

Key vocabulary

calypso

griot

soca

fusion

chantwell

Threats to our heritage

We are learning to:

- define relevant terms and concepts: endangered, economic development
- discuss the value of conservation and preservation for sustainability and social living
- threats to our heritage: endangered flora and fauna, illegal hunting.

Threats to our heritage ›

When we say that something is **endangered**, we mean that something is under threat and in danger of becoming **extinct** or totally destroyed. Human activities, such as growing cities, **threaten** the habitats or existence of our **flora** (plants) and **fauna** (animals).

In the Eastern Caribbean, each territory has agencies dedicated to looking after aspects of the natural heritage.

- The Environmental Protection Agency for Guyana was created under the Environmental Protection Act in 1996. Its responsibilities include protecting the environment from human activities, such as construction, and promoting the sustainable use of Guyana's natural resources. Additionally, EPA-Guyana is responsible for meeting national responsibilities under the UN Convention on Biological Diversity (protecting plant and animal life and variety), the Basel Convention (proper hazardous waste disposal and transport) and the Cartagena Convention (protection of marine ecosystems and wildlife).

- The Cayman Islands Department of Environment is a government department which manages and protects the environment and natural resources. This department works with non-governmental organisations such as the National Trust for the Cayman Islands to fund and structure environmental education programmes. One important programme is the Visiting Scientist Program, where international research scientists are able to receive approval for environmental studies after possible impacts of their study are considered.

The blue iguana is an endangered species of iguana found on Grand Cayman.

Research

Research the following protected natural sites: Anguilla's Marine Parks; Cabrits National Park; Dominica and Grand Etang Forest Reserve, Grenada. For each site write about 200 words and use photographs to illustrate your work.

Exercise

1. Name the three international agreements that EPA-Guyana has responsibility for.

2. Why do you think it is important for scientists to get approval by the Cayman Islands Department of Environment?

Discussion

In groups, discuss what you think is the greatest threat to our natural heritage today and why it needs to be preserved.

Illegal poaching »»

Poaching is the illegal hunting or capture of wild animals. In the Eastern Caribbean sea turtles are vulnerable to poaching since they nest on sandy beaches. Hawksbill and Green Turtles are still illegally hunted for their meat and eggs as they can sell for a high price on the black market. Both species are endangered.

Economic development »»»

Physical resources are valuable and essential to the **economic development** of a country. In the Eastern Caribbean our natural resources, such as oceans, lakes, waterfalls, flora and fauna have helped to develop the tourism industry and attract tourists.

However, this increased use of our natural heritage can having a damaging effect on the environment. Today, the threats to our natural habitats all result from human activities. For example:

- squatting, poaching and illegal hunting
- land clearing (fires), cattle grazing, logging, slash-and-burn agriculture, overfishing
- invasive alien species
- drilling for oil and gas, quarrying and **pollution** (such as oil spills and chemical leaks)
- global warming and climate change.

Infusion of external cultures »

The **infusion** of external cultures is also a threat to our natural heritage. This is where the influence of an external culture, for example North American culture, is introduced at the expense of our own cultural diversity in the Eastern Caribbean. This can be seen as a threat to the preservation of our heritage.

Exercise

3. Why do you think that illegal poaching takes place in the Eastern Caribbean?

4. In about 100 words, outline which human activities put our natural habitats at risk.

5. Create a vocabulary word map that outlines why economic development is important to a country.

The economic development of a country helps to:

- improve standards of living
- increase literacy rates
- increase life expectancy
- enhance economic activity/productivity in the community
- create and retain jobs
- change from an agricultural to an industry-based economy
- reduce poverty
- increase citizens' quality of life
- improve people's economic well-being.

Key vocabulary

endangered

extinct

threatened

flora

fauna

poaching

physical resources

economic development

pollution

infusion

Legacy for future generations

We are learning to:

- discuss the value of conservation and preservation for sustainability and social living.

Legacy for future generations ❯❯

Conservation and **preservation** of our resources now will enable our nation to leave a legacy for future generations to enjoy and benefit from. If we cut down all the forests, for example, many animals will lose their habitats and die.

Sustainability ❯❯❯

Unsustainable activities will make our heritage unavailable to future generations. Tourism is an important example of this. Tourists like to visit places that have interesting local culture and unspoilt natural environments.

Grand Etang Lake, Grenada.

However, tourism relies on developments such as hotels, transport and infrastructure. Building this infrastructure can damage the environment. Tourists also bring their own language and culture, which impacts local culture. Sustainable tourism must balance the immediate needs of the industry with the needs of the local community and of future generations.

Sustainable activities do not damage the resources that make them possible. For example, think about tourists visiting a waterfall or river. If they pollute and litter the environment, pick flowers or go fishing, they may destroy the natural environment for future generations. This type of tourism is not sustainable.

Ecotourism is a type of tourism that focuses on protecting the environment and local culture. Ecotourism means:

- travelling to undisturbed or unspoilt natural areas
- enjoying, studying or experiencing the natural environment without damaging it
- treating the environment responsibly and carefully
- benefiting local communities
- supporting conservation projects
- providing education to travellers and local communities.

Case studies

Coastal Zone Management Unit (CZMU), Barbados

The CZMU was formed in 1996. Its functions include monitoring coral reefs, consultation on coastal development, monitoring and control of beach erosion, regulating marine research, public education about coasts and managing the Carlisle Bay and Folkestone Marine Parks.

A noteworthy CZMU initiative was the Coastal Infrastructure Programme (2002–09). This project engineered the vulnerable west and south coast areas of Holetown Beach, Welches Beach and beaches from Rockley to Coconut Court. As a result beach access has improved, beaches have widened, flooding has reduced and landscaping has made these areas more attractive. This project has increased the value of the beach to locals, tourists and waterfront business owners while simultaneously conserving and preserving the beach.

Tobago Cays, St Vincent and the Grenadines.

Ecotourism in the Tobago Cays, St Vincent and the Grenadines

The Tobago Cays is a National Marine Park, managed by the Marine Park Authority. It is an ecotourism site which has special regulations to ensure that it can be preserved and conserved for future generations.

Only registered dive shops are allowed to operate in the area, fishing for lobster is seasonal, there is a speed limit on yachts and boats and dumping of wastewater is strictly prohibited, among other rules.

Activities include turtle- and bird-watching, hiking and snorkelling. Diving sites include the HMS *Purina*, a British gunship wreck, and a number of coral reefs.

A portion of the seaside walkway along Rockley to Coconut Court beach, Barbados.

Questions

1. In your own words, explain the term ecotourism.

2. Explain in your own words the role of the CZMU in Barbados.

3. How did the Coastal Infrastructure Programme benefit locals, tourists and waterfront business owners?

4. In your own words, explain why the Tobago Cays regulations are important.

Key vocabulary

conservation

preservation

sustainable

ecotourism

The value of conservation and preservation

We are learning to:

• discuss the value of conservation and preservation for sustainability and social living: employment; cultural transmission; standard of living.

Employment

We have seen that unsustainable activities will make our heritage unavailable to future generations. But we have also seen that the economy of a country can develop by using sustainable activities. This is **sustainable economic growth**.

The tourist industry in the Eastern Caribbean is an example of a sustainable industry. It also makes use of parts of our cultural heritage, such as our physical resources (forests, beaches, savannah, sea and so on). Tourists like to visit places that have interesting local culture and unspoilt natural environments.

Nevis peak, St Kitts and Nevis.

In turn, visitors to the Eastern Caribbean help to create jobs (employment). This helps to:

• improve **standard of living**
• increase economic activity in the community
• create more jobs, and retain them for the future
• reduce the poverty rate
• improve the people's economic well-being.

The Eastern Caribbean has a strong creative industry, which also contributes to the economy. The performing arts, publishing, design, music and music festivals have all grown in recent years. All have originated from the diverse cultural base of the region, which also helps to preserve our natural heritage. The development of the creative industry helps with employment, as well as maintaining the wide cultural diversity of the region.

Research

Choose one aspect of our natural heritage, for example an animal, plant or an ecosystem like forests or coral reefs. Write a report of about 350 words describing how it is threatened and what the region is doing to help.

Exercise

1. What term describes how it is possible to develop the economy of a country, while not harming that country's natural resources?

2. Name an industry in the Eastern Caribbean that is an example of a sustainable industry.

Cultural transmission >>>

One of the main characteristics of a culture is that it has to be transmittable. **Cultural transmission** refers to the way a group of people passes a society's culture from one generation to the next. If a culture is not transmitted, it will eventually die.

Culture can be passed from one person to another in the same generation, from one generation to the next between family members, or from one generation to the next where people are not related.

Examples of cultural transmission include language, religion, traditions and festivals, cuisine, dress, music and dance, culture and art, folklore and historical sites.

Standard of living >>>

A standard of living is how much money a person or family has, and the level of comfort that they have in the society where they live. Standards of living can also apply to whole communities.

The factors that affect a standard of living include: the wealth of a country and its economic development; how politically stable the country is; its level of education; and the quality and safety of the environment and climate.

Standard of living is closely linked to someone's **quality of life,** which is a measure of their overall well-being. The factors contributing to quality of life include financial and job security, health, family and the community.

One way to ensure a good quality of life is – as a country and as a community – to preserve cultural and biological heritage. This helps to strengthen citizens' sense of being connected to their national history and environment.

Cultural transmission refers to the way people pass a society's culture from one generation to the next.

Exercise

3. How can the creative industry of the Eastern Caribbean help to preserve our heritage?

4. In your own words, define cultural transmission.

5. Why is cultural transmission important to a society?

6. Can you think how culture is passed on to you by the members of your family? Give examples.

7. Define standard of living, using your own words.

8. What factors can affect standards of living and quality of life?

Activity

In groups, create a poster showing an example of each of these categories of cultural transmission that is in your country: language, religion, traditions and festivals, cuisine, dress, music and dance, culture and art, folklore and historical sites.

Key vocabulary

sustainable economic growth

standard of living

cultural transmission

quality of life

The role of the state and individual

We are learning to:

- explain the role of the individual and state in conserving and preserving our national heritage: survival of the species, global cooperation, interdependence, state initiatives, legislation.

Survival

All living things on Earth are **interdependent**. We rely on each other to survive. Human beings cannot **survive** without fresh air, water and other natural resources. In order to safeguard these resources, we must protect our natural heritage.

In the Eastern Caribbean, many groups live together. People have different religions, languages, cultures and ethnic backgrounds. **Tolerance** means allowing others to have their own views and practices.

Global cooperation

Cooperation means working together for a common goal at several levels. At a local and national level, communities may cooperate with local businesses and government to preserve their local resources and heritage. At an international level, governments of different countries need to cooperate in order to safeguard areas that are important for the world's population. At an individual level, we must preserve all the customs and traditions within our heritage, celebrate them and pass them down to future generations.

Countries that help each other or rely on each other are in interdependent.

Interdependence

Countries that help each other or rely on each other are interdependent. The leaders of states in the Caribbean see interdependence as the way forward and as a means of strengthening the development of states in the region. This interdependence started in the 1950s with the West Indian Federation and continues today through organisations like CARICOM and the Organisation of Eastern Caribbean States (OECS).

Exercise

1. Define the terms interdependence and cooperation.
2. What can we do as individuals towards conserving and preserving our heritage?

Initiatives and legislation ▶▶

Protecting our heritage includes many different activities, which can be done both by individuals and the state. For example:

- promoting sustainable development of the environment, economy and society through legislation
- identifying places that are of special natural or cultural importance
- restoring and maintaining heritage sites and buildings
- establishing and protecting nature reserves and sanctuaries where natural ecosystems can continue undisturbed
- establishing cultural centres and events so that local cultures, customs, art forms, languages and traditions do not disappear
- protecting records and artefacts at places such as museums, galleries and archives.

The OECS is a regional organisation which promotes sustainable development across the Eastern Caribbean. The Sustainable Energy, Ocean Governance and Fisheries, and Climate Change and Disaster Risk Reduction units within the OECS all deal with aspects of sustainable development. The OECS provides member states with valuable research, funding and support to meet their economic and social needs without damaging the environment.

There are large international organisations that are dedicated to identifying, protecting and preserving heritage sites around the world. Within each country, local organisations work towards the same aims. Examples include the United Nations Educational, Scientific and Cultural Organization (UNESCO) at international level and the National Trust of St Lucia at a local level.

Research

Using the internet, research the role and objectives of the OECS.

Project

Create a brochure/poster highlighting the need to preserve the heritage of your country.

Exercise

3. Name four ways in which our cultural heritage can be protected.

4. Identify a place in your neighbourhood that you think should be protected for future generations. Write a short piece of 100 words explaining why you think it should be looked after.

5. Name one organisation at both national and local levels that help to protect heritage sites.

Key vocabulary

interdependent/ interdependence

survive

tolerance

Questions

See how well you have understood the topics in this unit.

1. Identify which sector of our regional heritage the following icons contributed to:

Icon	Field
Kim Collins	political
H.N. Critchlow OBE	arts and culture
Sir Errol Barrow	track and field
Sir Viv Richards	sporting
Andrew Simmons	labour
Oscar Allen	environment
Dr John Hunte	science
Garth St Omer	social work
Professor Kathleen Coard	literature

2. Explain in your own words, what the following subcultures are:

   a) soca

   b) bouyon

   c) chutney

3. Write your own calypso song about any topic you like.

4. Name four threats to our natural habitats that result from human activities.

5. Which of these statements are related to the term 'ecotourism'?

- Travelling to towns and cities
- Experiencing the natural environment without damaging it
- Treating the environment responsibly and carefully
- Benefiting local businessmen
- Against conservation projects
- Providing education to travellers and local communities

6. Write a short essay (250 words) on the organisations listed below, describing how they function to protect our regional heritage:

- Environmental Protection Agency, Guyana
- Cayman Islands Department of Environment
- The Coastal Zone Management Unit, Barbados
- The Tobago Cays Marine Park, St Vincent and the Grenadines

7. Match the key vocabulary word (i–viii) with its definition (a–h).

   i) endangered

   ii) extinct

   iii) threatened

   iv) flora

   v) fauna

   vi) poaching

   vii) physical resources

   viii) economic development

   a) indigenous flowers or plants

   b) improving a country's standard of living

   c) in danger of extinction in the foreseeable future in a significant portion of its range

   d) indigenous animals

   e) the species no longer exists on Earth

   f) resources that are made by humans through their abilities and skills, such as buildings and technology

   g) likely to become endangered within the foreseeable future throughout all or a significant portion of its range

   h) when animals or birds are caught illegally

8. Complete these sentences:

   a) _____ refers to the way a group of people passes a society's culture from one generation to the next.

   b) _____ means working together for a common goal at several levels.

   c) Countries that help each other or rely on each other are _____.

   d) Protecting our heritage includes many different activities, which can be done both by _____ and the state.

   e) People have different religions, languages, cultures and ethnic backgrounds. _____ means allowing others to have their own views and practices.

9. Write a newspaper report of about 250 words, describing how the individual and the state can help to protect our heritage.

Checking your progress

To make good progress in understanding different aspects of your personal development, check to make sure you understand these ideas.

Identify the national heroes and icons in the history of the Eastern Caribbean who have made a significant contribution to our national heritage.

Describe how the people identified have made their contributions.

Write a short biography of an icon in the history of your country and present it to your class.

Explore the different subcultures of the Eastern Caribbean.

Describe the origins of musical subcultures in the Eastern Caribbean.

Research the history of national calypso competitions in the Eastern Caribbean.

Discuss the threats to our heritage, including our flora and fauna, and the impact of illegal hunting.

Consider the role of the Environmental Protection Agency Guyana and the Cayman Islands Department of Environment.

Identify how the Coastal Zone Management Unit and the Tobago Cays Marine Park have contributed to sustainable development and ecotourism.

Discuss the value of conservation and preservation for sustainability and social living.

Write a report on one aspect of our natural heritage and how it is threatened.

Consider the role of the individual and state in conserving and preserving our heritage.

Unit 2: Economic growth and development

In this unit you will find out ⟩⟩⟩

Understanding globalisation

- Explain and define the terms:
  - ○ globalisation, global village
  - ○ economy, trade
  - ○ technology, communicable disease
  - ○ communication, communication technology, information communication technology (ICT)

Impact of communication technology on globalisation

- Explain and define the terms:
- How new forms of communication technologies have an impact on globalisation and the economy of the Eastern Caribbean
- Positive and negative effects of modern communication technology: mass media, social media, music, the internet
- Negative effects of modern communication technology: cyberbullying

Relationship between transport and economic development

- Explain and define the terms: transportation, economic development
- Assess how transport has an impact on economic development

Global distribution of goods

- Define and explain relevant terms and concepts: consumer, consumerism, distribution, imports, foreign exchange, exports, marketing
- Evaluate the process of marketing
- Discuss the choices consumers have when purchasing goods
- Assess the importance of distribution as an agent of global economic change

Understanding globalisation

We are learning to:

- define and explain relevant terms and concepts: globalisation, global village, economy, trade, technology, climate change, communicable disease.

Globalisation

The word **global** means worldwide or relating to the whole world. **Globalisation** relates to things that take place all over the world. For example:

- opening up of world trading **markets**, through improvements in transport, communication and the removal of barriers to **trade**
- commercial activities – many businesses have branches in different countries and/or trade products all over the world
- social interactions in person or through social media like Facebook, Twitter and Instagram
- **climate change** and pollution, which are global problems
- **communicable diseases** can affect communities all over the world, and the whole world is responsible for trying to control them. A communicable disease is passed from one person to another, for example hepatitis, influenza or HIV/AIDS.

People connected in a global village.

An **economy** is a system of how industry, trade and finance are organised in a country, region or worldwide. In the Eastern Caribbean, globalisation offers opportunities such as:

- a greater range and quality of goods
- chances to export to new and bigger markets
- more exports, leading to an increase in employment
- more exports, resulting in increased business investments
- standards of living may increase, as can wages.

While economic globalisation has many positives, it can also mean that cheaper, imported goods can be bought by the population at the expense of locally produced goods. This can result in some companies going out of business.

Discussion

Do you rely on technology in your everyday life? What would happen if you were no longer able to use technology? Discuss this topic in groups.

Exercise

1. In your own words define globalisation and communicable diseases.

2. What are the advantages of globalisation in terms of trade?

Global village

The term **global village** is used to describe the way people all over the world have become connected through technology.

People who live in a village all know each other and communicate regularly with each other. In the same way, people all over the globe are now able to communicate with each other with technology, through **social media** such as Facebook and Twitter.

Distance is no longer a barrier to communication. The availability of news at our fingertips has encouraged us to become more involved in events around the world.

People in an internet café in the Philippines.

Technology

Technology consists of devices and systems which have been created for practical purposes. The technology that allows us to communicate with people all over the world is vast and complex. Satellites orbit the globe to relay weather reports and televised images to all parts of the world, and the internet connects people with friends and family as well as with business partners.

It is estimated that more than 40 per cent of the world's population now uses the internet to communicate and do research. The increase in access and usage over the last 20 years is quite staggering. In 1994 only 0.4 per cent of the world's population used the internet.

Many people have internet access in their homes or through their mobile phones. Others make use of public **internet cafés** to access the internet.

All big- and medium-sized enterprises rely on the internet to communicate with their customers and suppliers.

Activity

Make a poster or a drawing to illustrate your understanding of the term global village.

Key vocabulary

global

globalisation

market

trade

climate change

communicable diseases

economy

global village

social media

technology

internet café

Exercise

3. In your own words, define the terms global village and technology.

4. Why do you think the term global village is used?

5. Why do you think social media makes it easier to keep in touch with people in different parts of the world?

6. How many people in the world today have access to the internet?

7. In what ways can people today access the internet?

8. Why do you think businesses rely on the internet?

Impact of communication technology on globalisation

We are learning to:

- define and explain key terms and concepts: communication, communication technology, information communication technology (ICT).

Communication ⟩⟩

Communication is the transfer of information between a sender and a receiver. We communicate with people all the time in many different ways. We can talk, nod or shake our heads, wave, listen, write a note or letter, use a telephone, send an email, or use the internet to have a video call.

Good, fast communication is an essential part of any business, especially a global one. Businesses need computer networks, up-to-date software and reliable internet connections, as well as skilled employees to work within these communication systems.

Businesses need to invest in the latest communication technology. This allows their staff to provide an efficient service and enables customers to access information quickly and easily.

A common way people communicate in today's world is by using the internet.

Communication technology ⟩⟩

Communication technology is the transfer of information between a sender and receiver using technology.

Smartphones, **tablets** and laptop computers are examples of communication technology devices we use for communication and entertainment. Cell phones, computers, MP3 players, game consoles, tablets and **ebooks** have changed the way we communicate, work and play.

Discussion

How is it an advantage for students to have access to ICT at school and at home? Which types of ICT do you think students need access to, and why?

Exercise

1. Define the terms communication and communication technology.

2. Why do businesses need good communication?

3. What do businesses need if they are to have good communication?

Did you know...?

More than 204 million emails are sent every minute, and more than 46 000 Google searches are made every second.

ICT at work ▶▶▶

Information and communication technology (ICT)
is technology which transmit and store information
electronically.

ICT has changed the way people work. Computers and
machines have taken over many jobs that people used
to do, including bank tellers, call centre operators and
travel agents.

Technology has also created new jobs that did not exist
before, such as social media managers, video game
designers and computer technicians.

The ICT sector is one of the largest industries in some
countries. The development of ICT has created many
new careers and jobs, from computer programmers, web
designers and software developers to engineers, technicians,
support staff and sales people.

Amazon.com was one of the first and
largest online businesses. It began
as an online bookshop. Today it
sells everything from electronics to
clothing.

E-commerce ▶▶

ICT has changed how business can be done. An example of
this is **e-commerce** (short for electronic commerce), which
is buying and selling products and services via the internet
(**online**) and computer networks.

Think about a bookshop in your town:

- In the past, if you wanted to buy a book, you had to visit
  a shop, at its physical address, during opening hours and
  needed to deal with a person behind the counter.
- If you were looking for a particular book that wasn't
  in stock, you may have needed to order it through
  the bookshop.
- Today, you can go online and order a book through a
  website such as Amazon.

Exercise

4. Name some of the new types of jobs that the ICT
   sector has created.

5. Explain in your own words what e-commerce is.

6. What are the advantages of e-commerce?

7. Do you think it is easier to find a job today than it was
   100 years ago? Why/why not?

8. Define information and communication technology.

Research

Using the internet or
magazines, research the
terms communication;
communication
technology; and
information and
communication
technology (ICT). Find
pictures to illustrate your
definitions.

Key vocabulary

communication

**communication
technology**

smartphone

tablet

ebooks

**information and
communication
technology (ICT)**

e-commerce

online

Impact of communication technology: the internet and media

We are learning to:

- assess how new forms of communication technology have an impact on globalisation and the economy of the Eastern Caribbean: mass media, social media, music, the internet.

Mass media ⟩⟩

Mass media is a term used to describe the different media technologies that are used to reach large numbers of people (the masses). These include: print media, like newspapers; broadcast media, like radio, film and television; and electronic media, which is internet-based.

Mass media can have a positive impact. For example:

- It can offer personal development, by allowing people to share ideas, keep in touch and learn.
- Culturally, it can promote the way of life in the Caribbean region.
- It encourages cultural creativity, for example in music and films.
- It can help promote good values, freedom of expression, national pride and identity.
- It can help promote social and economic programmes.

Mass media can also have a negative impact. For example:

- It can present images of violence, sexual activity, promiscuity and other risky behaviours (such as drug and alcohol abuse), which can influence younger members of society.
- Overseas media do not represent national or regional views, and these could get overshadowed by the global media.

Mass media includes newspapers, radio, film and television and electronic media.

Research

Using the internet, research how communication technology has an impact on the economy of the Eastern Caribbean.

Exercise

1. Define the term mass media.

2. Give two examples of mass media and say how they are used.

3. Name two advantages and disadvantages of mass media to Eastern Caribbean society.

Social media ▶▶▶

Social media such as Facebook, Twitter and Instagram are popular ways for people to stay in touch with their friends and family. Social media can have a positive impact:

- It can keep people connected when physically apart.
- Communities can gather support for issues.
- Businesses can build relationships with communities.

There can be some disadvantages of social media:

- It can be addictive and distract people from their work and other activities.
- It can increase feelings of loneliness or depression.
- It can be used for cyberbullying, which can have serious consequences.

Social media such as Facebook, Twitter and Instagram help people to keep in touch.

The internet ▶▶▶▶

Whether you need to know today's weather or news, the starting time for a sports match or a detailed history of any country, you can find the information on the internet. The internet has changed the way people find information and has been a positive development in many ways:

- You can find a wide range of information and entertainment easily, for example you can watch live sports or movies.
- Online shopping is readily available, offering cheap products with fast delivery.
- It can raise awareness of news and issues with a wider audience.

Negative consequences of the growth of the internet include:

- the decline of publishing industry and use of libraries
- an increase in piracy (easy to download copyrighted music and movies)
- loss of local culture and knowledge as global culture spreads
- time-consumption, leading to a more **sedentary** lifestyle
- **information overload**, resulting in anxiety and stress.

Activity

Write a reflective piece titled 'How do communication technologies influence my life?' Write about 150 words.

Discussion

In groups, brainstorm ways that communication technology affects globalisation.

Exercise

4. Draw a graphic organiser showing the advantages and disadvantages of social media.

5. Which of the ICT mentioned on this page do you use?

6. Are there any which you do not use, and which you would like? Why/why not?

Key vocabulary

mass media

sedentary

information overload

The negative impact of communication technology

We are learning to:

- understand the negative effects of modern communication technology: cyberbullying.

Cyberbullying

Cyberbullying takes place when a person or a group of people uses the internet, mobile phones, online games or any other type of digital technology to threaten, tease or humiliate someone.

Types of cyberbullying

Online forums make it easy to bully or intimidate others by:

- sending abusive or nasty **emails**, or sending emails to a group of people who join in the bullying
- using **instant messaging (IM)** and **chatrooms** to send threatening or abusive messages to someone; asking others to join in
- writing nasty or upsetting comments on someone's profile on a **social networking site**; making jokes or comments about others on your updates or tweets
- setting up a fake profile dedicated to bullying someone else
- abusing or harassing someone through a multi-player **online gaming site**
- sending abusive texts, video or photo messages via mobile phones.

If you are being cyberbullied, you should:

- talk to someone you trust, such as a parent, teacher or counsellor
- keep copies of any abusive messages or comments, and record the dates and times
- try not to reply to any messages you receive, as it can encourage bullies and upset you more
- report the bullying to the site you are using (for example, Twitter, Facebook, Instagram); all social networking sites have help centres for people experiencing abuse.

Cyberbullying often takes place through mobile phones and the apps that people can get on them.

Activity

Write a short piece of about 100 words around the topic of responsible use of social media.

Case study

Cyberbullying can kill

Talisha, aged 13, begged her mother Arlene to set up an online profile for months before Arlene allowed her to do it. Soon, Talisha got a message from a boy. He said his name was Jason Khan. Talisha started emailing him regularly.

Soon, however, Jason – or someone using his account – started sending a chain of hurtful instant messages, calling Talisha a liar, calling her fat and other hurtful names. The **cyber abuse** became increasingly vicious, until one day Talisha went into her room and ended her own life.

'She felt there was no way out,' said Arlene. Six weeks later, Talisha's family discovered that their daughter was the victim of a hoax. Another girl had created the Jason Khan account as a trick, and sent the hate messages. An article in the *New York Times* wrote:

'Cellphone cameras and text messages, as well as social networking websites, e-mail and instant messaging, all give teenagers a wider range of ways to play tricks on one another, to tease and to **intimidate** their peers.'

And, unlike traditional bullying, high-tech bullying can happen anywhere, at any time, among lots of different people who may never actually meet in person. The victim can feel it is inescapable and the perpetrators are often **anonymous**.

Questions

1. In your own words, define cyberbullying.
2. Why do you think Talisha wanted an online profile?
3. **a)** How do you think Talisha felt when she started getting emails from 'Jason Khan'?
   b) How do you think she felt when Jason announced he didn't want to be friends with her anymore?
4. A hoax is a serious trick:
   a) Why do you think the girl who made up the Jason Khan account did it?
   b) How do you think she felt after Talisha's death?
5. Give four ways that cyberbullying differs from traditional bullying.
6. Talisha felt there was no way out. What other 'ways out' do you think Talisha could have found?
7. How do you think this event changed Talisha's community?

Project

In groups, create a poster that either describes the types of cyberbullying to look out for or gives advice about what to do if you are being cyberbullied.

Discussion

Discuss how the following behaviours and attitudes form an important part of using social media responsibly: cooperation, rationality, tolerance, freedom, respect.

Key vocabulary

cyberbullying

emails

instant messaging (IM)

chatrooms

social networking site

online gaming sites

cyber abuse

intimidate

anonymous

Relationship between transport and economic development

We are learning to:

- define relevant terms and concepts: transportation, economic development
- assess how transport has an impact on economic development.

Transport and economic development »

How can our **transportation** systems help economic development?

- Greater access to transport – transportation networks, such as roads, water (both inland and sea), air and rail, provide the **mobility** to move people and goods from one place to another. This in turn allows economic activity to flourish, which in turns leads to **economic development** – the improvement of a country's standard of living.

- Increased tourism – there are a number of attractions for tourists in Trinidad and Tobago, for example, beach holidays, cruise ship holidays and special events such as Carnival. Airports and seaports are needed, and must be able to handle large numbers of passengers, modern aircrafts and shipping.

- Distribution of goods – the transport networks help manufacturers to be able to transport their goods to where they can sell those goods. If they cannot do this, they will not be able to sell them. Without an **efficient** transportation network, an economy cannot develop.

Some of the advantages of an efficient transportation network are:

- an increased ability to buy and sell goods
- increased **competitiveness** – producing goods that are better or cheaper than goods produced by others
- increased production
- job creation – which, in turn, creates opportunities that lead to more jobs.

Transport systems, such as road networks in the cities, help to move people from one place to another.

Discussion

In groups, discuss how transport can help to boost economic activity. Consider how transport helps this process in your community.

Project

In groups, research magazines, newspapers or the internet to see how transportation has improved the lives of people around the globe.

Exercise

1. In your own words, define the term economic development.

2. Outline the advantages of an efficient transport system.

Here is a summary of how our transport systems help economic development.

ROADS
- Roads enable the movement of goods from the place where they are produced to places where they can be sold.
- Roads make remote areas more accessible.
- Different types of vehicles can use roads (for example, trucks, cars, buses).
- Roads allow workers to get to and from work, and traders to move goods.

WATER
- Water allows the transportation of heavy and bulky items.
- Goods can be imported and exported through **ports**.
- Inland waterways are often naturally occurring and generally do not need many repairs.
- Transporting by water means less traffic congestion.
- In the Caribbean, the presence of cruise ships encourages tourism.

HOW CAN OUR TRANSPORT SYSTEMS HELP ECONOMIC DEVELOPMENT?

RAIL
- Rail allows the transportation of heavy and bulky items.
- Rail travel can be relatively quick, as there is less congestion on the rail networks.
- The rail network can carry passengers and cargo.
- The rail network can carry large numbers of passengers in one trip, for example, to work.

AIR
- Air allows access to any part of the world in a relatively short amount of time.
- Cargo can easily be transported between countries or within large countries.
- Air travel encourages tourism.

Key vocabulary

transportation

mobility

economic development

efficient

competitiveness

port

Transportation networks like these give people and goods easier access to various parts of the country and the wider world. These goods can be bought and sold, and people can work to contribute to the economy and spend money. Both of these activities boost economic development.

Exercise

3. Name the different types of transport systems that we use.

4. Why are transport systems so important for economic development?

5. Which of the transport types do these refer to?

   a) access to remote areas
   b) can carry large numbers of people in one trip
   c) encourages tourism
   d) different types of vehicles can use it

Research

A car is manufactured in a factory in Japan and is going to be sold in Basseterre, St Kitts. Look at a map and try to work out what transport types could be used for this journey. Using a graphic display (for example, a poster, booklet or PowerPoint slides), show the possible route the car could take. Then write a short paragraph to describe the journey.

Global distribution of goods

We are learning to:

- define and explain relevant terms and concepts: consumer, consumerism, distribution.

Consumer and consumerism »

A **consumer** is a person who uses goods and **services**, which may satisfy the consumer's wants or needs. A large proportion of what many people buy satisfies their wants rather than their needs.

We need clothes to cover our bodies and keep us warm when it is cold. But most consumers buy more clothes than they need, buying several pairs of shoes, jeans or jackets because they want or like them. They may also buy new clothes every year because of changes in fashion. The older clothes are then discarded as the consumer wants new, fashionable clothes.

This is why many people describe the society we live in today as a **consumer society** (a society based on **consumerism**), which relies on consumers buying more than they actually need.

Most consumers buy more clothes than they need.

Distribution and marketing »

Distribution is the process through which a product or service is made available to consumers.

Distribution can sometimes be carried out directly by the producer or manufacturer (the person who makes the goods that consumers want or need). However, it usually involves a series of **intermediaries**, who link the producers with the consumers.

Typically, these intermediaries form a **distribution chain**, which involves the **producer**, a **wholesaler**, a marketing team, the **retailer** and the consumer.

Discussion

In groups, discuss the differences between a consumer and consumerism. Share your ideas with the whole class.

Activity

Working in groups, identify producers (farmers, factory owners), retailers, wholesalers and vendors (shops and street vendors) in your area. Interview some of these people to find out what they produce or sell. Find out where they get their goods from and who they sell their goods to. Report back to the class.

Exercise

1. In your own words, define consumer and consumerism.

2. Why is it said that today we live in a consumer society?

3. Explain the term distribution.

4. Before reading the next page, write down what you think these words mean: producer, wholesaler, marketing team, retailer. They are all related to the distribution chain. After you have read the text, compare your answers.

| **Producer** |
| A producer can be a single person or a factory. The producer can produce any goods – from food products to films and cargo vessels. Producers can also provide services that we need, like health care, or services that we might want, such as car repairs or hairdressing. |

| **Wholesaler** |
| A wholesaler is an intermediary in a distribution chain. A wholesaler buys and sells goods in bulk or in large quantities from producers. The wholesaler may have a **warehouse**, where the goods are stored. |

| **Retailer** |
| A retailer buys goods from a wholesaler. Retailers may sometimes buy only one item from a wholesaler, but very often they are required to buy certain quantities. Consumers are not usually allowed to buy directly from wholesalers. Retailers are **vendors**, as they sell goods to consumers. |

| **Marketing** |
| Marketing creates a **demand** for the goods or services that they produce or provide. |

| **Consumer** |
| The goods or services are sold to the consumer. |

Case study

Light Mobile Phones

Read this study of the distribution chain of an imaginary brand of mobile phones.

Light Mobile Phones are produced in a factory in China. They are packed in boxes and taken by truck to an airport for distribution to other countries. They are loaded onto a plane and flown to the Netherlands. They are then taken by truck or by rail to a wholesaler, who stores them in a warehouse. From the warehouse they are taken by plane, and then by truck, to retailers in Trinidad. Retailers in Trinidad buy the phones from the wholesaler and the consumers buy the phone in the shops, which are run by the retailers.

1. Complete these sentences.

    a) Wholesalers buy goods from ___ and sell goods to ___.

    b) Consumers buy goods from ___.

    c) Goods get from the producers to the consumers by means of a ___ chain.

    d) Distribution can be done by various means, such as ___ or ___.

2. How are goods and services made available to consumers?

3. Why is distribution a vital part of the process through which we buy our goods and services?

Key vocabulary

consumer

services

consumer society

consumerism

distribution

intermediaries

distribution chain

producer (manufacturer)

wholesaler

retailer

warehouse

vendor

demand

Global distribution of goods: imports

We are learning to:

- define and explain relevant terms and concepts: imports, foreign exchange.

Guyana's imports »

Guyana, like most countries, imports some of the goods and services that consumers need. **Imports** are goods or services that come into one country from other countries. All countries have to import some **products**, as they are not able to produce or manufacture everything themselves and they do not necessarily have the right natural resources. For example, some countries may not have land that is suitable for agriculture.

The main import into Guyana is refined petroleum. Excavation machinery; cars; chemical products such as fertilisers and cleaning products; and vegetable products such as wheat and corn account for its other main imports.

These products come from all over the world, but the biggest trading partners for Guyana are Trinidad and Tobago, the United States, China and Suriname. The total value of imports in 2016 was estimated to be around $1.62 billion.

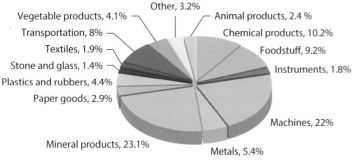

Imports into Guyana, 2016.

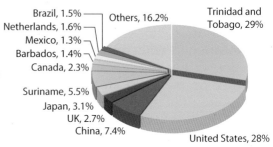

Countries from which Guyana imports, 2016.

Exercise

1. In your own words, define the term import.

2. Why does Guyana have to import goods?

3. Give some examples of the types of goods that Guyana imports.

4. Look at the pie chart showing imports. What are the three most popular goods/services?

5. Look at the pie chart that shows the origin of Guyana's imported goods. Name the three countries Guyana imports from the most.

Foreign exchange ⟩⟩⟩

All countries use goods and services from other countries. The purchase of these goods must be paid for with **foreign exchange**. This term refers to foreign currency obtained from the **foreign exchange system**. The foreign exchange system is a set of rules that each country sets to work out the value of its own currency against another country.

Countries can earn income from foreign exchange:

- by exporting goods, such as bananas, and natural resources, such as oil and bauxite
- from service industries such as tourism.

Balance of trade ⟩⟩⟩

As we have seen, countries can import a variety of goods. The difference in value between the exports and imports in one year is called the **balance of trade**:

- If the value of the exports is higher than the value of the imports, then the country has a favourable or positive balance of trade.
- When the value of the imports is higher than the value of exports, the country has an unfavourable or negative balance of trade.
- Trinidad and Tobago, for example, usually has a favourable balance of trade because of the high value of its exports. However, if the price of petroleum and natural gas drops, this could affect the balance of trade.

A favourable balance of trade is good for the economy of a country because:

- the country earns foreign exchange, which it can use to pay for imports
- the economy of the country is stable, which attracts investment and encourages entrepreneurs to invest in new businesses
- investment in turn creates more job opportunities.

Research

Working in groups, research online a list of products that your country imports.

Exercise

6. Define, in your own words, the term foreign exchange.

7. In 2015, the Cayman Islands exported $438 million worth of goods and imported $2.24 billion worth of goods. Did the Cayman Islands have a positive or negative trade balance?

Key vocabulary

imports

products

foreign exchange

foreign exchange system

balance of trade

Global distribution of goods: exports

We are learning to:

- define and explain relevant terms and concepts: exports.

Exports ⟩⟩

Exports are **goods** that are sent to other countries to be sold. Exports are usually subject to trading agreements between different countries and to national and international laws. For example, countries that manufacture military equipment may not be allowed to sell this equipment to countries that have disobeyed human rights laws in the past. Countries may also not be allowed to sell goods to countries on which **trade sanctions** have been imposed.

Countries export goods and products that they have in excess. If a country produces more meat than the people of that country can eat, then some of the meat is exported to other countries. Many countries also export natural resources like gas and coal to countries that do not have these resources.

Beer is one of St Vincent's top exports, Hairoun beer is brewed locally.

St Vincent and the Grenadines' exports ⟩⟩⟩

St Vincent and the Grenadines imports more than it exports and therefore has a negative balance of trade. In 2015, imports totalled $441 million while exports totalled $127 million. Main imports are refined petroleum and transportation, particularly sea vessels.

In 2015, St Vincent and the Grenadines' main Caribbean export partners were Barbados, St Lucia, and Antigua and Barbuda. Main international export partners vary. In 2015 Jordan, Sudan and Poland were the main partners while in 2014 Poland, Turkey, Italy and France topped the list. Exported goods in 2015 included petroleum gas, wheat, rice, cassava, beer, ships and boats.

Research

Work alone. Choose one product that St Vincent and the Grenadines exports. Find out where this product is exported to and the value of the export to St Vincent and the Grenadines.

Exercise

1. In your own words, define the term export.

2. What goods do St Vincent and the Grenadines export the most?

3. Give an example to show when trade sanctions may be imposed upon a country.

The following table shows the value of St Vincent and the Grenadines' top six exports in 2015.

.8

Export	Value (in US$)	% of total exports
Petroleum gas	47 200 000	37
Wheat	13 000 000	10
Passenger and cargo ships	5 950 000	4.7
Beer	4 990 000	3.9
Cassava	4 530 000	3.6
Animal food	3 440 000	2.7

This chart below shows the export destinations of goods from St Vincent and the Grenadines in 2015.

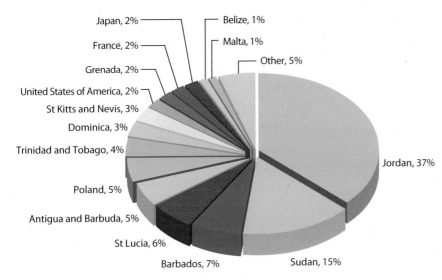

St Vincent and the Grenadines export destinations, 2015.

Exercise

Study the pie chart and table on this page. Discuss and answer these questions.

4. How important are passenger and cargo ships as exports to the economy of St Vincent and the Grenadines?

5. To which three countries does St Vincent and the Grenadines export the most? Which products do you think are exported to these countries?

6. What combined percentage of exports in 2015 was petroleum gas and beer?

7. Name the countries in the Caribbean which St Vincent and the Grenadines export goods to.

Key vocabulary
....

exports

goods

trade sanctions

Marketing

We are learning to:

• evaluate the process of marketing.

Marketing ▷▷

Marketing is the process through which producers, wholesalers or retailers create a demand for the goods or services that they produce or provide. Marketing involves the **advertising**, distribution and sale of goods. Marketing usually involves a number of procedures such as:

• identifying a product which is in demand by prospective consumers; if it is a new product, this is usually done through market research in the form of surveys and questionnaires

• agreeing on a selling price to make sure that the product is competitive with similar products on the market

• identifying where the product will be sold to consumers

• advertising the product to help increase sales and awareness of its availability

• following the distribution chain to get the product to the point of sale.

Advertising ▷▷▷

Advertising is when a producer tries to persuade consumers to buy their goods or services. Advertising usually takes the form of an advertisement (or advert) that looks to persuade consumers to buy the product by making it a desirable item, or service, to have.

Advertising can take the form of newspaper and magazine adverts, flyers, posters on billboards, ship fronts, television and radio adverts, and adverts on social media. Today, you can see adverts almost everywhere you go.

Exercise

1. In your own words, define the terms marketing and advertising.

2. Draw a graphic organiser to show the process of marketing and advertising.

Activity

Count how many examples of advertising you see on your way to school.

> **Did you know...?**
>
> There are two main types of adverts. Informative advertising tells consumers about a product and its benefits, whereas persuasive advertising tries to convince consumers to buy the product.

Advertising is when a producer tries to persuade consumers to buy their goods or services.

Project

Work in a group to create a product (for example, pepper sauce, chow, fruit juice). Develop and implement a marketing strategy to sell your product to other students and teachers. At the end of the exercise, submit the strategy that your group used to market the product, as well as the challenges experienced.

Marketing problems »»»

All businesses face challenges when they **market goods**. These may be related to **infrastructure** or perhaps local and international laws and trade agreements. Companies that have high profits can generally afford to market and advertise their goods and services. Smaller producers are the most likely to be affected by marketing problems, which can restrict their development. Some of the problems the smaller producers have in the Eastern Caribbean include:

- lack of access roads, which hinders distribution of products to markets
- limited **storage** space to store goods so that they do not perish
- competition from cheaper products, which means demand drops and the price a producer can charge is limited
- trade restrictions which prevent goods from being exported to some countries and imported from other countries, perhaps because of higher taxes (import duties)
- **bureaucracy**, a system of administration run by officials, which can be time-consuming, especially for smaller producers
- lack of time, skills or money to market their goods and find new markets for them.

A banana tree.

Case study

The banana industry

The banana industry was successful for the Eastern Caribbean in the 1970s and 1980s. Many farmers stopped growing other crops to grow bananas. The region was guaranteed a portion of the UK and European Union markets.

However, international competition from large companies, like Dole and Chiquita, has caused the industry to decline. These companies took advantage of cheap South American labour and land, and used political influence to fully take over the banana market.

One suggestion to regain lost profits is for Eastern Caribbean farmers to diversify the crops they grow, instead of growing only bananas.

Questions

1. Why do you think bananas were a good industry in the Eastern Caribbean?
2. How were international companies able to take over the banana industry?
3. How can farmers regain lost profits from the banana industry?

Research

Find out more about the banana industry. Which islands produce the most bananas? By how many tonnes has banana production declined? Do the islands still have a guaranteed market in the UK and EU? Are there any other barriers in this industry?

Discussion

In groups, brainstorm how consumers become aware of goods and services. Examine advertisements in magazines, newspapers and flyers to help you identify products and services that are being promoted.

Key vocabulary

marketing
advertising
market goods
infrastructure
storage
bureaucracy

Consumer choice

We are learning to:

- discuss the choices consumers have in purchasing goods: online shopping, imports, competition
- assess the importance of distribution as an agent of global economic change.

Online shopping ⟩⟩

In countries where there is sufficient internet connectivity, the economy can change significantly with the growth of e-commerce, or **online shopping**. People started using the internet to buy goods and services in the 1990s. This type of commerce has grown significantly since then, with many people relying on the internet to purchase things like train and air tickets, holidays and books, and to do their banking.

E-commerce businesses have websites with details of all the goods and services they sell. In order to buy goods online, a customer usually needs a debit card or a credit card, and a secure internet connection. This is a quick and easy way to shop, as goods purchased are delivered to your office or home, or via a post office.

Globalisation has helped to increase the number of cheaper goods that are available in supermarkets.

Imports of cheaper goods ⟩⟩

One effect of globalisation is an increase in the number of cheaper goods and services that are available. There can be a variety of reasons for this, including lower production costs, lower costs of raw materials and lower labour costs.

Large **transnational companies** (organisations that have business interests in more than one country) are able to use economies of scale to their benefit. This is where bigger companies are able to lower their unit costs, because they are selling more products. Having cheaper goods and services can be a good thing for the consumer, but the quality of goods may suffer, or the level of service may be lower than if you paid a little bit more elsewhere.

Research

Do your own research on the meaning of the term 'market'. This will broaden your understanding of how this term is used.

Exercise

1. What does e-commerce rely on to operate successfully?

2. How has online shopping changed the way people buy their goods?

3. Explain why having cheaper goods is not always a good thing.

Competition >>>

Globalisation and removal of barriers to international trade has led to increased **competition**. Competition exists when there are several producers who make the same or similar items, or who offer similar goods or services.

These producers compete with each other to make their products and services attractive to customers. Factors that affect competition include the quality, price and availability of goods and services.

Competition between producers can sometimes mean that:

- local producers who cannot compete against the buying power of big companies could go out of business
- local products can be thought of as too costly or they may become unavailable, limiting consumer choice.

The importance of distribution >>>

The 'Four Ps of Marketing' are the main things that you have to consider when marketing your goods. The four Ps are shown in the graphic on the right. Distribution ('Place' in the four Ps) is important because:

- if a product cannot reach the customer, or consumer, then the company who owns the product cannot sell any goods or make money – customers will just buy a rival product
- the price of a product is worked out according to several factors, including the cost of making and marketing the product, but effective and efficient distribution can help to keep the price down and therefore make the product more affordable to more people
- some online companies are more attractive to buy from, because they promise quick delivery – companies such as Amazon offer next-day deliveries; fast and efficient delivery helps to increase customer satisfaction and encourage repeat business.

Project

In groups, use the internet to identify the transnational corporations present in the Eastern Caribbean. Research the other countries where these organisations can be found. Present this information on a blank map of the world, using an appropriate key.

The Four Ps of Marketing

Product What are we selling?	**Price** How much will the product or service cost?
Place Where will we sell it and how will we get it there?	**Promotion** How will we let people know we are selling the product/service?

Exercise

4. Explain the advantages and disadvantages of competition.

5. In your own words, explain why distribution is important to a business.

6. If you were to produce a new brand of shampoo in your country, do you think you would face a lot of competition? From whom? What would you do about this?

Key vocabulary
....

online shopping

transnational company

competition

Questions

See how well you have understood the topics in this unit.

1. Match the key vocabulary word (i–vii) with its definition (a–g).

   i) global
   ii) globalisation
   iii) global village
   iv) communication
   v) communication technology
   vi) information and communication technologies (ICTs)
   vii) e-commerce

   a) the transfer of information between a sender and receiver using technology
   b) worldwide or relating to the whole world
   c) businesses that provide goods and services over the internet
   d) a process of making the world more connected, with goods and services being traded globally and people moving around freely
   e) technologies for transmitting and storing information electronically
   f) the way people all over the world have become connected through technology
   g) the transfer of information between a sender and receiver

2. Make a list of 10 goods or services that you use in a normal day.

3. Write a short essay explaining why you think that the mass media can have a positive impact on society. Use around 200 words.

4. Explain in your own words what sorts of things people should look out for if they think they are being cyberbullied.

5. Explain in your own words how globalisation can make goods cheaper for the consumer.

6. How can our road and air travel help economies develop?

7. Working in groups, choose one product that is commonly used by members of your group and is a local product. Each group should choose a different product.

   a) Research where in your country the product is produced and how it gets to consumers in the place where you live.
   b) Draw a distribution diagram or chart to show this process. Label the chart clearly.
   c) Find out how the product is marketed and what kind of competition there is for the product. How is the product priced? Is it more expensive or less expensive than competing products?
   d) Present your findings to the class.

8. Complete the sentences about the distribution chain.

   a) _____ creates a _____ for the goods or services that they produce or provide.

   b) The goods or services are sold to the _____.

   c) A _____ buys goods from a wholesaler.

   d) A _____ is an intermediary in a distribution chain.

   e) The _____ can be a single person or a factory.

9. Look at the pie charts below and answer the questions.

   a) Why do you think Guyana imports a high percentage of goods from the United States and Trinidad and Tobago?

   b) Using the pie charts, name three countries which Guyana imports from and three which St Vincent and the Grenadines export to.

   c) Why do you think that St Vincent and the Grenadines export a high percentage of goods to other Eastern Caribbean states?

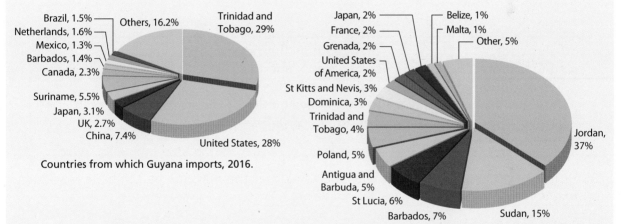

Countries from which Guyana imports, 2016.

St Vincent and the Grenadines export destinations, 2015.

10. Work in groups to create a product (for example, pepper sauce, chow, fruit juices) and develop and implement a marketing strategy to sell the product to other students and teachers. At the end of the exercise, submit the strategy that was used to market the product, as well as the challenges experienced.

11. Match these marketing terms to their definitions:

   a) Product   i)   How much will the product or service cost?

   b) Price   ii) How will we let people know we are selling the product/service?

   c) Place   iii) What are we selling?

   d) Promotion   iv) Where will we sell it and how will we get it there?

Checking your progress

To make good progress in understanding different aspects of economic growth and development, check to make sure you understand these ideas.

- Understand the terms global, globalisation and global village.

- Examine the role of technology in the modern world.

- Discuss what would happen if you were no longer able to use technology.

- Understand the terms communication, communication technology and information and communication technology (ICT).

- Assess how ICT has changed how business can be done, and the impact of mass media, social media and the internet on society.

- Explain the dangers of cyberbullying, and how to avoid it.

- Examine the relationship between transport and economic development.

- Consider why transport systems are so important for economic development.

- Research how transportation has improved the lives of people around the globe.

- Understand the terms consumer, consumerism and distribution.

- Examine the imports and exports of Guyana and St Vincent and the Grenadines.

- Evaluate the process of marketing.

Unit 3: Ethics and relationships

In this unit you will find out

Living in harmony

Prejudice and stereotypes

- Explain the terms
  - ethics
  - prejudice
  - stereotype
- The social impact of prejudice and stereotyping on society
  - national, regional and global
  - news media and social media
- The positive role that can be played by teachings from
  - religion
  - faith traditions
  - belief systems
  - influence of religion, faith tradition and belief systems
  - attitudes to prejudice

Conflict resolution

- Explain the terms
  - bullying
  - peer pressure
  - courage
  - mentorship
  - conflict resolution skills
- The impact of bullying and peer pressure on the lives of individuals
- Recognise the sources of influence in your own lives
- Understand the importance of mentorship in relation to virtuous living

Prejudice and stereotypes

We are learning to:

- define the terms ethics, prejudice and stereotype
- discuss the social impact of prejudice and stereotyping on society: national, regional and global.

Ethics, prejudice and stereotype ⟫

Ethics are rules for living in society according to what we consider to be right and wrong. We all have our own personal set of ethics, but groups of people (social, religious or professional groups) can also have their own set of rules.

Caribbean countries have a wide variety of cultures, embracing and encouraging diversity within their communities. But some people can show an unjustified dislike of other people, which is often no more than **prejudice** against other groups of people and believing in a **stereotype**.

Prejudice is an unreasonable dislike, negative belief or feeling about a particular group of people or things, or even a preference for one person or group of things over another that is not based on facts. Often a prejudice is passed on from one generation to the next. Someone who is prejudiced against someone else often shows hostility towards them.

Prejudice can cause racial discrimination – for example, if a person isn't given a job because of the colour of their skin. In South Africa, before it became a modern democracy, the white police showed prejudice against black people in the country. They treated them harshly and without dignity. Black people were imprisoned without cause.

Stereotyping is similar to showing prejudice, but involves holding a one-sided negative thought or belief about how another person, or a group of people, acts or behaves. A stereotype can often be related to **racism** (prejudice against a **race** or **ethnicity**) or **sexism** (prejudice against a member of the opposite sex). An example would be the belief that only men can be doctors and only women can be nurses.

Many people from different backgrounds come together to celebrate Carnival.

Discussion

In groups, discuss how ethics, prejudice and stereotypes can affect relationships – for example, peer friendships and relationships between parents and children and students and teachers. Share your ideas with the whole class.

Exercise

1. In your own words, define the terms prejudice, stereotype and ethics. Give an example of each.

2. Which is worse: prejudice or stereotype? Explain why.

Prejudice and stereotyping can have a negative impact on society. For example:

- It can put labels on people as to how they should live their lives according to their ethnicity, sex or religion.
- People can end up believing that what has been said about them is true, which can lead to low self-esteem, emotional problems and depression.
- It allows all prejudices, including racism and sexism, to grow in society, which creates ignorance.
- It denies opportunities to the victims of prejudice – for example, women can be badly represented in society, as they may be overlooked for a job, or paid less than a man for the same job role.

For some members of society, it makes them more determined to overcome prejudice and stereotype. For example, they work hard to get a good job or education despite people's prejudices.

Examples of prejudice on a regional and global scale include:

- Hitler's discrimination against and persecution of the Jews during World War II
- widespread racial discrimination in some countries – for example, the United States, throughout the slave trade in the eighteenth and nineteenth centuries, and for some time afterwards; some argue that it still is widespread in the USA
- women not being allowed to vote in many countries until the twentieth century
- discrimination against sexual orientation
- in Europe, increasing discrimination against immigrants.

Women can sometimes be overlooked for a job in favour of a man.

Activity

Your teacher will provide case studies of prejudice and stereotyping. For example, a woman gets overlooked for promotion, despite having the same qualifications and better experience than the man who got the job. You must identify the issue and suggest what should be the alternative behaviour.

Exercise

3. Explain why prejudice and stereotyping can have a negative impact on society.

4. Create a role play to clarify misconceptions about prejudice and stereotypes. For example, is it right that people should assume that only men can do certain jobs?

Activity

Create a PowerPoint presentation on prejudice and stereotyping for use with the lower form classes.

Key vocabulary

ethics

prejudice

stereotype

racism

race

ethnicity

sexism

Social impact of prejudice and stereotyping

We are learning to:

- discuss the social impact of prejudice and stereotyping on society: news media and social media.

Influence of news media and social media

One of the main places that children and adults learn stereotypes is from the mass media, which includes television, films, radio, adverts and social media (Facebook, Twitter, Instagram). The media are full of racial and gender stereotypes. Examples include the representation of:

- ethnic groups
- gender, girls/women, **femininity**; and boys/men, **masculinity**
- sexual orientation
- people with disabilities.

This photo shows how the media can often show gender stereotyping. The man is shown reading an economics newspaper, while the woman is shown with colourful shopping bags talking on the phone.

Gender

The media often displays gender stereotyping, particularly negative stereotyping of women. There are four basic types:

- Personality – women are shown as submissive and passive; men are shown as aggressive and dominant.
- Behaviour at home – women are portrayed as staying at home, cooking, doing the housework and child care; men earn the income.
- Occupations – women are shown as having a traditionally female job such as a nurse, secretary or librarian; men have more physical jobs, such as construction, or higher-skilled jobs like doctors or lawyers.
- Appearance – women are often shown as sexual objects and are defined by their perceived level of attractiveness; men are often shown as being **macho** (with a strong sense of masculinity).

Generally, women are portrayed as being weaker, less competitive and less adaptable than men.

Exercise

1. Name some of the racial and gender stereotypes represented by the media.

2. Draw a graphic organiser to show your understanding of the four gender stereotypes.

Case studies

Read the case studies and answer the questions that follow.

1. Adverts that encourage gender stereotypes like women cleaning up after their family, or men failing to do housework, face being banned under strict new watchdog rules.

   Following a year-long inquiry the Advertising Standards Authority (ASA) in the UK has found there was evidence to support stronger rules, on the basis that harmful stereotypes 'can restrict the choices, aspirations and opportunities of children, young people and adults'.

   Controversial adverts by Gap, KFC and Protein World, all of which received a number of complaints last year, are examples which could be affected by the crackdown.

A stranded victim of Hurricane Katrina is taken ashore by rescue workers after being rescued from her home in high water on 5 September 2005 in New Orleans, Louisiana.

2. In 2005, Hurricane Katrina struck the Gulf Coast, killing more than 1 000 people and leaving tens of thousands homeless.

   News media may have turned this natural disaster into a disaster for American race relations by repeatedly broadcasting images of black people who were often described as 'looting' in the catastrophic wake of the storm.

   According to a study these types of images lead white people to endorse harsh treatment of black evacuees (by, for example, not allowing them to seek refuge in another parish). Participants were not any less likely to help white evacuees, suggesting that racial stereotypes of blacks as criminals may have played a role.

Questions

1. What stereotype does the first case study highlight?
2. What reason for stopping stereotype adverts did the ASA give in their report?
3. What stereotype does the second case study highlight? How do you think the media influenced this stereotype?
4. Write a newspaper article of about 200 words about the dangers of prejudice and stereotypes.

Research

Using the internet, create a brochure on the importance of using social media and information from the news media responsibly.

Key vocabulary
....

femininity
masculinity
macho

Religion, faith traditions and belief systems

We are learning to:

- describe the positive role that can be played by teachings from religion, faith traditions and belief systems.

Influence of religion, faith traditions and belief systems

Religious prejudice, or discrimination, is the treatment of a person or group of people differently because of the religion that they belong to, or what they believe in.

However, a central principle of most religions is that we should love fellow human beings unconditionally. Many religious teachings include:

- understanding that differences between social groups are often caused by differences in circumstances, instead of differences between the people themselves

- advocating **religious pluralism**, which is a teaching that many different religious belief systems can coexist in the same society and accept that different religions, with different beliefs, can be equally valid

- challenging ideologies that are prejudiced against any form of religion

- encouraging contact, friendship and cooperation between different religious groups; and creating opportunities to explore the experiences of other groups imaginatively.

This photo of three friends of different religions standing happily together shows that religious pluralism can exist in the same society.

Religion has also played an important role historically in movements to challenge prejudice and unjust social hierarchies. For example, Farid Esack is a South African Muslim teacher who challenged racism and inequality in South Africa at a time when **apartheid** (a system in South Africa where people were kept apart on racial grounds) was the political system.

Exercise

1. In your own words, explain the term religious prejudice.

2. Why do you think religious pluralism is important?

3. What is the central teaching of most religions that should influence how all people live?

Attitudes to prejudice >>>

The largest religious groups in the world – **Christianity, Hinduism, Islam** and **Judaism** – all share similar views about prejudice and discrimination.

Christianity >>>>

Christians believe that each person is unique and that human beings are the highest form of life. Christians teach that all people are equal in the eyes of God and should be treated fairly, with respect and without prejudice.

People of different nationalities and religions together.

Hinduism >>

Hindus believe that the aim of life is **moksha** (to be spiritually liberated) and that the path to achieving this is through religious effort, working selflessly for others and living a good life. Hindus are taught not to show prejudice against anyone, including any other Hindus who may have different beliefs, and that all people should be treated with respect.

Islam >>

The holy book of Islam is called the **Qur'an** and it teaches Muslims to value human life and to live a righteous life. Muslims are taught that all people should get along with each other, that they should respect each other as fellow human beings and treat others in the same way that they would expect to be treated. Muslims are also taught not to speak badly about other people, to deal fairly with other people and to not let hatred of others lead them to sin.

Key vocabulary

....

religious prejudice

religious pluralism

apartheid

Christianity

Hinduism

Islam

Judaism

moksha

Qur'an

dignity

values

Judaism >>>

Judaism teaches that humans are created in the image of God, and because humans share the same characteristics of God they share the same **dignity** and **values**. The Jewish community is taught that everyone is equal in the eyes of God and that everyone should be treated in the same way. Judaism sees prejudice and discrimination as fundamentally wrong.

Exercise

4. In your own words, outline how the four major religions view prejudice and discrimination. Use a mind map if it would help you.

Bullying, peer pressure and conflict resolution

We are learning to:

- define the terms bullying, peer pressure, courage and mentorship
- analyse the impact of bullying and peer pressure on the lives of individuals
- recognise the sources of influence in our own lives
- understand the importance of mentorship in relation to virtuous living.

Conflict is a serious disagreement or clash between two or more people. Conflicts arise from differences of opinions, views, ideas or needs. However, conflicts can trigger very strong feelings.

Behind every conflict are powerful needs – the need to feel safe, to feel respected, recognised or loved, or the need for closeness and connection. Some of the main conflicts at school are caused by **peer pressure** and **bullying**:

- Peer pressure is when your peers (people of the same age – your classmates) try to influence you to do something that you do not want to do.
- Bullying occurs when an individual or group tries to intimidate others through physical or verbal abuse.

The impact of bullying and peer pressure 》》

Bullying can have a number of negative effects on the person being bullied, including:

- mental health issues, such as increased anxiety, depression, sadness and loneliness
- physical effects, such as changes in sleeping or eating patterns, tiredness
- students missing school.

Effects of negative peer pressure include:

- spending time away from the family and the values that they have
- lack of interest in school or academic study
- change of behaviour, such as disobeying and taking no notice of their parents
- smoking, alcohol abuse, drug abuse and sexual activity.

Bullying is a serious problem for those who are victims of it.

Project

Create presentations about bullying, peer pressure, courage and mentorship in terms of virtuous living (using skits, PPTs, etc.). You will show these to younger classes.

Discussion

In groups, discuss the connection between bullying, peer pressure, courage and mentorship in terms of virtuous living.

Sources of influence >>>

.4

The sources of influence in young people's lives include:

- relationships with their parents and family
- peer groups, who can offer empathy and understanding, but also offer negative influences, such as drugs, alcohol and risky behaviour
- cultural influence – a shared culture can lead to shared experiences
- the media and social media.

Importance of mentorship in relation to virtuous living >>>

A **mentor** – someone who gives advice and help to another person over a period of time – can be invaluable in helping young people. Some of the advantages of mentoring include:

- having someone who cares about them and is available to help them deal with day-to-day challenges
- increasing a person's sense of identity
- helping to decrease social violence, build respect for others and understand the importance of education and virtuous living.

Good mentoring, along with **courage**, can help improve:

- performance at school
- communication skills
- attitude and behaviour.

Conflict resolution skills >>

The process of ending a conflict and finding a peaceful way forward is known as **conflict resolution**. There are many ways of achieving conflict resolution. The steps in the flow diagram show good strategies to use when dealing with conflict.

One way to resolve conflict is through **mediation**. A mediator is a person who is not involved in the conflict but who can help guide the two sides towards an understanding.

Exercise

1. In a reflective journal, write two paragraphs about bullying, peer pressure, courage and mentorship.

2. Create anti-bullying posters and pamphlets for use in your school and your community. They should show how to resolve conflict.

Be able to empathise with the other person's viewpoint

↓

Be calm, non-defensive and respectful

↓

Be ready to forgive and forget, and to move on without holding resentment or anger

↓

Be willing to seek compromise and avoid punishing the other person

↓

Believe that facing conflict head-on is the best thing for both sides

Activity

Create a role play focusing on bullying, peer pressure, courage and mentorship, and conflict resolution skills. Invent scenarios where bullying and peer pressure are taking place. Work through how those situations could be resolved with a positive outcome.

Key vocabulary

conflict

peer pressure

bullying

mentor

courage

conflict resolution

mediation

Questions

See how well you have understood the topics in this unit.

1. Match the key vocabulary word (i–vii) with its definition (a–g).

i) prejudice	**a)** having a one-sided thought or belief of how another person, or group of people, acts or behaves
ii) stereotypes	**b)** features relating to the culture of a society that have an historical importance to that society
iii) racism	**c)** when prejudice is shown against a member of one gender and they are not treated fairly or equally
iv) sexism	**d)** an idea about someone or something that is not based on facts, but on preconceived ideas only
v) ethics	**e)** when prejudice, or discrimination, is shown against an individual or group of people based on their race or ethnicity
vi) ethnicity	**f)** groups into which human beings can be divided according to their physical features, such as the colour of their skin
vii) race	**g)** rules for living in society and what we consider to be the right and wrong things to do

2. Using the internet, research and write a newspaper article about the dangers of prejudice and stereotyping. Discuss what the terms mean and the impact that prejudice and stereotyping can have on society, and give examples of prejudice and stereotyping that are seen in society today. Write about 300 words.

3. Complete these sentences:

a) Prejudice and stereotyping can put _____ on people as to how they should live their lives according to their ethnicity, sex or religion.

b) Prejudice and stereotyping can lead to low _____, emotional problems and _____.

c) Prejudice and stereotyping allows racism to grow in society, which creates _____.

d) Prejudice and stereotyping denies _____ for the victims of prejudice – for example, because of the colour of their skin or gender.

4. Write and role-play some situations involving prejudice and stereotypes.

5. Match the definitions of gender stereotypes with their type:

a) Women are shown as passive and submissive; men are shown as aggressive and dominant.

b) Women are portrayed as staying at home, cooking, doing the housework and child care; men earn the income.

c) Women are shown as having a traditionally female job such as a nurse, secretary or librarian; men have more physical jobs, such as construction, or higher-skilled jobs, such as doctors or lawyers.

d) Women are often shown as sexual objects and are defined by their perceived level of attractiveness; men are often shown as being macho (with a strong sense of masculinity).

occupations   appearance   behaviour at home   personality

6. In your own words, explain how religion teaches us that we should love fellow human beings unconditionally.

7. Match the religious view (i–iv) to the religion (a–d).

i) each person is unique and human beings are the highest form of life   **a)** Islam

ii) the aim of life is to be spiritually liberated and the path to achieving this is through religious effort   **b)** Christianity

iii) to value human life and to live a righteous life   **c)** Judaism

iv) everyone is equal in the eyes of God and should be treated in the same way   **d)** Hinduism

8. Complete the graphic organiser about how to deal with conflict.

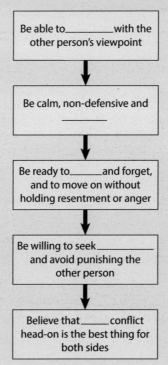

Be able to _____ with the other person's viewpoint

↓

Be calm, non-defensive and _____

↓

Be ready to _____ and forget, and to move on without holding resentment or anger

↓

Be willing to seek _____ and avoid punishing the other person

↓

Believe that _____ conflict head-on is the best thing for both sides

Checking your progress

To make good progress in understanding different aspects of ethics and relationships, check to make sure you understand these ideas.

Explain the terms ethics, prejudice and stereotype.

Understand the social impact of prejudice and stereotyping on society.

Discuss how ethics, prejudice and stereotypes can affect relationships.

Explore how the mass media portray prejudice and stereotyping.

Show how gender stereotyping is shown in the media.

Create a brochure on the importance of using social media and information from the news media responsibly.

Understand the term religious prejudice.

Explain the positive role that can be played by teachings from religion, faith traditions and belief systems.

Explain how the four major religions view prejudice and discrimination.

Understand the impact of bullying and peer pressure.

Understand the importance of mentorship in relation to virtuous living.

Explore how to resolve conflicts.

End-of-term questions

Questions 1–5 ⟫⟫

See how well you have understood the ideas in Unit 1.

1. Match the national icons with the contribution that they made.

i) Sir Errol Barrow	**a)** co-founder of the Barbados Dance Project
ii) Sir Lester Bird	**b)** 2003 World 100 m sprint champion
iii) Jeff Joseph	**c)** wrote *The Final Passage*
iv) Dr John Hunte	**d)** Prime Minister of Barbados following independence
v) Kim Collins	**e)** Prime Minister of Antigua and Barbuda
vi) Caryl Phillips	**f)** a pathologist
vii) Kathleen Coard	**g)** soca singer
viii) Toriano Edwards	**h)** Dominican musician

2. In your own words, explain the origins of musical subcultures in the Eastern Caribbean. Write 250 words.

3. Explain what conservation and preservation are and the role they have in creating a legacy for future generations. Write 150 words.

4. Identify some of the heritage areas in the Eastern Caribbean that are threatened by human activities. Name any flora and fauna that may be endangered in those areas.

5. Write a short essay of 150 words explaining how sustainable economic growth can help with preserving our heritage.

Questions 6–10 ⟫⟫

See how well you have understood the ideas in Unit 2.

6. Name four different ways in which we now live in a global world.

7. Name four opportunities that globalisation can offer the Eastern Caribbean.

8. Name some of the new types of technology that have helped with globalisation.

9. Look at the statements below and decide if they are positive or negative results of people using the internet.

   a) You can find a wide range of information and entertainment easily. _____

   b) There is information overload, resulting in anxiety and stress. _____

   c) It is time-consuming, which leads to a more sedentary lifestyle. _____

   d) It raises awareness of news and issues with a wider audience. _____

   e) It results in a decline in the publishing industry and in use of libraries. _____

f) Online shopping is easier, cheaper and faster. _____

g) Local culture and knowledge may be lost. _____

10. Match the key vocabulary word (i–viii) with its definition (a–h):

i) consumer

ii) distribution

iii) distribution chain

iv) producer

v) retailer

vi) services

vii) vendor

viii) wholesaler

a) the process of getting goods from producers to consumers

b) the person or factory that makes or grows products

c) a business that buys goods in bulk from a producer and then sells the goods to retailers

d) activities such as banking, hairdressing or tourism which are sold to consumers

e) the series of intermediaries who help to get goods from producers to customers

f) a person who uses goods and services

g) the person or the shop that buys goods in bulk from the wholesaler in order to sell the goods in smaller quantities to the consumer

h) a person or business that sells things

Questions 11–12 〉〉〉

See how well you have understood the ideas in Unit 3.

11. Write a short essay of about 150 words discussing the social impact of prejudice and stereotyping on society at national, regional and global levels. (Topic 3.1 will help you with this question.)

12. The media often displays four basic types of gender stereotyping. Match the type (i–iv) with the statement (a–d).

i) personality

ii) behaviour at home

iii) occupations

iv) appearance

a) Women are portrayed as staying at home, cooking, doing the housework and child care; men earn the income.

b) Women are often shown as sexual objects and are defined by their perceived level of attractiveness.

c) Women are shown as submissive and passive; men are shown as aggressive and dominant.

d) Women are shown as having a traditionally female job such as a nurse, secretary or librarian; men have more physical jobs, such as construction, or higher-skilled jobs like doctors or lawyers.

Unit 4: How we govern ourselves

In this unit you will find out

The electoral process in the Eastern Caribbean

- The electoral process, relevant terms and concepts
- The differences between government and politics
- Preparing for an election
- The factors influencing a political choice
- The process on Election Day
- The formation of a new government
- Free and fair elections and universal suffrage
- The importance of a free and fair election process
- The constitution and constitutional reform
- The significance of constitutional reform

Humanitarian law – consequences of war and conflict

- How war disrupts normal life
- How gangs affect local communities
- The action necessary to reduce or prevent the suffering caused by war
- The promotion of respect for human dignity
- Strategies for making a difference

Humanitarian law – the need for justice

- Justice and why it is needed
- Universal Declaration of Human Rights
- Ways in which justice can be served
- Who judges the accused
- The reasons for international tribunals
- The International Criminal Court
- The role and functions of the Caribbean Court of Justice

The electoral process in the Eastern Caribbean

We are learning to:

- define and use appropriately relevant terms and concepts: elector, electorate, candidate, independent candidate.

Governments of the Eastern Caribbean are **representative democracies,** which means that people are elected by voters to serve in the government.

Elections are held regularly to choose people who will serve in national and local government. People are chosen according to an electoral process, which is described in the constitution of the state.

Political rallies are a major part of elections.

Elector

An **elector** is a person who has the right to **vote** in an election. In order to have the right to vote, you have to be **eligible** and you must also be registered as a voter. In order to be eligible to vote, you must:

- be 18 years old
- be a citizen of the country you are voting in
- be a Commonwealth citizen who has lived in the country you want to vote in for at least one year
- have lived in your constituency (election district) for at least two months.

You need to have a **National Identification Card** in order to register as a voter.

> **Did you know...?**
>
> In the 2016 election in St Lucia, 161 883 individuals were registered to vote but only 86 475 (53%) actually voted.

Electorate

The **electorate** is all the people in the country who are eligible and registered to vote in an election. The electorate in Caribbean countries has increased over the years. For example, in St Lucia in 1982, three years after gaining total independence from Britain, 48 507 votes were counted, while in 2016, the most recent election year, 86 475 votes were counted.

Exercise

1. How old do you have to be in order to vote?

2. Do you have to be a citizen of the country you intend to vote in to be able to vote in elections?

3. What was the size of the electorate in St Lucia in 1982? How does this compare to the size of the electorate for the most recent election?

Candidates ▶▶▶

A **candidate** in an election is a person who seeks to be nominated or elected to a position in the national or local government.

If the candidate gets enough **votes** and is elected, he or she **represents** the people who have voted. This is a principle of **democratic government**.

Candidates in elections in St Lucia have to:

- be aged 21 years or older
- have been born in St Lucia or have lived in the country for 12 months immediately before nomination
- be able to speak English, to allow them to take part in the proceedings in the House
- be **nominated** by at least six registered electors in the country
- be registered with an established political party or stand as an independent
- register and pay a deposit before they can start their campaigns to win **supporters** who will vote for them.

Candidates can be members of political parties or they can be **independent candidates**. You have to be 18 years old to be eligible to vote in most democratic countries around the world. Some countries, for example Brazil, Argentina, Cuba and Austria allow citizens to vote from the age of 16.

The red mark on the finger shows that these people have voted in the election. This is to prevent people having more than one vote.

Discussion

Why is it important to get a National Identification Card? Why do you think that registered voters do not always cast their votes in an election? Discuss these questions in class.

Exercise

4. What is the difference between a candidate and an elector?

5. In one sentence, describe what is meant by 'the electorate'.

6. Would you be allowed to nominate a candidate for your government? Give a reason for your answer.

7. Are you, or members of your family, eligible to vote? Why/why not?

8. Who is the Prime Minister of St Lucia now, and which political party do they lead?

9. How many members of this party are in the House of Representatives?

Research

You are going to create a portfolio in your notebook about the electoral process. Go to www.caribbeanelections.com, use the 'Country Browser', find your country, click 'Education'. Find the section on elections and research the rules for people who want to be nominated as a candidate in an election in your country.

Key vocabulary

representative democracy

election

elector

vote

eligible

National Identification Card

electorate

candidate

votes

represents

democratic government

nominated

supporters

independent candidate

Constituents and constituencies

We are learning to:

- define and use appropriately relevant terms and concepts: constituency, constituent, campaign, manifesto.

Constituents and constituencies ⟩⟩

Eastern Caribbean countries are divided into a number of areas known as **constituencies**. The people who live in this area, the **constituents**, vote for who they want to represent them in local and national elections.

The person who receives the majority of votes from that area is the winner. He or she then represents that constituency at local or national level in government.

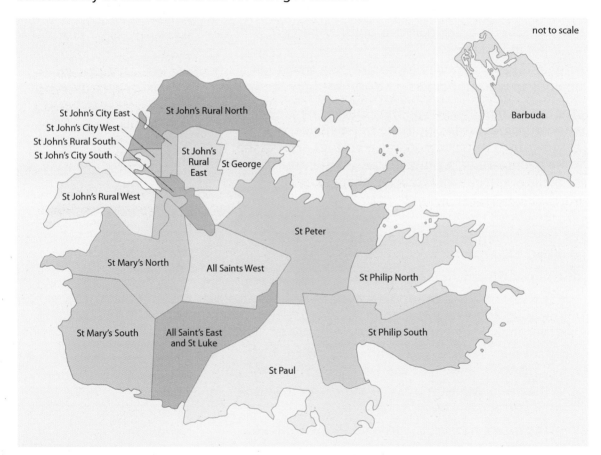

There are 17 constituencies in Antigua and Barbuda (data taken from 2014).

Discussion

What ideas would you like your elected representatives to include in their manifestos? Think about issues that affect your life or the lives of your families and friends. Make a list of five ideas.

Antigua and Barbuda is divided up into 17 constituencies. Each constituency elects one Member of Parliament (MP) to sit in the House of Representatives, which is part of the national government.

For example, St John's Rural North is a constituency in the north and St Mary's South is a constituency in the south of Antigua. In 2014, Barbuda was a single constituency.

Campaign

A **campaign** is a series of events that are organised to help a candidate get elected. During a campaign, candidates try to convince voters about why they should get their votes.

Candidates present their ideas about matters that concern the people of the constituency and the country as a whole. They use the media as well as personal appearances to get their messages across to voters.

Manifesto

All candidates put together a **manifesto** before they begin their campaigns. A manifesto states publicly what the candidate's views are on certain issues and explains the policies they support or will introduce if they are elected. The manifesto will reflect the policies of the political party that the candidate represents. Manifestos are very important to the electoral process in all countries.

Did you know...?

You can also make a personal manifesto in which you publicly declare what you would like to achieve. Here are some things that people have written in personal manifestos:

- Live up to my potential!
- See the world!
- Work out regularly.

Exercise

1. In your own words define the terms constituency, constituent, campaign and manifesto.

2. How many constituencies are there in Antigua and Barbuda? Name five of them.

3. Who do constituents vote for?

4. Name five types of campaign activity that a candidate could engage in while running for election to national or local government.

5. Explain what you would expect to see in a manifesto.

6. Find out the name of the constituency in which you live.

7. Choose five constituencies in your country. Find out who has been elected to represent these constituencies in national government as an MP. Find out which political party each MP belongs to. To help you get this information, you can log onto the www.caribbeanelections.com website. Add the information you have found to your portfolio.

Research

Work in pairs and find out the meaning of the expression 'to be on the campaign trail'. Find examples of what happens on the campaign trail, then report back to the class with your ideas.

Key vocabulary

constituency

constituent

campaign

manifesto

Nomination Day

We are learning to:

• define and use appropriately relevant terms and concepts: franchise, adult suffrage, nomination, Nomination Day.

Franchise ❯❯

To have the **franchise** means to have the right to vote. People who have the right to vote are enfranchised. In most modern democracies all adult citizens are enfranchised.

In Dominica, a limited franchise existed before 1951. To qualify, individuals had to earn over $30 annual income and male labourers receiving one shilling (12 pence) a day did not qualify. In 1951 full adult suffrage was introduced.

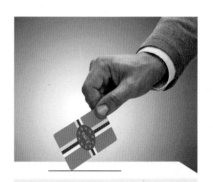

Adult suffrage ❯❯❯

Adult suffrage is the right that adults (people over a certain age) have to vote in political elections. Until the 1920s adult suffrage was a privilege that was reserved for some people only. In most countries, only wealthy men were allowed to vote. People who did not own land, and women, were not enfranchised.

Today suffrage is seen as a right, and most democracies allow all adult citizens over the age of 18 to vote. Adult suffrage was granted to all the British colonies in the Caribbean in the 1940s and 1950s. St Lucia and Antigua were granted adult suffrage in 1951 along with Dominica.

In 1951, all adults in Dominica were able to vote in national elections for the first time. Finally, all citizens of the country had a real say in choosing their own government. Previously excluded adults, such as labourers and farm workers, were able to vote for the first time. This encouraged people to take an active interest in their own country and how it was governed.

In 1951, all adults in Dominica were able to vote in national elections for the first time.

Discussion

Why should electors nominate candidates? Why should candidates have to pay a deposit in order to be officially declared a candidate? Discuss these questions with your teacher.

Exercise

1. Explain in your own words what the terms franchise and adult suffrage mean.

2. Make this statement accurate: all adults in Dominica have been enfranchised since the 1920s.

3. How did voting change in the 1940s and 1950s in the Caribbean?

Did you know...?

In the nineteenth and twentieth centuries in the UK, women known as suffragettes fought for their right to vote in elections.

Before they can stand for election, all candidates who represent political parties, as well as independent candidates, have to gain formal **nomination** as candidates.

Nomination means that candidates have to follow a certain procedure in order to be able to stand for election. These procedures take place on **Nomination Day**.

Read the following newspaper article about Nomination Day in a recent general election.

Case study

Today is Nomination Day in Dominica

The process begins at 9 a.m. and ends at 4 p.m. Each candidate must make a statutory declaration that indicates that they are a person who is properly qualified to be nominated as a candidate in Dominica. Anyone who wishes to stand for election must be nominated on an official nomination paper.

Candidates are expected to present themselves to returning officers in their respective constituencies and should be recommended by six electors from their constituencies in order to be nominated. Candidates can stand either for an established political party or as an independent.

Additionally, each candidate is expected to make a deposit of $500, which at the end of the day is deposited into the treasury. Candidates lose their deposit if they do not secure a specified number of votes in the election.

When all the documents are in order, the information is then sent to the Electoral Office, where the process of printing the ballot papers with the names of those who have been properly nominated takes place.

Questions

1. List three things that you have to do if you wish to become a candidate in an election in Dominica.
2. To whom do candidates have to apply for nomination?
3. What does the Electoral Office do?
4. Who can nominate a candidate?
5. What happens to the nomination fees collected?
6. What happens to the candidate's fee if they do not get a reasonable number of votes?
7. What effect do you think the granting of adult suffrage has had on the people of the Caribbean?

Research

Go to www.caribbeanelections.com, use 'Country Browser', find your country, click 'Education'. Find the section on elections to find out more about Nomination Day and how nominations work in your country. Add the information you have found to your portfolio.

In the UK, suffragettes were women who fought for the right to vote.

Key vocabulary

franchise

adult suffrage

nomination

Nomination Day

Ballots

We are learning to:

- define and use appropriately relevant terms and concepts: ballot, ballot box, secret ballot.

Ballots

A **ballot** is a vote or a piece of paper on which a person records his or her vote. When people talk about winning 'the ballot', they mean the total number of votes cast in an election.

Ballot paper

A **ballot paper** on which you cast your vote has the names of the candidates and the political parties with which they are associated.

In some countries there are also photographs of the candidates on the ballot papers. In order to cast your vote, you make a cross next to the name of the person for whom you are voting.

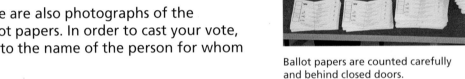

Ballot papers are counted carefully and behind closed doors.

The candidate

The candidate in an election is the person who seeks to be nominated or elected to a position in the national or local government. Voters have to decide who they are going to vote for. Their choice may depend on a number of factors, such as:

- what party the candidate belongs to
- if they are currently in national or local government, and are doing a good job
- whether they agree with the candidate's policies, for example their economic, education and health policies
- whether they have the necessary qualities to be a leader, for example are they honest or a good communicator?
- does the voter like the candidate?

Ballot boxes are sealed so that people cannot tamper with them.

Discussion

In groups, discuss the reasons why you would vote for someone in an election. Make a list and then share them in a class discussion.

Exercise

1. Define the terms ballot and ballot box.
2. What would you expect to see on a ballot paper?
3. What do you do with a ballot paper?
4. What does it mean if a candidate wins the ballot?

Ballot box

Once you have chosen the candidate for whom you wish to vote, you place your ballot in a **ballot box**.

A ballot box is a special box which is sealed so that people cannot tamper with it. Voters put their ballot papers in the ballot box. The box is only opened when the votes are counted.

Secret ballot

When you vote or cast your ballot in an election, you do so in secret. You do not have to tell anyone who you have voted for and nobody should watch you while you make your cross on the ballot form.

Eastern Caribbean constitutions state that voting in elections has to be by means of a **secret ballot**.

Secret ballots allow people to vote anonymously and freely. This helps to make sure that you have a real choice when you vote, as it stops other people from intimidating or bribing you to vote for someone else. This helps to prevent electoral fraud.

Show of hands

Another way of voting is by means of a show of hands. This method is sometimes used in schools or clubs. People are asked to raise their hands to vote for a person or to agree with a proposal.

This method is not secret, as everyone can see how you vote. It is not appropriate in general elections, as it would be difficult to check votes afterwards and it could also lead to corruption and voter intimidation.

Voting in elections in the Eastern Caribbean has to be by means of secret ballot.

> ### Did you know...?
>
> The word ballot comes from an Italian word *ballotta*, which means 'a small ball'. It refers to an old system of voting in which people cast their ballots by placing small coloured balls in a container.

Exercise

5. Write a sentence explaining what a secret ballot is.
6. Why does a ballot box have to be sealed?
7. What are the advantages of a ballot by show of hands? Are there any disadvantages?
8. Which of the following are advantages/disadvantages of a secret ballot?
   a) You can vote for whom you choose without fear of intimidation.
   b) It makes it difficult to bribe people to vote for a certain candidate, because you cannot be sure who they will really vote for.
   c) Some people may be anxious about having to complete the process by themselves.
   d) You don't have to tell others who you have voted for.

Key vocabulary

ballot

ballot paper

ballot box

secret ballot

Voting systems

We are learning to:

- define and use appropriately relevant terms and concepts: floating voters, first-past-the-post system, Election Day, hung parliament.

Floating voters

Some voters always support one political party, while others are sometimes unsure who to vote for. These voters are called **floating voters** in an election. Floating voters can affect the outcome of an election, because political parties cannot guess who they are going to vote for. Their votes can also help to decide an election that is closely contested.

First-past-the-post system

There are two types of electoral system: the **first-past-the-post system (FPPS)**, and the **proportional representation (PR)** system. The difference between the two relates to how votes are counted and the way candidates win elections.

The first-past-the-post system is used to elect Members to the House of Representatives in the Eastern Caribbean. In this system, one candidate is elected for each constituency. The candidate who wins is the candidate who gets the most votes in that constituency. In some systems, candidates have to win a **majority** of the votes – in other words, more than 50% of the votes. The winning candidate becomes the constituency representative in the House of Representatives, and wins a seat in Parliament.

The party that wins the majority of seats in Parliament wins the overall election and therefore forms the government. The Prime Minister is selected from the winning party and the leader of the opposition is selected from the party with the second-highest number of seats.

Proportional representation

In some countries, like Guyana, candidates are elected through a system of proportional representation (PR). In a PR electoral system, voters vote for a political party. Each party draws up a list of candidates for an election. The number of candidates elected from each party is directly proportional to how many votes were cast for that party.

Floating voters can be influenced by party political advertising.

Research

Work in groups. Find out:

- on which date the last general election was held in St Kitts and Nevis
- which political parties contested the election
- which political party won the election
- the names of five candidates who were elected to serve in the House of Representatives.

Election Day ▶

Candidates who are elected to serve in the House of Representatives serve for four to five years at a time. This means that new elections have to be held at least every four to five years.

The Prime Minister, Premier, President or Chief Minister can call for elections before the five years have been completed. This sometimes happens when one party does not have a clear majority or when there are important issues that need to be resolved.

A country may have an Electoral Department, Electoral Office or Elections and Boundaries Commission, which along with the government will notify voters when elections will occur. On that day, **Election Day**, people cast their votes. The votes are counted and the results are usually announced the following day, as counting the votes can take a long time.

Hung parliament ▶▶

A **hung parliament** is when no party has gained the overall majority of seats in Parliament to take control and to form a government. When this situation occurs, two (or more) parties may join forces to create a government. Alternatively, the election may be held again.

Activity

You have been asked by your local newspaper to write an article explaining the terms first-past-the-post system and proportional representation for Form 3 students. Write about 100 words.

Exercise

1. Go to www.caribbeanelections.com and under 'Education' select 'Democratic Electoral Systems' to find out the electoral systems used in the following Eastern Caribbean countries: Anguilla, Antigua and Barbuda, Barbados, Dominica, Grand Cayman, Grenada, Guyana, Montserrat, St Kitts and Nevis, St Lucia, St Vincent and the Grenadines.

   What do you notice about these countries' electoral systems? Add the information you have found to your portfolio.

2. In your own words, define floating voter.

3. What is Election Day?

4. Explain the term hung parliament.

5. In your own words, compile a glossary of terms used so far in Units 4.1–4.5. Write at least 15 definitions.

Key vocabulary

floating voters

first-past-the-post-system (FPPS)

proportional representaion (PR)

majority

Election Day

hung parliament

Preparing for an election

We are learning to:

- understand the differences between government and politics
- outline the steps in preparing for an election in the Eastern Caribbean
- discuss the factors influencing a political choice.

Differences between politics and government

It is important to understand the differences between politics and government. Politics refers to the beliefs or theories people hold about the way a country should be run, while government is the body, or institution, that runs the country. This is why we have different political parties, which have different ideas as to how a country should be run.

Politicians often address citizens publicly to gather support and promote their party's manifesto.

Steps in preparation for an election

There are a number of legal steps involved in setting up a national election before polling day in the Eastern Caribbean:

- The government announces the intention to hold an election and Parliament is dissolved.
- Electoral registration – the electorate (voters/electors) check that they are registered to vote.
- The dates for Nomination Day and the election are set.
- Political parties nominate their candidates on Nomination Day. Candidates have to be nominated by at least six people.
- Venues for polling stations are identified. The buildings must be safe, a public or community-owned building with facilities for the disabled and elderly voters, and located within the electoral district.
- A notice about the polling stations is published in a newspaper, detailing the date of the election, hours when the polling station is open, its address and station number, and information about the candidates.
- Poll cards are sent out. These contain the details of the elector, date of the election and location of the elector's polling station.

Following Nomination Day, the candidates and parties begin their campaign. First they decide their policies and publish their manifesto. The campaign that follows typically has public meetings and rallies, **house-to-house canvassing** and **opinion polls**.

Activity

In groups, imagine that you are a youth officer with a political party. Brainstorm a five-minute speech in which you aim to encourage people to vote for your party. Outline your manifesto and say why people should vote for you. Then one member of your group presents your speech to the rest of the class.

Factors influencing a political choice >>>

In the Caribbean, all citizens aged 18 and over can vote in a national election. There are many different factors that determine the party or candidate a voter may choose to vote for:

- Gender – men and women sometimes vote differently based on certain issues, as particular things will be more important to men or women. A party's manifesto may contain promises that appeal particularly to men, or more to women.

- Race/culture – voters from a particular ethnic group may choose to vote for a candidate from the same ethnic group; in countries that are dominated by one ethnic group, the party that has the support of that group often wins the election.

- Religion – some religious denominations do not allow people to vote in elections, but when they do they often vote for a candidate or political party that shares their religious views.

- Emotions – people may be biased by responding emotionally to a particular candidate's or party's campaign. They may not like the other candidates, not agree with a political party's view or feel unhappy with the performance of the government.

- Family – family members often vote for the same party that their family has voted for across several generations, as they often share the same value systems and outlook on life.

- Political socialisation – political parties attract loyal followers, who will always vote for a particular party.

- Tolerance of different political views to your own.

- The media have a responsibility to give accurate, balanced and unbiased coverage of an election, allowing all parties equal access to advertising opportunities. However, newspapers, television and radio can influence public opinion. Sometimes they can present a biased view of a certain political party, either in a positive or negative way, and in some countries governments own particular media outlets.

Voting booths are separated at polling stations.

Activity

Write a paragraph to describe why someone might change their mind about which political party to vote for.

Discussion

As a class, your teacher will lead a discussion on why people give support to different political parties.

Exercise

1. Draw a flow diagram that outlines the steps in preparation for an election.

2. Why do you think people from the same ethnic and/or religious groups often vote for the same party?

Key vocabulary

house-to-house canvassing

opinion polls

The process on Election Day

We are learning to:

- explain the process to be followed on Election Day.

Before Election Day

It is important before polling day that voters do the following:

- make sure that they have registered to vote – if they are not registered they cannot vote
- make sure that they know where their polling station is – voters are usually given these details
- make sure that they know what time the polling station opens and the time it closes – voters have to be in the queue to vote before closing time to be allowed to vote
- make sure that they take something with them to prove their identity (for example some countries have a National Identification Card), otherwise they will not be able to vote.

The police are often at polling stations to make sure voting is fair and peaceful.

The process on Election Day

Polling stations open at different times in different countries, for example in Barbados it is from 6 a.m. to 6 p.m. and in Dominica the times are 7 a.m. to 5 p.m. Voters are allowed to go and cast their vote at any time during those hours. If a voter is still queuing to get in the polling station at the final hour they are allowed to vote, but no one who joins the queue after this time is allowed to vote.

The voting process: Barbados

- The presiding officer shows those at the polling station the empty ballot boxes to prove they are empty, before sealing and locking the boxes.
- Voters are directed to provide their name to the presiding officer or polling clerk who checks their name against the **voter list** (or register).

Exercise

1. Does Election Day occur before or after Nomination Day?
2. Between what times are you allowed to vote?
3. What should you bring with you to the polling station?

- The voter is given an official ballot paper which is marked by an official mark to show it is genuine.
- The voter enters a private voting booth. The ballot lists the candidates in alphabetical order. An X is placed next to the candidate selected and the ballot paper folded and put into the ballot box.
- Ballot boxes are taken to a central place in the constituency where each ballot is counted in the presence of the candidates.
- When all the votes are counted the results are announced by the Returning Officer.

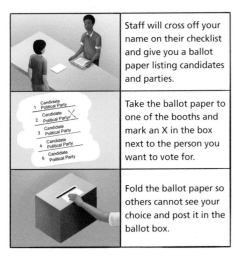

Staff will cross off your name on their checklist and give you a ballot paper listing candidates and parties.

Take the ballot paper to one of the booths and mark an X in the box next to the person you want to vote for.

Fold the ballot paper so others cannot see your choice and post it in the ballot box.

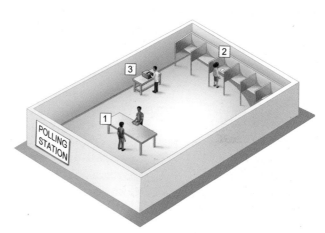

The illustrations above show what happens once you are inside the polling station.

The voters are supervised by a number of staff at the polling station:

- the presiding officer – responsible for the running of the polling station
- poll clerks – who are responsible for managing the queue, asking the elector for his or her ID card, checking the documents to determine that the elector is entitled to vote and ticking off the elector's name to say they have voted
- officers in charge of the ballot box
- information officer(s) (where considered necessary) – who help to give general information to the electors and answer questions.

Project

In groups, role-play the steps involved in a general election. Include the selection of candidates, the campaign, the casting of ballots, the declaration of a winner and the victory and losing speeches.

Exercise

4. What are the roles of the presiding officer and poll clerks on Election Day?
5. Draw a flow diagram that outlines what happens on Election Day.

Key vocabulary

polling stations

voters list

A new government

We are learning to:

- discuss the activities following an election in the formation of a new government.

Formation of a new government

Following the declaration of the result of the general election, the party with the largest proportion of the vote begins the process of forming a new government.

The member who commands the majority in the **House of Representatives** becomes the Prime Minister. Candidates who get the most votes in a constituency become members of the House of Representatives.

It is the Prime Minister's role, in their capacity as head of government, to appoint ministers and junior ministers to the **Cabinet**. If they feel it is necessary, they restructure the ministries that they may have in their government.

Parliament Building, Bridgetown, Barbados.

The Opposition

The Opposition to the government is led by the largest party that did not form the government after a general election.

The role of the Opposition is to hold the government to account for the decisions that it makes and to scrutinise their policies.

Appointment of Senators: Dominica

Dominica's House of Assembly is **unicameral**. **Senators** and constituency representatives make up one house of parliament. Senators are appointed by the **President**, five on the advice of the **Prime Minister** and four on the advice of the Leader of the Opposition.

The President is elected by members of the **House of Assembly**.

Activity

Use the internet to research the current Senate in your country. Do the senators have expertise in particular areas? How do you think having appointed members of government and elected members benefits your country?

Exercise

1. Write a short paragraph describing how a new government and Opposition are formed after a general election.

2. After a general election, who appoints the new Cabinet?

3. What is the role of the Opposition?

4. Explain how senators are selected in Dominica.

People who are elected to national and local government in a democracy have a responsibility to carry out the duties and services for which they have been elected.

The citizens who have elected these representatives also have a responsibility to make sure that these representatives do their jobs correctly.

There are several ways in which citizens can be involved.

- When Parliament is discussing new proposed bills, which may later become laws, members of the public are invited to comment and to give their views.
- Government representatives also hold meetings from time to time, which citizens can attend.
- There are websites from which citizens can get information freely and through which they can contact government representatives.

If government officials do not do their work in a satisfactory manner, there are ways of removing these officials from their jobs:

- Elected officials will not be re-elected if they have not performed well.
- Officials who are found to be corrupt can be removed from office.

All government officials, including the Prime Minister, are subject to the laws of the country, like any other citizen.

Grenadian Prime Minister Keith Mitchell.

Exercise

5. Name two ways in which citizens can scrutinise the role of the government.
6. How can government officials be removed from office if they are not doing their job satisfactorily?
7. Do you think the Prime Minister can be removed from office? How and why?
8. Research, compare and contrast the roles of:
   a) The Governor General (St Lucia, Antigua and Barbuda)
   b) The Prime Minister and Opposition Leader (St Kitts and Nevis, Barbados)
   c) The President (Guyana, Dominica)

Key vocabulary

House of Representatives

Cabinet

unicameral

senator

President

Prime Minister

House of Assembly

Free and fair elections

We are learning to:

- define and explain relevant terms and concepts: free and fair elections, universal suffrage
- recognise the importance of a free and fair election process.

Universal suffrage in Guyana 》

Universal suffrage is the term used to show that all competent adult persons in a country have a right to vote. The right to vote is not restricted by race, sex, belief, wealth or social status.

Guyana was under **Crown Colony** rule from the British. This system had a Governor and a Legislative Council. The Council was made up of people nominated by the Governor. Under this system, citizens did not have the right to vote.

In 1928, a **limited franchise** was introduced. This is a system where not all the population was allowed to take part – in Guyana 14 members of the legislative council were elected, but 16 others were appointed. Women and people who did not own land could not vote. Limited educational prospects also meant that rules regarding reading and writing English further limited the franchise.

A strong trade union movement developed after civil disturbances in 1920 and 1921, and the outcome of the 1938 Moyne Commission report resulted in full adult suffrage.

In 1953 Guyana held its first general elections under adult suffrage. In 1966 Guyana became independent and became a republic in 1970.

Universal suffrage was the result of protests and agitation of common people against unfair treatment.

Research

Using the internet, research situations around the world where elections have not been free or fair. For example, you could research occasions in the past when people have been excluded from voting or other countries around the world that are not democracies. You could use the search phrase 'unfair elections in history'. Write an essay of 200 words outlining your findings. Add any consequences for countries that have not had fair elections.

Exercise

1. In your own words, define the term universal suffrage.

2. How were officials selected under Crown Colony government?

3. What were the terms of the limited franchise in Guyana in 1928? Were these terms good for the nation's citizens?

4. What factors resulted in adult suffrage in Guyana?

Free and fair elements ▶▶▶

An election should adhere to the principles of universal adult suffrage and has to be **free and fair**.

A free and fair election occurs when the parties taking part in the election do not try to persuade citizens to cast their votes in their favour by using force or intimidation. It should also ensure that the counting of the votes is accurate and not open to abuse.

Elections, at both national and local level, also require the following conditions to make them free and fair:

- universal suffrage for all eligible men and women
- freedom to register as a voter or as a candidate
- freedom of speech for candidates, their parties and the freedom to hold political rallies and campaigns
- polling stations accessible to everyone and supplying a private space for people to cast their vote.

Registering to vote.

Importance of free and fair elections ▶▶▶▶

It is in the interests of all political parties to make sure that general elections are **transparent**:

- to avoid voters being persecuted or prevented from voting, by threats of violence or attacks on polling stations
- to avoid voters being intimidated or bribed to vote for a candidate or a party
- to avoid voters being excluded from voting based on race, sex, beliefs, wealth or social status
- to ensure that the counting of votes is transparent and independent and not tampered with
- to ensure that ballot papers are not deliberately miscounted, lost or destroyed.

Exercise

5. List four conditions that make an election free and fair.

6. List four scenarios that would make an election unfair.

7. Do you think it is fair that people should be excluded from voting because of their race, sex, beliefs, wealth or social status? Explain why/why not.

8. Write a paragraph explaining why an election should be free and fair. Write about 50 words.

Discussion

In groups, discuss this statement: 'Elections should be free, fair and free from fear.' Do you agree with this? Discuss as a group, then outline your conclusions to the rest of the class.

Did you know...?

Article 21 of The Universal Declaration of Human Rights states that 'everyone has the right to take part in government'.

Key vocabulary

universal suffrage

Crown Colony

limited franchise

free and fair

transparent

The constitution

We are learning to:

- define and explain relevant terms and concepts: constitution, constitutional reform
- discuss the significance of constitutional reform.

Constitutional reform

The **constitution** is a written document that sets out the laws by which a country is governed. It outlines:

- the structure and powers of government
- the rights and responsibilities of its citizens
- how governments are chosen
- the role of the civil service.

Constitutional reform is the process of changing or renewing the constitution. Reform usually comes about when a law, or an aspect of the law, is unfair to the country's citizens, or if the concerns of the country's citizens are not being fairly heard.

The coat of arms of St Lucia.

There has been a long history of constitutional reform in the Eastern Caribbean which is still ongoing today. As colonial powers captured, lost and used treaties to manage the region's resources, constitutions changed. The abolition of slavery meant that new laws regarding labour had to be written.

In the nineteenth and early twentieth century, changes to constitutions across the Eastern Caribbean were focused again on labour, but more specifically on the relationship between adult suffrage and working conditions. During this time, trade unionism became a powerful force in Eastern Caribbean politics and party politics emerged.

Post-British rule, some territories became republics and further changes were required to encourage regional integration, such as the West Indies Federation and CARICOM.

Exercise

1. In your own words, define the terms constitution and constitutional reform.

2. Why has constitutional reform been an ongoing issue in the Eastern Caribbean?

Research

Research the constitution of your country. If you had the power to change the constitution, what would you change? Write no more than 250 words.

Independence and reform ▶▶▶

When Eastern Caribbean territories gained independence from Britain, the British constitution was adopted. The day-to-day running of the country was more secure in the hands of its citizens. However, it became evident that the new economic, social and cultural issues that each country faced would need to be addressed.

Some countries such as Guyana, Trinidad and Tobago and Dominica turned to republicanism, which meant that their constitutions were no longer tied to that of Britain.

A statue of Sir Vere Cornwall Bird, father of Antigua's independence.

This increased constitutional freedom and allowed these countries to reshape their parliaments and affairs to better suit their needs, in more large-scale ways. Other territories continued to use the British constitution as a base and made small changes over time to reflect their needs.

Constitutional reform is a change to the fundamental laws of a country and therefore changes are debated in Parliament and are subject to party politics.

The significance of constitutional reform ▶▶▶

Constitutional reform is important because it helps people have a greater say in how the country is run, giving them the opportunity to participate in forming the foundational laws of their country. This is significant, as it brings together the collective energy and expertise of different groups and organisations, which the government is likely to respect more than an individual organisation. A common voice on issues adds strength to the advocacy position.

It is also important for the country because it can move away from laws made under the British constitution that are not necessarily applicable to the modern-day needs of every a country.

Discussion

In groups, discuss how constitutional reform can be used by political parties to promote a particular political idea. For example, how can constitutional reform promote stricter rules for businesses or reduced rights for some individuals?

Exercise

3. Which constitution was adopted by Eastern Caribbean territories after independence?

4. Why has the constitution needed to change and be updated?

5. In your own words, explain why constitutional reform is needed in your country. Write 50 words.

Key vocabulary

constitution

constitutional reform

Humanitarian law

We are learning to:

• describe how war disrupts normal life.

The consequences of war 》》

War disrupts the lives of ordinary people and causes terrible suffering and hardship. Some **conflicts** are short and quickly resolved, while others drag on for years and are challenging to resolve. It is difficult to remain neutral and impartial when discussing these conflicts.

Case study

Israeli–Palestinian question

The Israeli–Palestinian conflict is a struggle between the Israeli and Palestinian peoples that has been going on since the end of World War II. The struggle has its origins in events that took place before that.

Because their home was destroyed by bombs, this family has to live among the rubble and under a tent.

Despite many attempts to resolve this conflict, it continues today. The conflict has caused widespread suffering among the people who live in the Middle East. Families have been split up, thousands of people have died and been injured, and thousands have lost their homes. There are constant attacks on both sides.

The struggle is about the rights of the Jewish and Arab people who live in the area and their rights to sovereignty and land.

At the end of World War II, Jewish people were given land in part of Palestine. This created the state of Israel on this land. Many of the Arabs who lived in Palestine had to move.

The main areas that are contested are the areas of Gaza and the West Bank. The Israelis do not want to allow the Palestinians to have their own state, and the Palestinians do not recognise Israel as a legitimate state.

Discussion

Discuss the Israeli–Palestinian conflict with your teacher. Think about this question: what do you think you would feel if you were an ordinary Palestinian or Israeli citizen?

Questions

1. Which areas do the Israelis and Palestinians contest?

2. What do the Palestinians want?

3. What do the Israelis want?

4. When did the main conflict begin?

5. How has the conflict affected people's daily lives?

Jamaat al Muslimeen is an organisation that operates in Trinidad and Tobago. In 1990, they attacked the Red House in Port of Spain in an attempt to overthrow the government. They claimed that the government had oppressed them. They stormed the television and radio stations as well as the Red House, where Parliament meets.

For six days they held the Prime Minister (A.N.R. Robinson) and some members of his Cabinet hostage. When the Prime Minister ordered the army to attack them, he himself was beaten and shot. A state of emergency was declared.

The attack lasted six days, and there was looting and chaos in Port of Spain during this time. The members of the Muslimeen group finally surrendered when they were offered **amnesty**. They were taken into custody and tried. However, the Supreme Court ordered them to be released, as they had been promised amnesty.

This attempted **coup d'état** had several consequences:

- More than 20 people died during the unrest.
- Hundreds of people were injured and taken to hospital.
- There was widespread looting and arson in Port of Spain.
- Millions of dollars' worth of damage was done to properties in Port of Spain.
- The people of Trinidad and Tobago were shocked by the events.
- A commission of enquiry was set up 20 years later in an attempt to work out what had happened.
- Properties belonging to Jamaat al Muslimeen were taken away to compensate for the damage done during the unrest.

Research

Using the internet, research places that have experienced war and conflict, and their effect on ordinary people, for example the recent Syrian conflict or the Israeli–Palestinian conflict. Write a short report of about 250 words and use photos to illustrate your report.

Exercise

1. Why did Jamaat al Muslimeen attempt a coup d'état?
2. How did they break the law?
3. Were they punished for breaking the law?
4. Was this an example of justice?
5. What effect did this attack have on different communities?
6. How did ordinary people feel about the attack?
7. How did the attack affect Trinidad's democratic way of life?

Key vocabulary

conflict

amnesty

coup d'état

How gangs affect local communities

We are learning to:

• describe how war disrupts normal life: gangs.

How gangs affect local communities ❯❯

A **gang** is an organised group of criminals. People join gangs because they are seen as a way of making money and becoming powerful.

Gangs are involved in all sorts of crimes, from murder and robbery to internet scams that cheat people out of their money. Gang wars in the Caribbean, and in particular Trinidad and Jamaica, have a damaging and devastating impact on their surrounding areas and people's normal life.

A number of factors lead youths to crime, such as poverty, unemployment, abuse at home and lack of education.

Gang life can appeal to vulnerable youths because of promises of money, drugs and weapons.

Vulnerable youths are lured into gang life first by the promise of money, drugs and weapons. If they refuse, threats are made against them until they join the gang. Once in the gang – with money in their pocket and possibly armed with a gun – they then feel **empowered**, perhaps something they have never felt before.

What solutions could help to prevent Caribbean youth from falling into gang culture?

• Education: ensure that the curriculum gives the opportunity to leave school with qualifications.
• Employment: the government provides opportunities for training, career advice, finance for start-up businesses.
• Money: investment by governments into solving social problems.

Exercise

1. Are gangs a problem in your area? What do gangs do?

2. Why are some people tempted into joining gangs?

3. What possible solutions are there to prevent people from forming and joining gangs? Use the internet to research your suggestions further.

Discussion

Your teacher will lead a class discussion about the effects of gangs in the local community. Discuss ways to prevent young people from engaging in gang activities.

Case study

Gang 'war zones'

Some areas in Trinidad and Tobago have been declared 'war zones', as citizens become fearful to visit those areas as part of their normal everyday lives. Here are some examples:

2005: Fear and tension shroud the once-peaceful village of Spring View, Petit Valley. The few residents who spoke with the media yesterday said they were scared, following the declaration of an all-out gang war.

Their fear follows Sunday's shooting dead of Jamaat al Muslimeen member and reputed gang leader Glenroy 'Malick' Charles. Vows to avenge Charles' death were made openly on Sunday morning by several residents said to be his associates, in the presence of policemen and soldiers.

Less than three hours later, 26-year-old Marlon 'Tall Paul' Scott was gunned down in front of his mother at Powder Magazine, Cocorite. Charles' murder has left residents afraid to go out, even to the shops. Threats by angry gang members on Sunday are not being taken lightly.

By evening that day, a self-imposed curfew had taken effect, except for those whose jobs demanded late hours. Villagers were indoors well before 5 p.m. The only sign that residents were in their homes yesterday were opened windows.

2013: A series of **arson** attacks in Laventille by gangs left dozens of residents without a home. One theory for these attacks was that wealthy businessmen who had an interest in the real estate of the area had hired the gangs to commit the attacks in an attempt to drive people out.

2015: Rival gangsters from 'Rasta City', based in Laventille, fought with gangsters from the 'Muslims' in Central Trinidad, making residents fearful for their safety after a series of shootouts, violence and murder.

Questions

1. Who was Glenroy Charles?
2. Why do you think 'Tall Paul' Scott was killed?
3. How did the gang violence in these three cases affect the local residents?
4. Do you think the residents could have reacted in any other way? Give a reason for your answer.

Gang members can be armed with weapons, which escalates the violence.

Key vocabulary

gang

empowered

arson

The response to war

We are learning to:

- identify the action necessary to reduce or prevent the suffering caused by war.

Efforts required to respond to the consequences of war

When a war breaks out or there is unrest in a country, other countries sometimes send in military support and **humanitarian aid**. The United Nations often sends **peacekeepers** into conflict areas to try and keep the peace, protect civilians, and help to get food and medical supplies to the civilians. They also help rebuild infrastructure like roads and bridges.

CARICOM has been involved in peacekeeping missions in the Caribbean since it was formed in 1973, for example in Haiti from 1993 to 1996. Military personnel from CARICOM countries have also provided humanitarian assistance to countries after natural disasters. After Hurricane Ivan hit in 2004, Trinidad and Tobago sent soldiers to assist the people of Grenada.

Military personnel from Barbados unload humanitarian aid for the people of Grenada after Hurricane Ivan.

Other responses include:

- supporting long-term development by using non-governmental organisations (NGOs) and community groups to help people improve their community
- creating institutions for at-risk young people, to help combat the gang culture of Trinidad and Tobago
- governments introducing anti-gang legislation.

Dilemmas in providing humanitarian aid

People who provide assistance in conflict areas face many dilemmas. They face dangerous situations and have to deal with the suffering of the people they are trying to help. The people are often injured or ill, have lost their homes and their families, and do not have food and water. People who provide humanitarian aid also have to be neutral and impartial in the way they deal with the population.

Exercise

1. How has CARICOM participated in peacekeeping and humanitarian missions? Give two examples.
2. What is humanitarian aid?

Did you know...?

United Nations peacekeepers wear blue helmets so that they can be recognised easily.

Peacekeepers in Haiti

Jean-Claude Duvalier, a dictator who had ruled Haiti for many years, was overthrown in 1986. In the years that followed, elections were held, but the government was not stable or strong. Jean-Bertrand Aristide was elected President and then removed in a coup d'état.

The country experienced a great deal of violence and corruption. Therefore, in 1993, the United Nations Security Council voted to send a multinational force to Haiti. This force – which consisted of 20 000 support staff and soldiers – arrived in the country in 1994.

CARICOM sent soldiers and other qualified people to join this mission. The mission helped to stabilise the country and restore democracy, safety and economic progress, to a certain degree.

After his second term in office, Jean-Bertrand Aristide was forced to step down as President again in 2004 and there was widespread unrest in the country.

The United Nations sent another peacekeeping mission to Haiti – called MINUSTAH (United Nations Stabilization Mission in Haiti) – whose aim was to stabilise the country.

A Brazilian peacekeeper patrols an area in Haiti as part of MINUSTAH.

Questions

1. Why did the United Nations send a second mission to Haiti in 2004?

2. Work in groups. Imagine you have been sent on a peacekeeping mission to an area where there is conflict. What would you do in the following situations? Role-play each scene and your reactions.

   a) You come across a group of women and children. They have no food or water. You only have your own bottle of water with you. What do you do?

   b) A wounded fighter asks for medical assistance. You know that this fighter has killed innocent women and children. Should you give assistance?

   c) You have been given some boxes of food to hand out to people in need. However, there is not enough for everyone and people start to push and grab parcels of food.

Research

Work in groups and research the role of CARICOM in one of these missions: Haiti (1993–6) after the overthrow of Duvalier or Grenada (2004–5) after Hurricane Ivan.

Key vocabulary

humanitarian aid

peacekeepers

Human dignity

We are learning to:

- promote respect for human dignity
- develop strategies for making a difference.

Promotion of respect for human dignity 》》

If people showed more respect for the dignity of other people, it is possible that there would be fewer conflicts. Here are some things that can be done to help promote respect for the dignity of others.

Respecting human dignity 》》

In 1994, there was **genocide** in Rwanda, a country in Africa. Between 500 000 and 900 000 Tutsi people were killed by Hutu people, who lived in the same state. The slaughter continued for 100 days and during this time terrible crimes were committed.

Rwandan Hutu Jean-Paul Akayesu in court in January 1998.

The genocide in Rwanda prompted the United Nations to set up an International Tribunal to deal with the violations. It also made the establishment of an international criminal court more urgent.

One of the accused in the genocide was Jean-Paul Akayesu. He worked as a teacher and school inspector and was a member of a political party called the Republican Democratic Movement (MDR).

Akayesu served as mayor of Taba Commune from April 1993 to June 1994. He was accused of supervising the bodily and mental harm, torture, and murder of people in the commune. He was convicted, and is now serving a lifetime prison sentence.

Exercise

1. Explain what human dignity is. Give an example of how human dignity can be violated.

2. Why should you not be silent if you see someone's rights being violated?

3. Can you violate someone's dignity if you respect them?

4. Look at the statements in the word cloud to the right. How do you think these statements help to promote respect for human dignity?

Treat others the way you would like them to treat you.

Don't be silent when you see a violation.

Listen to what others have to say.

Find out what the facts are, don't jump to conclusions.

Accept that there will be disagreements.

Strategies for making a difference ▶▶▶

Organisations like the United Nations High Commission for Refugees (UNHCR) and the International Committee of the Red Cross develop strategies to deal with the consequences of war, conflict and natural disasters.

- Providing humanitarian aid like food, shelter and medical care is a priority for these organisations. They also help **refugees** who have fled their countries to settle in new countries or to return to their own countries when it is safe to do so.

- Another important aim is to **reunite** members of families who have been separated as a result of conflict. The National Red Cross and Red Crescent societies also help with this important work.

- They help families get in touch with other family members and have developed databases containing names and photographs of people who have lost family members. These organisations use this information to connect people with their loved ones.

- Organisations not only provide immediate aid in the form of food, water and medical care, but also help people to live normal lives again. For example, they help them to build new homes and repair infrastructure that is needed in order for the economy of an area to get started again.

- Children often suffer the most during and after armed conflicts. Several organisations have been set up around the world to support such children. Some organisations provide food, medical care and safe places for the children to live. They help to trace their parents or support them in finding new homes if their parents have died. Organisations like the Red Cross, the United Nations Children's Fund (UNICEF) and Save the Children are a few examples.

Members of the Red Cross build new homes in Haiti, 2011.

Discussion

What can be done to help prevent people suffering as a result of war and conflict? How would you feel if you were separated from your parents or family for 12 years? Discuss these questions with your teacher.

Exercise

5. Name two organisations that help to reunite families separated by war or conflict.

6. What is a refugee? Give an example from current conflict areas.

7. Name some of the strategies adopted by organisations that can help people affected by war or conflict. Produce a poster showing these strategies.

8. Write a poem expressing your feelings for people who have been affected by war and conflict.

Key vocabulary

genocide

refugee

reunite

The need for justice

We are learning to:

- define and explain relevant terms and concepts: justice, the need for justice
- understand the Universal Declaration of Human Rights.

What is justice? 》

We all have a need for **justice** when we are wronged or when we see others are wronged. Justice means giving each individual what he or she deserves with reference to a standard of rightness.

Justice must be reasonable. For example, if someone is killed or injured during a conflict, decisions have to be made about who should take responsibility for the death and how they should be dealt with.

Courts of law exist in all countries to deal with people who have **violated** the laws of the state. There are also international courts of law, which deal with international violations of humanitarian laws.

We demand justice!

Treat people equally – that is real justice.

Give people what they deserve – that is justice!

Justice means being fair!

Justice is not about punishment – it's about putting things right.

Justice is not the same as revenge.

Exercise

1. In your own words, write a definition of justice.

2. Work in groups. Read the statements above about justice and discuss what each statement means.

3. Research an example in the history of your country in which justice was not carried out. Discuss, and explain why.

The **Universal Declaration of Human Rights (UDHR)** was adopted by the General Assembly of the United Nations in 1948. It was the first international statement about human rights and the need for justice. It has since been built into the constitutions and laws of most countries around the world.

The Declaration was drawn up to promote basic rights and freedoms for all people. All countries that are members of the United Nations signed the Declaration, and in doing so they agreed to promote respect for human rights.

There are 30 articles in the Declaration. In Form 1, we looked at the first five articles. Here is a reminder of some of those, along with some further examples:

Article 1 All human beings are born free and equal in dignity and rights.

Article 3 Everyone has the right to life, liberty and security of person.

Article 5 No one shall be subjected to torture or to cruel, inhuman or degrading treatment or punishment.

Article 13 (1) Everyone has the right to freedom of movement and residence within the borders of each state.

(2) Everyone has the right to leave any country, including his own, and to return to his country.

Article 18 Everyone has the right to freedom of thought, conscience and religion.

Article 19 Everyone has the right to freedom of opinion and expression.

Article 30 Nothing in this Declaration may be interpreted as implying for any State, group or person any right to engage in any activity or to perform any act aimed at the destruction of any of the rights and freedoms set forth herein.

Exercise

4. In your own words, define the term Universal Declaration of Human Rights.

5. Why was the Universal Declaration of Human Rights drawn up?

6. Why do you think the first article is 'All human beings are born free and equal in dignity and rights'?

7. True or false?

   a) Only certain people have the right to free movement.
   b) No one has the right to free thought.
   c) Everyone can have their own opinion.
   d) It is wrong to harm or try to destroy people's freedom.

Key vocabulary

justice

violate

Universal Declaration of Human Rights (UDHR)

How justice can be served

We are learning to:

- explore the consequences of dealing/ not dealing with the violators of society after an armed conflict has ended
- understand ways in which justice can be served
- understand the institutions that judge the accused.

If there is to be justice for all people living in a country, there have to be laws describing how people should be treated and how they should behave. There also have to be ways to enforce these laws and to resolve conflicts if they arise.

Ways in which justice can be served

The Defence Force and the police protect people during times of conflict. The Courts of Law are responsible for making sure that justice is served by:

- proper punishment or fair treatment through the judicial system
- ensuring human rights are not denied or neglected and dealing with those who have violated laws
- ensuring that all groups in society (regardless of gender, ethnicity, class, religion, and so on) are treated equally
- ensuring equal access to all resources and opportunities
- minimising corruption and discrimination
- helping people gain access to an improved quality of life, such as proper medical care and education.

A judge in his chambers.

If someone is accused of having committed a crime or a violation of the law, they can be fined or sentenced to community service as a punishment. In more serious cases, such as fraud or murder, offenders are put on trial. If there is evidence that they are guilty of the crime as charged, they will be punished according to the laws of the state. This could include fines or a prison sentence.

Exercise

1. What role do the police have in the justice system?

2. How do the Courts of Law make sure that justice is served fairly?

3. How can people who have committed minor crimes be punished?

4. What sort of crimes will result in the accused person being put on trial in a court of law?

Discussion

In groups, find out what the word sedition means. Then discuss if you think that laws against sedition and treason can be used to oppress citizens. If so, how? Then discuss your ideas with the rest of the class.

The people who judge the accused ⟫

Most democratic countries have an independent arm of government called the **Judiciary**.

This arm of the government works to resolve conflicts in society, to suggest and apply remedies to situations in which there is conflict, and to punish those who break the laws of the country if necessary. They ensure that there is equal justice for all people under the laws of the country.

The Judiciary consists of:

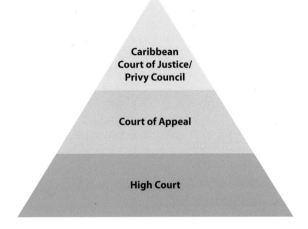

Discussion

Your teacher will lead the class in a discussion about the impact of not dealing with violators of individuals, families and society as a whole. Consider:

- By not dealing with offenders, did the crime rate increase?
- Do we have more gangs?

- The Magistracy deals with all **criminal** and **civil offences** and refers very serious cases to the High Court. Magistrates listen to evidence and pass judgements in the Magistrates Courts throughout the state.
- The Supreme Court is presided over by the Chief Justice and judges and is made up of the Court of Appeal and High Court. The judges preside over serious cases and listen to appeals when there is disagreement about the way in which justice has been served.
- Some countries have a Family Court, which seeks to resolve conflicts that arise in families, mainly by providing support and expert assistance.

Exercise

5. In your own words, explain the purpose of the Judiciary.

6. What is the role of the Supreme Court?

Key vocabulary

Judiciary

criminal offence

civil offence

International tribunals

We are learning to:

- define the reasons for international tribunals
- examine the reasons for the introduction of the International Criminal Court
- explain the role of Mr A.N.R. Robinson in the creation of the International Criminal Court.

Sometimes conflicts and violations of law are so serious that organisations like the United Nations have decided that violators need to be dealt with at an international level.

The reasons for international tribunals ≫

At the end of World War I, there was a feeling that certain leaders should be prosecuted for their actions at an international level and that an International Court should be set up to deal with such matters. However, it was only after World War II that the first **international tribunals** were set up. These were not permanent courts, but courts set up to serve justice in particular conflicts.

One court was set up in Nuremberg to judge German leaders and military personnel for humanitarian law violations during World War II. Another court was set up in Tokyo to judge Japanese leaders for their violations of law during the same war. Civilians like doctors, judges and businesspeople who committed serious crimes were also put on trial.

In 1993, an international tribunal was set up to deal with war crimes committed when Yugoslavia broke up into separate countries. In 1994, another tribunal was set up to deal with war crimes committed during the Rwandan genocide.

In 1994, a tribunal was set up to deal with war crimes committed during the Rwandan genocide.

Exercise

1. Why were international tribunals initially set up?

2. In your own words, explain what an international tribunal does.

3. What types of crime do international tribunals deal with?

4. In small groups, research one of the examples of international tribunals given above. Outline when the tribunals took place, who was on trial and the outcome of the tribunal. Discuss your findings with the rest of the class.

Did you know...?

Pol Pot was the Prime Minister of Cambodia (then called Kampuchea) between 1976 and 1979. He was a **dictator**. It is estimated that during his rule up to three million people (a quarter of the country's population) died as a result of his policies.

In 2002, the **International Criminal Court (ICC)** came into existence. This court has the authority to prosecute people all over the world for crimes like genocide, crimes committed during wars and any other crimes against humanity. The ICC sits at The Hague in the Netherlands.

In 2003, the first judges were appointed and sworn in. Then the work began. The first judgment was against the rebel Congolese leader Thomas Dyilo. He was accused, and found guilty, of war crimes relating to the use of child soldiers.

To date, more than 30 people have been convicted of international crimes by this court. These include people like the Ugandan rebel leader Joseph Kony, who was convicted of committing war crimes and crimes against humanity. His rebel movement was accused of abducting young children and using them as slaves and child soldiers.

A.N.R. Robinson with Archbishop Edward J. Gilbert in Tobago, 2001.

The role of A.N.R. Robinson in the creation of the ICC

A.N.R. Robinson served Trinidad and Tobago as Prime Minister from 1986 until 1991 and then as President from 1997 until 2003.

In 1989, as Prime Minister of Trinidad and Tobago, he proposed that an International Criminal Court should be set up. This was not a new idea, but he gave the idea impetus again. His proposal was that the world needed an international court to deal specifically with crimes associated with the international drug trade.

His idea was accepted and the United Nations started the process of setting up the laws to establish such a court. Robinson received widespread international recognition for his role in this. He served as a consultant in the setting up of this new court, and in 1979 as a member of the United Nations Expert Group on Crime and Abuse of Power.

Exercise

5. When did the International Criminal Court come into existence?

6. Explain how Thomas Dyilo and Joseph Kany violated Humanitarian Law.

7. In your own words, outline the role A.N.R. Robinson played in establishing the ICC.

Discussion

Discuss one of the topics below and explore how justice was done. Identify what crime or crimes had been committed and how people tried to seek justice for these crimes:

- Adolf Hitler and the mass murder of millions of Jewish people, Romanians, homosexuals and disabled people.
- Jamaat al Muslimeen
- Yugoslavian civil war (1990s)
- Rwanda genocide (1990s)
- Pol Pot and the Khmer Rouge in Cambodia.

Key vocabulary

international tribunal

dictator

International Criminal Court

The Caribbean Court of Justice

We are learning to:

- describe the role of the Caribbean Court of Justice.

The history of the Caribbean Court of Justice

The **Caribbean Court of Justice (CCJ)** is located in Port of Spain, Trinidad and Tobago. This country is referred to as the 'seat' of the Court, because the Court's headquarters are based there.

The CCJ was set up to settle disputes related to the Revised Treaty of Chaguaramas. The Court is also the highest court of appeal on civil and criminal matters for the national courts of Barbados, Belize, Dominica and Guyana.

In 1970, at a meeting of Caribbean Commonwealth heads of government, Jamaica proposed that the region should establish a Regional Court of Appeal. However, it was not until 1989 that heads of government agreed to this. In 1999, it was agreed that the CCJ would be located in Port of Spain.

The CARICOM states of Antigua and Barbuda, Barbados, Belize, Grenada, Guyana, Jamaica, St Kitts and Nevis, St Lucia, Suriname, and Trinidad and Tobago signed the agreement to establish the CCJ in 2001. Dominica and St Vincent joined them in 2003. In April 2005, the CCJ first opened its doors and began operating.

The seal of the Caribbean Court of Justice.

The reasons for the Caribbean Court of Justice

The aim of the CCJ is to provide high quality justice to the people of the Caribbean by 'guaranteeing accessibility, fairness, efficiency and transparency' and 'delivering clear and just decisions in a timely manner'. The CCJ helps to reinforce regional integration by settling commercial disputes. It also brings a single vision to the development of law in the Caribbean region, which has lots of different cultures and historical backgrounds.

> **Did you know...?**
>
> The vision of the CCJ is to be:
>
> - a leader in providing high-quality justice
> - responsive to the challenges of our diverse communities
> - innovative, fostering jurisprudence that is reflective of our history, values and traditions, and consistent with international legal norms
> - inspirational, worthy of the trust and confidence of the people of the region.

Exercise

1. Why was the Caribbean Court of Justice set up?
2. Which country initially suggested the idea of a Caribbean Court of Justice?
3. Which countries are part of the CCJ?

The CCJ is two courts in one, and has two functions:

- **An original jurisdiction** – it deals with citizens' rights to move between CARICOM countries freely and their right to move money and business. This is the basis of the CARICOM Single Market and Economy (CSME) and the Revised Treaty of Chaguaramas (an agreement in 2001 between CARICOM countries, to promote efficiency in the production of goods and services in the region).

  Under the original jurisdiction, disputes can be brought to the CCJ by referrals from:

  - member states' courts of tribunals
  - member states
  - private individuals or groups
  - businesses
  - the community.

- **An appellate jurisdiction** – it hears appeals from lower courts in civil (including family), criminal cases or constitutional matters. This jurisdiction can only be accessed by citizens of those countries who have signed on the CCJ as their final court of appeal.

The CCJ brings a single vision in the development of law in the Caribbean region.

The CCJ can have a total of nine judges. Judges are appointed from candidates who respond to advertisements that are placed throughout the Commonwealth, and are interviewed by the Regional Judicial and Legal Services Commission (RJLSC).

CCJ judges must have high moral character, intellectual and analytical ability, sound judgment, integrity, an understanding of people and society and must be distinguished in their careers.

As of December 2017, the CCJ has seven judges from St Kitts and Nevis (where the President of the CCJ is from), St Vincent and the Grenadines, the United Kingdom, the Netherlands Antilles, Jamaica, and two judges from Trinidad and Tobago.

Discussion

As a class, discuss the reasons for, and role of, the CCJ. Consider why it is important to the Caribbean region.

Exercise

4. In your own words, outline the functions of the CCJ.

5. Who can bring a dispute to the CCJ?

6. Create a timeline of the history of the CCJ.

7. Using the internet, research the current CCJ judges.

Key vocabulary

Caribbean Court of Justice (CCJ)

Questions

See how well you have understood the topics in this unit.

1. Match the key vocabulary word (i–viii) with its definition (a–h).

   i) election   **a)** the ballot of voting papers on which you choose your candidate in an election

   ii) elector   **b)** a person who lives in a constituency

   iii) electorate   **c)** a process during which voters choose candidates by voting for them

   iv) candidate   **d)** proposed as a candidate

   v) votes   **e)** a voter or person who has the right to vote in an election

   vi) nominated   **f)** people who are registered to vote in an election

   vii) constituency   **g)** an area in a country where voters elect a representative to a local or national government body

   viii) constituent   **h)** a person who seeks election

2. Explain the difference between a ballot, a ballot paper, a ballot box and a secret ballot.

3. What is Nomination Day?

4. How often does a general election happen in the Eastern Caribbean?

5. In your own words, explain the terms first-past-the-post and proportional representation.

6. Name five factors that can affect how a person chooses to vote.

7. Who forms a new government after an election?

8. Explain why a general election should be free and fair.

9. Read the results in the table from an imaginary parliamentary election. Answer these questions:

Results
Candidate A (Blue party): 14 780 votes
Candidate B (Green party): 17 890 votes
Candidate C (Red party): 11 301 votes
Total number of votes cast: 43 971 votes

   a) Which political party won this seat in Parliament?

   b) Did any candidate win a majority of the votes?

   c) Which system was used to declare the winner of this election?

10. Write a short paragraph explaining how gangs can affect communities.

11. What is the purpose of the Universal Declaration of Human Rights?

12. Describe the role of each of the following:

     a) Magistrates Court
     b) The Supreme Court
     c) Family Court

13. Look at the diagram and describe what is occurring at each location (1–3).

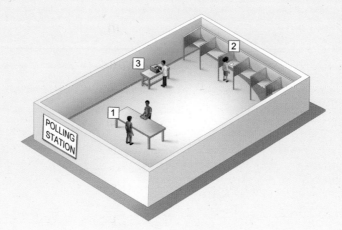

Checking your progress

To make good progress in understanding different aspects of how we govern ourselves, check to make sure you understand these ideas.

Understand the electoral process in the Eastern Caribbean.

Explain the process on Election Day.

Role-play the steps involved in a general election.

Understand the importance of universal suffrage and the importance of a free and fair election process.

Understand the significance of constitutional reform.

Research the constitution of your country and write what you would change about it.

Understand the consequences of war and conflict.

Explain how war disrupts normal life and how gangs affect local communities.

Discuss ways to prevent young people from engaging in gang activities.

Understand the promotion of respect for human dignity, and why and how justice can be served.

Understand the role of international tribunals.

Discuss the role of the Caribbean Court of Justice and why it is important to the Caribbean region.

Unit 5: Our environment

In this unit you will find out 》》

Scientific and technological developments and our environment

- Define and explain relevant terms and concepts
- Examine scientific and technological developments in society; grow crops, build houses, transport, the internet, cellular phones, medicine
- The positive influence of scientific and technological developments on the environment
  - easy movement of people
  - better quality food
  - better communication
  - cures for diseases
- The negative influence of scientific and technological developments on the environment
  - health problems
  - environmental problems: pollution, ozone layer depletion, climate change, deforestation, GM crops

Humans and our environment

- Discuss the reasons for urbanisation
  - better standard of living
  - access to health care
  - availability of jobs
  - migration
  - education
- The positive and negative effects of urbanisation
  - positive: better opportunities, higher standard of living, services
  - negative: health issues, pollution, unemployment and underemployment, shortage of housing/overcrowding, commuting issues, poverty and crime
- The ways high population density can be controlled
- Family planning
- Improvement of services: education, water supply, transport, electricity, communication, health care services, hospitals, availability of jobs

Scientific and technological developments and our environment

We are learning to:

- define and explain relevant terms and concepts
- examine scientific and technological developments in society; grow crops, build houses.

The main goal of **science** is to build knowledge and understanding, with the aim of making life easier for humans. The term **technological** describes something that is based in science and can be applied to everyday life to solve problems. Scientific development and advances can help us in how we use our environment for our benefit.

Technology and crop growing

There have been a number of significant scientific developments in farming in recent years. Some of the most important include:

- **Genetically modified (GM) crops** – where scientific techniques have been used to change the DNA of the crops, allowing them to grow in more difficult climates or environments. This has allowed crops to grow in areas/countries that have never been productive before.

- **Pesticides and fertilisers** – these are improving all the time. Pesticides are used to kill insects that would damage the crops, and fertiliser is used to help crops grow.

A tractor sprays crops with pesticide.

Technological developments in farming

Other examples of new technology that are used to help farmers get the most out of their land include:

- **Irrigation** equipment – sprinkler systems allow farmers to water their crops when there has been a lack of rainfall. This type of technology is particularly useful in countries that have drier climates, such as the USA, Australia and many African countries.

- **Software and mobile apps** – these are used for all sorts of practices in farming now, from ordering seeds to checking the weather to monitoring the movement of **livestock**.

- **Global positioning systems (GPS)** – farmers are able to locate their exact positions in fields. This allows them to create maps to measure and record **terrain**, features in the fields (such as a river) and moisture levels.

Research

Using the internet, and working in groups, explore the topic 'How to build a Caribbean eco home'. Research the materials that you would need, the type of energy to use and the features it would have. Write a report of about 250 words, with illustrations, and share it with the rest of the class.

- **Drones** – are now used to take photos of the farm to show land use. They can also be used to produce 3-D maps for soil analysis, which allows more efficient planning of seed planting. Drones are also used for spraying crops. According to some experts, using drones can be up to five times quicker than traditional methods of crop spraying. Drones can be more accurate, as well, as they adjust the amount of chemical used to suit the changing geography of the area.

- **Cloned animals** – the first successful clone was a sheep named Dolly, cloned from her mother in 1996. Since then pigs, deer and horses have also been successfully cloned.

House building ▶▶▶

An **eco-friendly** house is one that is designed to be **sustainable** while having a low impact on the environment. Eco-friendly houses are built using sustainable materials and aim to conserve and use less energy and water. This can be achieved by:

- using sustainable energy, such as wind turbines or solar panels
- ecological materials, such as reclaimed bricks, wood, stone or bamboo, which is available on many Caribbean islands
- a thatched roof to catch rainwater and a cistern to collect the rainwater and recycle it
- waste management – low-flush toilets, which use less water when flushing
- growing your own food, such as vegetables and herbs, and keeping livestock such as chickens and goats; also keeping compost
- employing local craftspeople, who use local materials for interior furniture.

Using solar panels on roofs is one way to make a house more eco-friendly.

Key vocabulary

science

technological

genetically modified (GM) crops

pesticides

fertilisers

irrigation

livestock

global positioning systems (GPS)

terrain

drones

cloned sheep

eco-friendly

sustainable

Exercise

1. In your own words, explain the terms science and technological.

2. What are GM crops?

3. Give examples of technological developments in farming.

4. Explain the term eco-friendly.

5. Describe how an eco-friendly house is different from a normal house.

Technological developments in society

We are learning to:

- define and explain relevant terms and concepts
- examine scientific and technological developments in society: transport, the internet, cellular phones, medicine.

Scientific and technological developments in transport 》》

People are becoming more connected as transport methods improve.

- Aeroplanes have been around for just over 100 years, but people have only flown all over the world in the last 50. It is estimated that there are over 100 000 flights every day across the world.
- Japan is the leader in train technology. Their Shinkansen train lines are a series of high-speed 'bullet trains' that travel at speeds of up to 320 km/h.
- Electric cars are becoming more and more popular as an environmentally friendly way to get about. Autonomous (driverless) cars are the new developments in vehicle transportation. This type of car uses sensors to navigate the roads with no driver.

The Japanese Shinkansen train, known in English as the bullet train, at Kyoto station.

The internet 》》

Up until the 1990s people used books to research information, and if they wanted to keep in touch with friends and family the only option was a letter or phone call. Now the internet has completely changed our daily lives.

The internet is a global network that anybody can access, providing they have a computer and internet connection. All sorts of information is available online now, which makes researching by any other method outdated and time-consuming. **Emailing** has fast become the method of choice when communicating with others as it sends messages and information instantly rather than having to wait for the postal system. This has revolutionised society.

Exercise

1. What are some of the most recent developments in transportation?
2. What is the internet?
3. How has the internet changed people's lives?

Research

In groups, using the internet, research two of the topics covered on these two pages. Explain how each has impacted on modern, everyday life. Write a report of about 500 words, with illustrations, and share it with the rest of the class.

Cellular phones >>>

As with the internet, up until the 1990s **cellular phones** (or cell/mobile phones) were not commonplace. Some people had them – mainly businesspeople and the wealthy – but after the 1990s it became the norm to carry around a cell phone.

Carrying a cell phone has many advantages, the most important one being the ability to communicate with people on the go, 24-7. That is especially important for parents with children, as both can get in touch if needed.

Since the 1990s, cell phones have continued to evolve and now they do far more than simply make a phone call.

People are able to send emails and text messages, take photos, connect to the internet, use social media sites – even pay for things when you're out.

You can now pay for things with your cellular phone.

Medicine >>

Scientific and technological developments within the medical sector are huge. Scientists are constantly finding cures and treatments for illnesses and conditions. This allows many diseases such as smallpox, measles (in many countries), rubella and polio to be eradicated. The medicines that are being developed allow people to live much longer.

Furthermore, major technological developments are being made all the time in medicine, such as:

- MRI scanners – machines used to produce images of the inside of the body
- Pacemakers – devices placed in the chest to control the rhythm of the heart
- Brain–computer interfaces – paraplegic and quadriplegic people are able to control computer cursors using only their brain
- Prosthetic limbs – artificial limbs made with computer technology can recreate all the functions of normal limbs.

Discussion

Your teacher will divide your class into four groups and will allocate one of the topics (transport, the internet, cell phones and medicine) from these pages to each group. Each group will argue why they think their topic is the most important technological development to today's society. Once every group has presented to the class, carry out a vote to see which one was most persuasive.

Exercise

4. What was the most important use of a cellular phone when they were first invented?

5. Make a list of all the things you use your cell phone for.

6. List some examples of technological developments in medicine.

Key vocabulary
....

email

cellular phone

109

Technological developments in the environment

We are learning to:

- evaluate the positive influence of scientific and technological developments on the environment.

The positive influence of scientific and technological developments

The scientific and technological developments that have taken place in the last 50 years have completely changed society. There are many arguments supporting these developments, and others that raise important concerns.

Easy movement of people

There have been several technological developments that allow people to travel all over the world. There are few countries that remain **inaccessible** and difficult to reach. Examples of these are South Georgia and the South Sandwich Islands, which are found to the north of Antarctica, and Naurau in the Pacific Ocean. Both of these countries are very remote and difficult to reach.

Aeroplanes, trains and cars all allow people to reach destinations that previously had been inaccessible to them.

One advantage of technological developments is that they have made international travel to many destinations much easier for people.

Better quality food

Farming is becoming more efficient due to the improvements in science and technology in this field. The introduction of new farming methods and techniques allows for greater productivity of crops. The introduction of genetically modified crops means that crops are now able to grow in countries and areas where previously they could not.

Before the introduction of farming methods such as precision farming, drone fertilisation and genetically modified crops, the crops that were grown were not necessarily of the best quality. Often poor weather conditions would affect both the quality and quantity of the crops grown.

These methods help to improve the quality of crops, and therefore the food that we eat. However, there are arguments that GM crops are not necessarily a good thing.

Better communication

Keeping in touch with friends and family has never been easier:

- Email allows instant messages to get through to people on the other side of the world.
- Text messaging using cell phones is a quick and easy way to keep in touch.
- The internet is used to make calls via FaceTime and Skype.

There are also software **apps** such as WhatsApp and Snapchat that allow messages and photos to be sent instantly.

These developments make communicating today far more efficient and effective.

Cures for diseases

Scientific research into diseases is one of the most well-funded areas of medical research.

Hundreds of millions of dollars' worth of funding is raised every year across the world to help scientists find cures for some of the world's biggest killer diseases, such as cancer, heart disease and HIV. Scientists are devoted to finding cures for these diseases.

Because science continues to find cures for diseases, people will live longer and longer. Many diseases that used to be deadly are now curable due to scientific research. Diseases that are now curable include:

- chickenpox
- malaria
- polio
- tetanus
- smallpox.

Activity

Think about your daily routine. In your notebook, record all the technology in the categories that we have looked at (transport, food, communication, medicine) that you use during the day. Think how it helps you. Then, as a class, discuss your findings and decide if technology is a good thing.

Scientific research into diseases, if successful, will help people to live longer.

Exercise

1. What has been the biggest factor in allowing people to move easily around the world?
2. What affects the quality of crops being grown?
3. Other than those mentioned here, can you name any other ways of communicating with people?
4. Name some diseases that scientists have found cures for.

Key vocabulary

inaccessible

apps

Technological developments in the environment

We are learning to:

- evaluate the negative influence of scientific and technological developments on the environment.

The negative influence of scientific and technological developments

There are many advantages to new technological and scientific developments, but these also bring some concerns.

Health problems

Using a computer, cell phone and tablet to access the internet or play games is a great way to entertain ourselves, but there are health risks associated with too much **screen time** (time spent looking at an electronic device), particularly with children. These include:

The amount of time children use a tablet to play games is on the increase.

- **Obesity** is when someone is overweight (or **obese**). When you sit at the computer or on a mobile device, you are not using any energy and therefore you are not burning any calories. Over a long period of time this can cause you to become overweight, which could lead to obesity. It is thought that for an average pre-school child, one hour of screen time each day means they are 52% more likely to be overweight than those that do less than this. Being overweight can lead to further health problems, such as diabetes, heart disease, stress, anxiety and depression.
- Lack of sleep – using mobile devices and computers stimulates your brain, so using these just before bed can make it far more difficult for you to get to sleep.
- Sight problems – eye pain can occur from staring at a screen for long periods of time. This can lead to problems with vision in the future.
- Aches and pains – since the invention of cell phones and other mobile devices, doctors have had to invent new medical terms to describe some of the aches and pains caused by too much screen time. These include **text thumb** and **phone neck**.

Exercise

1. How can too much screen time lead to obesity?
2. What other health problems are associated with too much screen time?

Discussion

Your teacher will divide the class into two groups to take part in a debate. One group will argue the positive contributions that scientific and technological developments make to society, while the other group will make the case for the negative contributions. After the debate, your teacher will decide which group argued their case most effectively.

Environmental problems ⟫⟫

- Pollution – the most harmful types of pollution for the environment are water and air pollution. Technology, such as aeroplanes and vehicles, is one of the biggest causes of air pollution. Ferries, ships and tankers can cause an increase in water pollution, as oil and petrol are leaked into the sea water.
- Ozone layer depletion – the **ozone layer** is a protective layer around the Earth's atmosphere that stops harmful ultraviolet rays from the sun reaching the Earth. Ultraviolet radiation can cause skin cancer. Human activity has caused the ozone layer to deplete. The biggest contributor is chlorofluorocarbons (CFCs), which are found in vehicle air conditioning systems, solvents and refrigeration systems.
- Climate change is the change of the Earth's temperature and weather patterns as a result of increased carbon dioxide in the air (caused by human activity). Many scientific and technological developments have harmful effects on the environment. Air travel contributes 4–9% of climate change, and vehicle use is one of the biggest contributors to carbon dioxide emissions. Increased use of aeroplanes, rail and vehicles means that more carbon dioxide is emitted into the atmosphere with a resulting increase in global warming and climate change.
- **Deforestation** – the removal of trees and vegetation to create open spaces for human activities – can be harmful for the environment, as it can lead to increased global warming and climate change. Trees breathe in carbon dioxide, which warms our planet. Fewer trees leads to more carbon dioxide, so temperatures increase.
- Genetically modified crops can be harmful to the environment, because they require a lot of fertilisers to help them grow. Fertilisers can cause pollution to nearby rivers and streams, which can ultimately get into local water supplies and make people unwell.

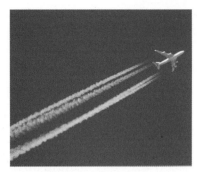

Aeroplanes cause large amounts of pollution in the atmosphere.

Activity

Write an essay outlining the positive and negative influences that technological development has on our everyday lives. Use about 250 words.

Exercise

3. Explain how various forms of transportation contribute to climate change.
4. What is the main concern with using GM crops?
5. What connects all the environmental problems caused by scientific and technological developments as outlined above? (Clue: they are all caused by _____ _____.)

Key vocabulary

screen time

obesity/obese

text thumb

phone neck

ozone layer

deforestation

Urbanisation

We are learning to:

- discuss the reasons for urbanisation.

What is urbanisation? 〉〉

Urbanisation is an increase in the number of people living in **urban** areas as opposed to **rural** areas.

In developed countries, most people live in urban areas – in some cases, 90% of the population. However, in developing countries, only around 50% live in urban areas.

However, as countries **industrialise**, more and more people move away from the countryside in search of new opportunities in the cities. Developing countries have some of the fastest-growing urban populations.

Bridgetown in Barbados in an example of an urban area.

Better standard of living 〉〉〉

There is a far better **standard of living** (level of comfort and wealth that a person or family may have) in urban areas than in rural areas, particularly in developing countries.

Rural areas in the developing world may not have access to clean, running water or electricity, although most urban areas will have both facilities.

Sanitation is also far better in urban areas, as there are proper methods of rubbish disposal and sewers. These may be absent from rural settlements.

Access to health care 〉〉〉〉

Rural areas in developing countries have very little access to good medical facilities. Hospitals and medical facilities tend to be in the cities. Some people move to urban areas to access better medical facilities.

In rural areas, there may only be the most basic medical care. A rural community may only have someone who is trained in basic medical ailments and first aid, while urban areas have considerably more medical facilities, including doctors, nurses and hospitals.

In many countries, people living in urban areas have a higher life expectancy than those living in rural areas. This is partly to do with the increased medical care that is available there.

Availability of jobs

The countryside has very few job opportunities. Most people living in rural areas farm the land. They generally do this on a **subsistence** basis, meaning they farm enough food to feed themselves and their families.

Urban areas have many more employment opportunities, as this is where all the offices and businesses locate, so people move here looking for work. Not only is there a wider variety of job opportunities in urban areas, but there are also better-paid jobs.

Farming in the countryside is mainly subsistence; therefore little or no money is generated from this method of farming. In contrast, in the cities, people are employed in different sectors of industry and receive a weekly or monthly wage. Wages can differ massively between vocations, but they are generally much better paid than those in the countryside.

Migration

Urbanisation refers to the increased number of people living in urban areas. Most of these people have **migrated** to the cities from the countryside.

Most people that move to the cities are people considered 'economically active', aged between 15 and 65, although most of them are in their twenties and thirties. The migration of young adults to the cities is mainly for employment purposes, but also for the other opportunities that are available, such as medical care and education.

Education

Rural areas tend to have few schools, particularly in developing countries. Therefore young people move to urban areas to attend higher or further education institutes.

Discussion

In groups, discuss the reasons for urbanisation. In a role play, interview a member of the group who explains their reasons for urbanisation. Then place the main reasons for urbanisation in order of importance. Finally, share your findings with the other groups, to see if you agree.

Modern office buildings in Castries, Saint Lucia.

Exercise

1. In your own words, define the term urbanisation.
2. What are the main causes of urbanisation?
3. Why do you think urban areas can offer better standards of living?
4. Explain why urban areas have more job opportunities.
5. Suggest some reasons why young people move to cities.
6. Where do you think you would find a university – in a rural or urban area? Why?

Key vocabulary

urbanisation

urban

rural

industrialise

standard of living

subsistence

migrate

Urbanisation

We are learning to:

- describe the positive and negative effects of urbanisation.

Positive effects of urbanisation

The positive effects of urbanisation are outlined below.

Better opportunities

There are more, and better, opportunities for people living in urban areas. For example:

- There are more schools/universities for people wanting to study – urban areas will most likely have at least one university and several colleges, as well as high schools and primary schools. Education in rural areas can be much more limited, particularly in developing countries. In poorer countries, rural communities might only have the most basic of education facilities, offering only primary level education

- More employment opportunities – in rural areas, these may only be in the farming sector, whereas in the cities there are far more jobs in a variety of sectors, such as offices, medical centres and call centres.

Inner cities can have clean and pedestrianised areas for shopping and working.

Higher standard of living

Urban areas tend to be more affluent. They have more services and amenities for people living there, such as running water, electricity, heating, flushing toilets, waste disposal, refuse collection. These make living in these areas far nicer.

Services

Services such as education, health and social care are far more accessible in the cities than they are in the countryside. In urban areas, services can also be more efficient, because providing amenities such as fresh water and electricity is easier due to the more concentrated population.

Project

Using the internet, collect pictures that show the positive and negative effects of urbanisation. Then create a slide show presentation that shows the positive and negative effects of urbanisation.

Exercise

1. Describe the better opportunities that people have when they live in urban areas.

2. What makes people living in urban areas have a higher standard of living than those in the countryside?

- **Health issues** – the movement of people from one area to another can lead to spread of disease. For example, malaria is often spread by the migration of people. Poor conditions in urban areas, with overcrowding and poor sanitation, can lead to many diseases, such as typhoid and malaria.

- **Pollution** – with large numbers of vehicles in urban areas, as well as factories, **air pollution** can be a big problem. Vehicles and factories emit harmful gases that can lead to health problems such as asthma.

- Unemployment (when someone does not have a job) and **underemployment** (having work but not fully using one's skills or abilities) are problems in urban areas. Consequences include homelessness and crime.

Overcrowded roads cause problems such as congestion, pollution and delay to people's journeys.

- **Shortage of housing/overcrowding** – because people are attracted to urban areas, often there are not enough houses. This can lead to overcrowding in the houses that are available. Housing shortages in developing world cities, such as Mumbai, is a major problem – 18 million people live in Mumbai, but there are not enough houses for this population, so temporary housing has popped up. This type of temporary housing is known as **shantytowns** or **slums**. The standard of living here is very, very poor.

- **Commuting issues** – the increased number of people owning a vehicle in urban areas creates problems such as congestion and pollution. People can spend long periods of time travelling between their homes and work every day, particularly if they live in the more affordable suburbs. Car travel can also lead to problems of air and noise pollution in urban areas.

- **Poverty and crime** – poverty and crime become major problems. There are large numbers of people living in urban areas and the gap between rich and poor is very obvious in many cases. The lack of jobs, money and housing can lead people to turn to crime.

Activity

Write an essay debating the positive and negative effects of urbanisation. Use about 250 words. In your conclusion, decide whether the positive effects outweigh the negative ones, or vice versa.

Exercise

3. Describe some of the problems associated with urbanisation.

4. Why do you think unemployment and underemployment can lead to social issues such as homelessness and crime?

5. Why is commuting a problem in urban areas?

Key vocabulary

air pollution

underemployment

shantytown/slum

Humans and our environment

We are learning to:

- explain the ways high population density can be controlled.

How population density can be controlled ⟩⟩

Population density is the average number of people living in one square kilometre. Population density tends to be much higher in urban areas than in rural ones. Areas or countries with high population densities are often **overpopulated**. Overpopulation can cause a number of problems:

- Increasing numbers of young people make the provision of education more difficult.
- There are not enough jobs, and unemployment can lead to poverty, and then crime and other antisocial activities.
- A shortage of houses can lead to overcrowding, as well as high rents and house prices.
- There can be more pressure on amenities such as water and electricity.
- Rural–urban migration may take place, which leads to further overcrowding in urban areas.

Solutions to controlling population density include:

- family planning
- improvement of services offered in rural areas, such as education, amenities and communication.

Family planning clinics play an important role in reducing birth rates.

Family planning ⟩⟩⟩

Access to **family planning** clinics is one of the best methods of reducing birth rates. Family planning is the practice of controlling the number and frequency (spacing) of children in a family.

Family planning usually involves some form of contraceptive, such as a condom or a contraceptive pill, which lowers the risk of an unwanted pregnancy. Condoms are the only form of birth control that can also protect a couple against transmission of sexually transmitted diseases (STDs).

Exercise

1. In your own words, define the term overpopulation.
2. Explain why overpopulation of an area is a problem.
3. What is the best way to keep birth rates down?

Improvement of services ⟩⟩⟩

One important way to reduce high population densities in urban areas is to improve services offered in rural areas. This includes developments in:

- Education – it is often difficult for central and local government to provide quality schools in rural areas. Initiatives can include improving the smaller schools that already exist, and offering distance learning courses. A distance learning course is a form of education where the students work at home and send in their work to a teacher by the internet.

- Water supply – rural areas often have problems with water distribution and quality, because they are too far from national distribution systems. Solutions include collecting rainwater, water recycling and well construction.

- Transport – in rural areas, roads are often poor and prone to flood or storm damage. Building better-quality roads would improve the infrastructure from rural to urban areas, and also be much more reliable.

- Electricity – supplies in rural areas can be difficult, partly due to distances but also the terrain. Initiatives to improve electricity connection in rural areas include using local generators by using solar power.

- Communication – internet, mobile phone network and telephones. The provision of wireless communication and internet services in rural areas would help those areas to connect better with the outside world. For example, it would help businesses.

- Quality health care services, hospitals – as for education, it can be difficult to provide quality health care in rural areas. Government-subsidised health programmes, such as immunisation and health centres, can improve health services.

- Availability of jobs – diversifying the economy into other sectors, such as tourism, energy, food sustainability, information and communication technologies (ICT), culture and creative industries, maritime industries and finance.

In rural areas, roads are often poor and prone to flood or storm damage.

Research

In groups, prepare a newspaper article that discusses the problems caused by overpopulation and ways to prevent high population densities. Provide examples to show how services to rural areas in your country have been improved. Add illustrations, if available. Then present your article to the rest of the class.

Exercise

4. Name two ways in which the provision of education can be improved in rural areas.

5. What effect do you think better roads and better communication would have for a rural area?

Key vocabulary

population density

overpopulated

family planning

Questions

See how well you have understood the topics in this unit.

1. Match the key vocabulary word (i–viii) with its definition (a–h).

    i) science

    ii) technological

    iii) genetically modified crops

    iv) pesticides

    v) fertilisers

    vi) livestock

    vii) eco-friendly

    viii) sustainable

    a) describes something that is based in science and can be applied to everyday life to solve problems

    b) not damaging to the environment; sustainable

    c) chemicals that kill insects, weeds and fungi that damage crops

    d) able to continue at the same level without destroying the resources it relies on

    e) build knowledge and understanding, with the aim of making life easier for humans

    f) chemicals that promote fast plant growth

    g) animals used in farming

    h) where scientific techniques have been used to change the DNA of the crops, allowing them to grow in more difficult climates or environments

2. How would you keep in touch with people in the 1990s, compared to nowadays (using new technology)? Write about 200 words.

3. Name four positive influences on society that have come about through scientific and technological developments.

4. Name four negative influences on society that have come about through scientific and technological developments.

5. Write an essay comparing the positive and negative influences on society that have come about through scientific and technological developments. Decide whether you agree with this statement: 'Scientific and technological developments cause more harm to society than help.'

6. Complete these sentences:

a) The time people spend looking at electronic devices such as computers, laptops, phones or tablets is known as _____.

b) If someone is overweight, they are described as _____.

c) An injury to one of the digits on your hand caused by the overuse of electronic devices is known as _____.

d) You can get _____ neck by using electronic devices too much.

7. Write a short report outlining the reasons for urbanisation.

8. Explain the role that migration has in relation to urbanisation.

9. Answer 'urban' or 'rural' to these questions:

a) There are fewer job opportunities here.

b) The standard of living is higher.

c) The health care facilities tend to be more basic.

d) Sanitation is usually better in these areas.

e) There are more sectors of industry here.

f) Jobs tend to be better paid.

10. Why is the shortage of housing in urban areas a problem?

11. Explain, in your own words, how family planning can help to control population density.

12. Match the two parts of these sentences, (i–vi) to (a–f):

i) A distance learning course is a form of education

ii) Rural areas often have problems with water distribution

iii) Building better quality roads would improve the

iv) Initiatives to improve electricity connection in rural areas

v) The provision of wireless communication and internet services in rural areas

vi) Government-subsidised health programmes,

a) infrastructure from rural to urban areas and would also be much more reliable.

b) where the students work at home and send in their work to a teacher over the internet.

c) such as immunisation, and health centres, can improve health services.

d) would help those areas to connect better with the outside world.

e) and quality, and because they are too far from national distribution systems.

f) include using local generators by using solar power.

Checking your progress

To make good progress in understanding different aspects of our environment, check to make sure you understand these ideas.

Examine scientific and technological developments in society.

Research a topic and explain how it has impacted on modern, everyday life.

Discuss which technological development has had the most impact on society.

Evaluate the positive influence of scientific and technological developments on the environment.

Explain how communication and medicine are beneficial to society.

Record how technology impacts on your everyday life.

Evaluate the negative influence of scientific and technological developments on the environment.

Explain the health problems that technology can cause.

Explain the environmental problems that technology can cause.

Discuss the reasons for urbanisation.

Explain the positive and negative effects of urbanisation.

Write a newspaper article about overpopulation and ways to prevent high population densities.

Unit 6: The physical Earth and human interactions

In this unit you will find out

Earth's structure
- Describe the internal layers of the Earth; major crustal plates
- Identify the features found at crustal plate margins or boundaries
- Explain the relationship between plate boundaries and earthquakes, rock types, volcanoes, fold mountains, tsunamis
- Explain the formation of the three types of rocks

Earth's natural disasters
- Define terms and concepts: earthquake, seismic, focus, epicentre, magnitude
- Locate on a map major earthquake zones in the Caribbean
- Describe the use of seismographs and the Richter scale in measuring the occurrence and magnitude of earthquakes
- The effect of earthquakes on the physical and human environment
- Mitigation strategies against earthquakes
- Define the term volcano; the structure of a volcano
- The effects of volcanic eruptions on the physical and human environment
- Interpret photographs to analyse the impacts of earthquakes and volcanoes

Weather and climate
- Differentiate between weather and climate
- State the elements of the weather and climate
- Seasonal types experienced in the five climatic zones
- The ways climate influences ways of life
- Interpret line and bar graphs and isohyet maps
- Classification of hurricanes according to the Saffir-Simpson Scale
- The effects of hurricanes in the Caribbean
- The weather conditions associated with the passage of a hurricane (before, during and after)
- Precautions to minimise the effects of hurricanes; practise responsible behaviour

The structure of the Earth

We are learning to:

- describe the internal layers of the Earth: crust, mantle and core.

The crust

The Earth has three main layers: **crust, mantle** and **core.**

The crust is the outermost layer of the Earth, and it is the thinnest layer. It is the part that we live on. The crust floats on top of the mantle. It ranges from 5 km to 70 km in depth. There are two types of crust:

- **continental crust** – the part that the continents are on; it is 20–70 km in depth and extends into the mantle
- **oceanic crust** – found under the seas and oceans (about 6 km in depth).

The crust is not one solid piece but it is split into different parts called **tectonic plates**.

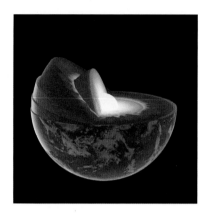

An illustration of the internal layers of the Earth.

The mantle

The mantle is the thickest layer of the Earth and has an average thickness of 2 880 km. Temperatures in the mantle are very hot – approximately 900 °C. In the mantle there are both liquid and solid rocks. The liquid rock is known as **magma**.

The core

The core is the very centre of the Earth. It is split into two parts, the **inner core** (about 2 400 km thick), which is solid and made of iron, and the **outer core** (about 2 200 km thick), which surrounds the inner core and is liquid nickel. Temperatures in the core can reach 6 000 °C.

Exercise

1. Using your own words, define crust, mantle and core.
2. Look carefully at the text.
   a) Which is the thickest part of the Earth's layers?
   b) Which is the hottest part?
   c) Which part is exposed to the Earth's surface?
   d) Name the two types of crust.

An apple is an easy way to understand the structure of the Earth:

- The skin of the apple is the crust.
- The fleshy part, nearest to the core of an apple, is a little softer than the rest of it.
- The core of an apple is similar to the outer and inner cores of the Earth.

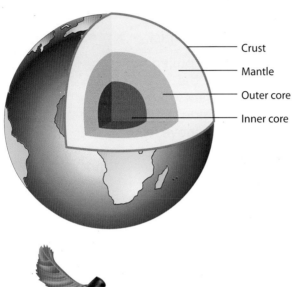

Crust

Mantle

Outer core

Inner core

Exercise

3. Which part of the apple represents the crust?

4. Why do you think we use an apple to help us understand the structure of the Earth?

5. Draw your own diagram to show the structure of the Earth. Label your drawing, and add labels for the oceanic and continental crusts.

Key vocabulary

crust

mantle

core

continental crust

oceanic crust

tectonic plates

magma

inner/outer core

Major crustal plates

We are learning to:

- describe major crustal plates
- locate the major crustal plates inclusive of the Caribbean and neighbouring plates on a world map.

Tectonic plates

The Earth's crust is split into seven main plates and many more smaller plates. These are called tectonic plates and they float like rafts on top of the liquid rocks in the mantle.

The plates move because they are being pushed and pulled in different directions by **convection currents** inside the mantle. Convection currents are very similar to currents that are found in rivers, seas and oceans but they are inside the Earth. Because of these currents, the tectonic plates move in different ways.

Boundary margins

Where two tectonic plates meet it is called a **plate boundary** or **plate margin.** There are four different types of plate margins, depending on the direction the plates are moving in:

- Constructive (or divergent) plate margins. This is when two plates move away from each other. Magma from the mantle rises to the surface in between the two plates and hardens to form new land. **Volcanic eruptions** are common at constructive plate margins.

- Conservative (or transform) plate margins. This is when two plates slide past each other. **Earthquakes** occur here as the two plates move past each other.

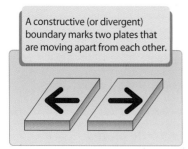

A constructive (or divergent) boundary marks two plates that are moving apart from each other.

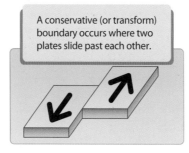

A conservative (or transform) boundary occurs where two plates slide past each other.

- Destructive (or convergent) plate margins. This is when two plates move towards each other. In this scenario, one plate is made of continental crust and the other of oceanic crust. When they move towards each other, the oceanic crust is pushed underneath the continental crust, where it melts. Both volcanic eruptions and earthquakes are found at destructive plate margins.

- Continental plate collision. This is when two continental plates move towards each other. The continental crust cannot sink, so the land is pushed upwards instead and forms very high mountains, called **fold mountains**.

The Caribbean and plate tectonics

The Caribbean Plate has four plate margins, which makes it a very active area. The North American Plate is above it and the South American Plate is below. The Nazca Plate and the Cocos Plate are both to the left of the Caribbean Plate.

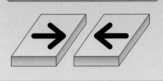

A destructive (or convergent) boundary occurs where two plates made up of continental and oceanic crust are pushing towards each other.

Continental plate collision occurs when two continental plates move towards each other.

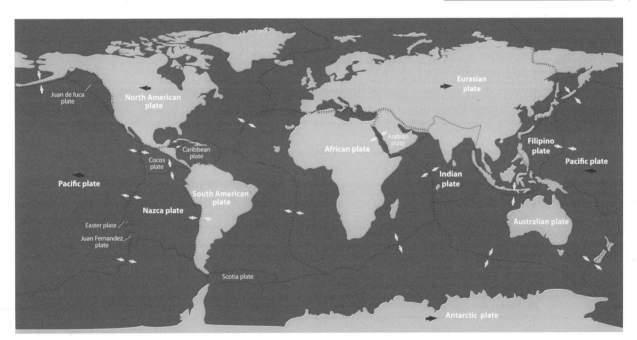

Tectonic plates of Earth.

Exercise

1. In your own words, define the term plate boundary/margin.

2. Name the four types of plate margin.

3. How many plate margins are in the Caribbean? Name them.

Key vocabulary

convection current

plate boundary/margin

volcanic eruption

earthquake

fold mountains

Plate margin features

We are learning to:

- identify the features found at crustal plate margins or boundaries
- explain the relationship between plate boundaries and earthquakes, rock types, volcanoes, fold mountains and tsunamis.

The features found at plate margins ⟩⟩

The type of features found at the different plate margins depends on the direction that the plates are moving in. There are many examples of tectonic activity, but not all occur at all plate boundaries. The table summarises the features that are found at each.

Plate margin	Description	Features	Two plates where this happens	Example
Constructive (or divergent)	Two plates move away from each other	Volcano Volcanic islands/ new land Earthquake	North American Plate and Eurasian Plate	Iceland
Conservative (or transform)	Two plates slide past each other	Earthquake	Pacific Plate and North American Plate	San Andreas Fault, USA
Destructive (or convergent)	A continental plate and oceanic plate move towards each other	Volcano Earthquake	Cocos Plate and Caribbean Plate	Mexico
Collision	Two continental plates move towards each other	Fold mountains Earthquake	Eurasian Plate and Indo-Australian Plate	Himalayas

Exercise

1. Name four different features that are found at destructive plate boundaries.

2. Give an example of a country or area where two plates move away from each other.

3. What features are found at collision plate boundaries?

4. Give an example of two plates that form a conservative plate boundary.

One of the volcanic Aeolian Islands near Sicily in Italy.

Some of the less well-known features of plate margins are:

- Volcanic islands – areas of new land that have been created at constructive plate margins. As two plates move away from each other, magma rises up and erupts over the sea or land. Here it forms solid rock. More and more rock is created every time an eruption happens. The volcano gradually gets higher, until it rises above the surface, forming an island.

- Folding and faulting – folds in the Earth's surface occur when there has been a huge amount of force put on it. The best examples of this are fold mountains. As two continental plates move towards each other, the plates cannot sink, so they are pushed upwards.

- **Faults** – cracks in the Earth's crust. They form when stress is put onto the rocks, usually by the movement of plates. As the plates move, rocks crack.

- **Subduction zones** – subduction is the downward movement of an oceanic plate underneath a continental plate into the Earth's mantle.

- Tsunamis – a series of waves that form in the oceans following an earthquake or underwater volcanic eruption. These waves are different from normal sea waves because of their size and the speed at which they move towards land. These waves travel at speeds of more than 950 km per hour.

- Rock types – there are many different types of rock on the Earth's surface and they are all formed from different processes. Most rocks can fall into one of three categories: igneous, sedimentary or metamorphic.

Discussion

In groups, discuss where earthquakes and volcanoes are found and the relationship between the movement of plates and the features found there. Share your discussion with the rest of the class.

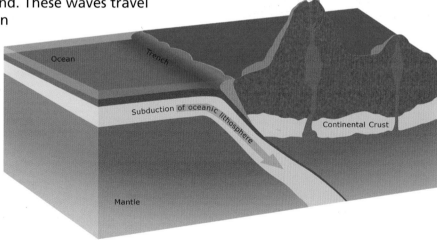

Volcano

Ocean

Trench

Subduction of oceanic lithosphere

Continental Crust

Mantle

Subduction zone – the downward movement of an oceanic plate below a continental plate and into the Earth's mantle.

Exercise

5. Describe how volcanic islands form.

6. What is the difference between a fold and a fault?

7. Where do subduction zones occur?

8. What are the three main causes of tsunamis?

Key vocabulary

faults

subduction zone

Types of rock

We are learning to:

- explain the formation of the three types of rocks and give examples.

Rock types

There are three main rock types found on the Earth: **igneous**, **sedimentary** and **metamorphic**. These rocks have been formed by different processes, known as the rock cycle – a process through which the major rock types change into each other.

Igneous rocks

Igneous rocks are the most common rock type found on Earth. They are formed when magma from the mantle rises to the surface, then cools and hardens. This hardened rock is called igneous rock.

There are many examples of igneous rock, such as basalt, granite and obsidian. All igneous rocks contain crystals. Some rocks will have larger crystals than others – the size of the crystals depends on how quickly the magma cooled. The larger the crystal, the slower the magma **solidified**.

There are two types of igneous rock: **intrusive** and **extrusive**. Intrusive igneous rocks form inside the Earth – most igneous rocks are formed beneath the surface. These rocks have much larger crystals, because it has taken a long time for the rocks to cool.

Granite is the most well-known intrusive igneous rock. Extrusive igneous rocks form above the surface. These rocks generally form from a volcanic eruption as lava is ejected from a volcano. These rocks have much smaller crystals, because they have cooled very quickly. Examples of extrusive igneous rocks are obsidian, pumice and basalt.

Obsidian is an igneous rock.

Activity

Use the internet to research the term 'rock cycle', then draw a diagram to show the cycle.

Did you know...?

- Igneous rock can change into sedimentary rock or into metamorphic rock.
- Sedimentary rock can change into metamorphic rock or into igneous rock.
- Metamorphic rock can change into igneous or sedimentary rock.

Exercise

1. Name the three main rock types.
2. Explain how igneous rocks form.
3. If an igneous rock has large crystals, has it cooled quickly or slowly?
4. What are the two types of igneous rock. How do they differ?
5. Give examples of both types of igneous rock.

Sedimentary rocks >>>>

Sedimentary rocks form under the seas and oceans. They form when the sediment that was **transported** (carried) by rivers into the seas and oceans is **deposited** (laid down) at the bottom of the sea floor. This sediment includes things such as sand and pieces of rock – even the skeletons of sea creatures.

The weight of the sediment squeezes down on the previous layer and squeezes out the water (**compaction**), which allows salt crystals to form. The crystals help to glue all the sediment together, forming a rock (**cementation**).

This process will continue with more layers added on top, so sedimentary rocks have very clear layers. Examples of sedimentary rock include limestone, chalk and sandstone.

Prehistoric fossil found in sedimentary rock.

Slate is a metamorphic rock.

Metamorphic rocks >>

Metamorphic rocks are formed by pressure or heat under the surface. They are formed from igneous and sedimentary rocks. Igneous and sedimentary rocks can be heated under the surface of the Earth. This will usually happen if they are close to rising magma. These rocks do not melt, but change chemically.

The heating of these rocks puts them under huge pressure and the crystals become arranged in layers. There are many examples of metamorphic rock. Slate and marble are possibly the most well known. Slate is formed from shale; marble from limestone. Others include:

- quartzite – formed from sandstone
- gneiss – formed from granite
- granulite – formed from basalt.

Exercise

6. Describe how sedimentary rocks are formed.
7. Give two examples of sedimentary rocks.
8. How are metamorphic rocks formed?
9. Give two examples of metamorphic rock and state what rock they originated from.

Activity

Your teacher will give you 10 different rocks. Identify the different rock types.

Key vocabulary

igneous rocks

sedimentary rocks

metamorphic rocks

solidified

intrusive rock

extrusive rock

transported

deposited

compaction

cementation

Earth's natural disasters

We are learning to:

- define terms and concepts: earthquake, seismic, focus, epicentre, magnitude
- locate on a map major earthquake zones in the Caribbean
- describe the use of seismographs and the Richter scale in measuring the occurrence and magnitude of earthquakes.

Earthquakes ≫

An **earthquake** is a sudden shaking of the Earth's crust. The shaking happens when tectonic plates move. Earthquakes happen at all plate boundaries.

At constructive plate margins, the plates are moving away from each other. Magma then rises to the surface. An earthquake can occur as the magma moves its way through the crust.

Earthquakes happen at all plate boundaries.

- At destructive plate boundaries, two plates are moving towards each other. As they push against each other, the oceanic plate is forced underneath the continental plate. The sudden downward movement of the oceanic plate causes the land to shake violently.

- At conservative plate margins, the plates are sliding past each other. This is not a smooth process and the two plates often jolt and judder suddenly as the move causes the land to shake.

- At collision plate boundaries, two plates are moving towards each other. These two plates are made of continental crust, so the land is pushed upwards. Often the upward movement of the crust can cause it to shake.

The term **seismic activity** is used to refer to the movement of tectonic plates and the activity that results, such as earthquakes or volcanic eruptions.

When an earthquake happens, the point at which it happens underground is called the **focus.** The point directly above the focus on the Earth's surface is called the **epicentre.**

Magnitude refers to the size of the earthquake. The **Richter scale** shows the strength of an earthquake.

Recording and measuring an earthquake ▶▶▶

When an earthquake happens, **seismic waves** are sent out from the focus and travel through the crust. These waves are then picked up and recorded on instruments called **seismographs**. Seismographs are able to detect strong earthquakes anywhere in the world. They can also record the time and location. To pick up smaller magnitudes, local seismographs are used.

The size of the earthquake is then shown using the Richter scale. The Richter scale goes from 1.0 to 9.9, with 9.9 being the strongest. There has never actually been an earthquake measuring 9.9. The most powerful earthquake ever recorded was 9.5 – occurring in Chile, in 1960.

Activity

Using a shake table, explain how different structures respond to earthquakes.

Usually not felt, but can be recorded by topography	1.0-1.9	Micro
Vibrations detected	2.0-2.9	Minor
	3.0-3.9	
	4.0-4.9	Light
Windows rattle or break, light damage	5.0-5.9	Moderate
Crack in buildings, falling branches	6.0-6.9	Strong
Buildings collapse, landslides	7.0-7.9	Major
	8.0-8.9	Great
Devastation, many deaths	9.0 and greater	

Earthquake magnitude scale.

Exercise

1. Explain how earthquakes occur at constructive and destructive plate boundaries.
2. What is the difference between the focus and the epicentre?
3. What is the difference between magnitude and the Richter scale?
4. What do seismographs pick up?

Key vocabulary

earthquake

seismic/seismic activity

focus

epicentre

magnitude

Richter scale

seismic waves

seismographs

Effects of earthquakes

We are learning to:

- examine the effects of earthquakes on the physical and human environment
- interpret photographs to analyse the impacts of earthquakes on the environment.

Effects of earthquakes 》》

The damage caused by an earthquake depends on a number of different factors, however the strength of the earthquake is possibly the most important factor.

Earthquakes with a magnitude of less than 6.0 generally don't cause a lot of damage. However, earthquakes with a magnitude over 6.0 can be highly destructive.

Effects of earthquakes on the human environment 》》

Strong earthquakes can have devastating effects on the human environment. The most common effects include:

- buildings and infrastructure (roads and bridges) collapse
- loss of life and property
- injury
- homelessness
- broken gas and water pipes
- fires break out
- contaminated water supplies
- spread of disease.

Effects of earthquakes on the physical environment 》》》

As with the human environment, there are many effects of earthquakes on the physical environment such as:

- tsunamis and flooding
- **aftershocks** – small earthquakes following the main one
- **landslides** – sudden movement of rock, earth or debris down a slope
- **mudslides** – wet soil or sand moves suddenly downhill
- farmland and vegetation destroyed by tsunamis, landslides, mudslides and flooding.

A road damaged during an earthquake.

Research

Using the internet, research photographs and newspaper articles documenting different earthquakes. Analyse the impact of earthquakes on the environment.

Case study

Haiti earthquake

On 12 January 2010, an earthquake measuring 7.0 on the Richter scale affected the countries of Haiti and the Dominican Republic. The epicentre of the earthquake was 16 km west of Haiti's capital of Port-au-Prince. The focus was only 8 km beneath the surface.

Haiti lies on the boundary of the Caribbean and North American Plates. This is a conservative plate boundary – the Caribbean Plate is moving in one direction and the North American Plate goes in the opposite one.

The human effects of the earthquake were devastating. It is estimated that, as a result of the earthquake, approximately 220 000 people were killed and 300 000 were injured. It is believed that 250 000 homes were destroyed and, as a result, 1 million people were made homeless. In total, 3 million people were affected.

Transport and communication links – such as roads and railways – were destroyed or badly damaged. This meant that emergency services could not get through to certain areas. More than 50 hospitals are thought to have been badly damaged, as well as 1 300 schools.

Following the earthquake, experts identified that two tsunami waves affected Caribbean regions, with waves approximately 3 m high. The waves affected the coastline along the Bay of Port-au-Prince and the southern coast of the island of Hispaniola. It is believed that the tsunamis killed three people and destroyed several homes.

Following the initial earthquake, there were 52 aftershocks measuring 4.5 or more on the Richter scale, These lasted until 24 January – 12 days after the first earthquake.

Building damage during an earthquake in Turkey, 2011.

Questions

1. Name five effects of earthquakes on the human and physical environment.

2. What caused the earthquake in Haiti in 2010?

3. In total, how many people are thought to have been affected by the earthquake?

4. How many aftershocks followed the initial earthquake?

5. Study the photographs below showing the effects of an earthquake. Analyse the impact of the earthquake in these photographs.

Activity

Write three paragraphs explaining how you felt (or think you would feel) if you were in an earthquake.

Key vocabulary

aftershock

landslide

mudslide

Planning against earthquakes

We are learning to:

- demonstrate an understanding of the mitigation strategies used against earthquakes.

A **mitigation strategy** is a plan to reduce the loss of life and property by lessening the impact of disasters. There are a number of things that people can do to minimise the damage caused by earthquakes.

What can you do?

When people live in areas that are prone to earthquakes, they are well educated in what to do in the event of an earthquake:

- At school, students are taught and regularly practise what to do in the event of an earthquake. Earthquake drills are often used in school in order to prepare the students. These might be rehearsed once a month.
- People stock up on food, water and medical supplies.
- Any business or organisation responsible for many people will also want to educate their employees on what to do in the event of an earthquake.
- There is a worldwide strategy called 'Drop, Cover and Hold' that helps to educate people all over the world in what to do during an earthquake.
- Most schools and businesses will also have a tsunami evacuation plan if they are in areas that are vulnerable to natural disasters.

Preparedness kit

People in areas prone to earthquakes and tsunamis are also encouraged to have a disaster supply kit in their houses and businesses. This is usually a rucksack filled with belongings that will be useful in the event of a natural disaster. Some of the things that people might put in their disaster supply kit include:

- first-aid kit and medications
- torch
- water and canned/tinned food
- emergency contact numbers
- cash.

If you are in a building, you should:

DROP to the ground (before the earthquake drops you!),

Take **COVER** by getting under a sturdy desk or table

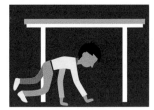

and **HOLD ON** to it until the shaking stops.

If you are outside, move away from buildings, trees, street lights and power lines, then 'Drop, Cover and Hold' until the shaking stops.

Building design ▶▶▶

There are a number of things that countries can do to minimise the damage caused by earthquakes. One of the best things they can do is alter the design and materials used on new buildings and roads.

Traditionally, buildings and roads are made from concrete, which will collapse during an earthquake. Countries such as Japan, which experience a lot of earthquakes, have found that by building with materials that gently sway with the movement of the earthquake, buildings are far more likely to stay standing. Therefore all new buildings and roads are being built in this way.

Insurance ▶▶

People can take out insurance on homes, property and possessions, so that the insurance company will pay out to replace anything that is damaged in an earthquake. This can be great for replacing possessions, but will not make up for sentimental items lost or damaged during an earthquake or tsunami.

Earthquake-resistant skyscrapers in Tokyo.

Early warning systems ▶▶▶

As earthquakes cannot be predicted, it is only possible to alert people after the earthquake has already happened. Early warning systems send out alerts to people all over the country to say that an earthquake has been detected. Even a few seconds can minimise the damage and loss of life caused by an earthquake, so they are seen as very useful.

When people are alerted of an earthquake, they can follow the 'Drop, Cover and Hold' procedures, move to safe locations and the emergency services can be put on standby. All of these steps should help to reduce the number of people killed or injured during an earthquake.

Exercise

1. What is the 'Drop, Cover and Hold' procedure?
2. Give examples of things that should be included in a disaster supply kit.
3. Describe how building design can help to reduce damage.
4. Why is it beneficial for people to take out earthquake insurance?

Activity

Outline at least three strategies that could be used by individuals or communities to reduce the amount of damage caused during an earthquake.

Activity

Your teacher will give you a copy of your school's evacuation plan. Study the plan and then, in groups, role-play what you would do in the event of an earthquake.

Key vocabulary

mitigation strategy

An earthquake action plan

We are learning to:

- create an action plan to assist people affected by earthquakes
- practise responsible behaviour in times of disaster.

Action Plan ⟩⟩

In countries where earthquakes are very common, emergency Action Plans will be created so that everybody knows what to do during an earthquake. The following is an example of a school's Action Plan for an earthquake situation. Your school will have one that is very similar.

OBJECTIVES

The main objectives are to:
- ensure the safety of all students, staff and visitors during and after an emergency
- prepare students, staff and visitors for an emergency
- plan a safe and well-designed response to emergencies
- protect the school building and facilities
- provide the school with a coordinated approach to restoring normal conditions following an emergency.

IDENTIFY TASKS

There are a number of tasks that need to be completed before, during and after an earthquake. These include making sure that:
- every member of staff and all students are aware that an emergency is imminent/taking place/has occurred
- all staff/students follow the emergency procedures
- the emergency services are notified
- students are reassured during and after an emergency
- first-aid treatment is given to those who need it
- all staff and students are accounted for following an emergency, and anyone missing is reported immediately
- other members of staff and students are helped
- order is restored.

DELEGATE TASKS

Some members of staff will have more responsibility than others – for example, senior management (headteachers, for example) will be expected to take on more responsibilities before, during and after an emergency. Classroom teachers are expected to follow the emergency procedures thoroughly.

SUCCESS CRITERIA

For a school to measure the success of an emergency situation, the following must be considered:
- the time taken for a drill to be issued and time taken to evacuate the school
- whether all staff and students followed procedures

- the number of casualties
- the time taken for emergency services to respond.

TIME FRAME

The time frame depends on the nature of the emergency. Procedures should be carried out as quickly as possible, ensuring that all staff and students find a safe place or are evacuated from the building as quickly as possible.

RESOURCES NEEDED

It is recommended that the following items are supplied to all classrooms:

- first-aid kit
- blankets
- blank class register
- pens
- whistle
- drinking water
- portable radio
- torch.

EVIDENCE OF COMPLETION

Following an emergency, the headteacher must complete an Emergency Response Form detailing the incident, making specific mention to the success criteria of the emergency.

Project

Imagine that an earthquake situation is about to happen. In groups, write your own Action Plan, using the following headings: Objectives, Identify tasks, Delegate tasks, Success criteria, Time frame, Resources needed, Evidence of completion. Use the example Action Plan to help you.

Being responsible >>>

Above all else, there are things that people should do during an emergency:

- stay calm and try not to panic
- follow instructions that are given to you
- put into practice safety procedures – for example, find a safe place to take cover
- help others where possible, but not at the expense of your own safety
- stay where you are until you are absolutely sure that the disaster is over.

Exercise

1. What are the main objectives of an Action Plan?

2. How is the success of an emergency situation measured?

3. What resources must all classrooms have?

4. Why do you think it is important for schools to have an Action Plan?

5. Why do you think you need to act responsibly during an emergency?

Volcanoes

We are learning to:

- define the term volcano
- name and locate on a world map three active volcanoes within the Caribbean and other areas of the world
- draw an annotated diagram to show the structure of a volcano.

Volcanoes

Volcanoes are hills or mountains that allow lava, gas and ash to escape. Volcanoes can come in three different states:

- **active** – could erupt at any time
- **dormant** – has not erupted in 10 000 years, but could do again
- **extinct** – has not erupted in the last 10 000 years and will not erupt again.

There are two different types of volcano, depending on where and how they are formed:

- **Shield volcanoes** form at constructive plate boundaries. As two plates move away from each other, magma rises to the surface. As it reaches the land, the lava explodes over the land as a volcanic eruption. The lava is very thin and runny, so it spreads out over the land. Eventually the lava hardens to form igneous rock. As more and more eruptions occur, the lava builds up, forming a low-lying, wide hill known as a shield volcano.

- **Composite volcanoes** form at destructive plate boundaries. As the oceanic plate is pushed down into the mantle, magma rises to the surface and explodes over the land. The lava here is very thick, so doesn't flow very fast. The best example of this is pahoehoe lava. The lava and ash build up to form a cone-shaped volcano with alternating layers of lava and ash. As more and more eruptions occur, the volcano becomes higher.

Nevis Peak is a potentially active volcano on Nevis, St Kitts and Nevis.

Exercise

1. Name the three different states in which a volcano can exist.

2. What are the differences between a shield volcano and a composite volcano?

Structure of a volcano ▶▶▶

All cone (composite) volcanoes have a similar structure:

- a magma chamber underneath the Earth's surface
- a cone-shaped hill or mountain built by layers of lava, rocks and ash
- a conduit (pipe) that runs up the centre of the volcano from the magma chamber to the vent, as well as a crater at the top.

Active volcanoes in the Caribbean ▶▶▶

- Soufrière Hills volcano in Montserrat is a composite volcano formed on the margin of the North Atlantic Plate and the Caribbean Plate. Soufrière Hills volcano has had a number of devastating eruptions over the years, the most recent being in 2010, when an eruption led to a **pyroclastic flow** that affected the surrounding area. In 2009, Soufrière Hills had a number of eruptions, also creating pyroclastic flows. One of the eruptions even led to a **lahar** ripping through the Belham Valley.

- Mount Pelée is another composite volcano in the Caribbean. It is located in Martinique in the West Indies. One of its most deadly eruptions was in 1902, when the entire city of Saint-Pierre was destroyed by the eruption and pyroclastic flow that occurred on 2 May. There were only a handful of survivors in the whole city. In 1929, the volcano began to erupt again, triggering pyroclastic flows and lahars. However, this was not nearly as deadly as the eruption in 1902, as authorities evacuated the area quickly.

- Morne Watt is a composite volcano found in Dominica. It is a very tall volcano, reaching heights of 1 224 m, which makes it one of the highest peaks in Dominica. There was a major eruption that took place 1 300 years ago, as well as a small eruption in 1997.

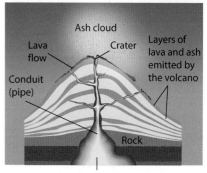

The structure of a volcano.

Project

Using the internet, choose one volcanic eruption that has taken place in the Caribbean and research it fully. Produce a PowerPoint presentation or a poster on the eruption of the volcano.

Exercise

3. Define the terms pyroclastic flow and lahar.
4. Where is the magma chamber in a volcano?
5. What is the cone-shaped hill of a volcano made out of?
6. What type of volcano is Mount Pelée?
7. Draw a diagram or create a model, to show the structure of a volcanic cone.

Key vocabulary

volcano

active

dormant

extinct

shield volcano

composite volcano

pyroclastic flow

lahar

Materials ejected by volcanoes

We are learning to:

- describe the materials ejected by volcanoes.

Materials ejected by volcanoes 〉〉

Not all volcanoes eject the same materials: some volcanoes erupt lava, while others have no lava eruption at all. There are a number of different volcanic materials that may be ejected from a volcano during a volcanic eruption.

Lava 〉〉〉

Lava is the most common type of volcanic material. When it is below ground, it is known as magma. It is not until it has been erupted from a volcano that it becomes known as lava.

Lava is different depending on the type of volcano it is erupting from. Shield volcanoes have thin, runny lava, and are often referred to as having **low viscosity**. **High viscosity lava** is the opposite. This is very thick lava that is ejected from composite volcanoes.

Molten lava coming from Eyjafjallajökull eruption, Iceland.

Ash 〉〉〉〉

Volcanic ash is made from rock and volcanic glass. It is formed during a volcanic eruption when the rock and glass are pulverised.

Volcanic ash is very different from ash made from burning wood, as it is much harder and coarser. Also, unlike ash from burning wood, it doesn't dissolve in water. It has a sand-/grain-like appearance. Volcanic ash can be very harmful.

Volcanic bombs 〉〉

A volcanic bomb is a large piece of molten rock that is ejected from a volcano during an eruption. In order to be classed as a volcanic bomb a rock has to be more than 6.4 cm wide, but they can reach sizes of over 5 m.

Exercise

1. What is the difference between high viscosity lava and low viscosity lava?

2. What is volcanic ash made from?

3. What is a volcanic bomb?

Gases

There are a number of gases that are emitted during a volcanic eruption. In fact, some volcanoes only eject gases during an eruption. The most common of these gases are:

- Carbon dioxide – can be deadly. Volcanoes quite often emit carbon dioxide (not just during an eruption). Small amounts of this gas in the air are not harmful to people. However, if the concentration increases, it can lead to headaches, dizziness and even death.
- Sulphur dioxide – more of an irritant than a deadly gas. Emissions of sulphur dioxide can cause irritation to your eyes, nose and throat.
- Hydrogen sulphide – a highly toxic gas. In small concentrations, it can be sensed in the air by our noses, as it has a rotten egg smell. As the amount in the atmosphere increases, its smell disappears. This is a problem, because high concentrations of hydrogen sulphide can very quickly lead to death.

People watching the volcanic ash cloud from Eyjafjallajökull eruption, Iceland.

Pyroclastic materials

A pyroclastic flow is a cloud of extremely hot gas and ash that erupts from a volcano and then travels down volcanic slopes, destroying everything in its path. They are very dangerous, as they can reach temperatures of up to 1 000 °C and can travel at speeds of 720 km per hour.

The extremely high temperatures, combined with the high speeds, mean that pyroclastic flows are one of the deadliest effects of volcanic eruptions. Pyroclastic flows can be life threatening:

- In AD 79, the eruption of Mount Vesuvius and subsequent pyroclastic flow killed everyone in Pompeii (now Naples), in Italy.
- In 1991, over 40 people were killed in Japan when a pyroclastic surge erupted from Mount Unzen.
- In 1997, 19 people were killed on the Caribbean island of Montserrat from a pyroclastic flow down Mosquito Ghaut.

Activity

Your teacher will select documentaries, case studies, DVDs and internet resources of volcanic eruptions for you to review in class.

Exercise

4. Give three examples of volcanic gas.
5. What is a pyroclastic flow?

Project

Your teacher will divide the class into three or four groups. They will give you a worksheet and all the materials to create a model volcano and show how an eruption happens.

Key vocabulary

low viscosity

high viscosity

The negative effects of volcanoes

We are learning to:

- examine the effects of volcanic eruption on the physical and human environment
- interpret photographs to analyse the impact of volcanic eruptions on the environment.

Negative effects of volcanic eruptions

Volcanic eruptions can have devastating effects on an area and can also cause widespread death and destruction.

Damage to buildings

Buildings can be completely destroyed during a volcanic eruption. The eruption itself will not cause too much damage to buildings. However, a pyroclastic flow or lahar can be devastating. Pyroclastic flows can completely destroy anything in their path, including buildings and roads.

A house is buried by lava on Mount Etna, Sicily, Italy.

Lahars can also be devastating, as these are fast-moving flows of water, and volcanic debris can completely bury buildings and roads. As they travel, lahars also pick up a huge amount of debris that is then able to cause even more damage to structures such as buildings, roads and bridges.

Volcanic ash can be particularly problematic, because when it is mixed with rainwater it becomes very heavy and **dense**. This can cause roofs to collapse.

Destruction of vegetation

As with damage to buildings, volcanic eruptions can also destroy **vegetation** in the area.

Pyroclastic flows will burn or singe plants, trees and other types of vegetation, since they are not able to withstand the very high temperatures. Lahars have the power to uproot trees and transport them as they travel downhill.

Exercise

1. Which causes most damage to buildings – the volcanic eruption or the pyroclastic flow?

2. How do volcanic eruptions cause damage to buildings?

3. How is vegetation destroyed by volcanic eruptions?

Key vocabulary

dense

vegetation

Effects on the climate

Volcanic eruptions can have significant effects on the climate. During a volcanic eruption, large quantities of gases (such as sulphur dioxide) and dust are ejected into the atmosphere. The presence of large amounts of gas and dust in the atmosphere can stop sunlight from getting through and therefore lowers temperatures at the Earth's surface.

Loss of life and property

Volcanic eruptions are not necessarily the deadliest of natural disasters. However, there have been a number of deadly volcanic eruptions over the years. The eruption of Mount Vesuvius in Pompeii (now Naples) is probably one of the deadliest volcanic eruptions, as it killed the entire population of Pompeii.

More recent deadly eruptions include the eruptions of: Krakatoa, in 1883, which killed 36 000 people; Mount Lamington, which killed 2 942 in 1951; and Mount Pinatubo in 1991, which killed 847. Most people killed during a volcanic eruption are killed by pyroclastic flows.

Chances Peak, part of the Soufrière Hills (on the island of Montserrat in the Caribbean) is a volcanic area. In 1995, when it erupted, it had been dormant for almost 300 years. When the volcano began to erupt, it continued to do so for five years. During these years while the eruption continued, the small island population was evacuated.

Travel disruption

Volcanic eruptions can completely disrupt air travel. In 2010, after the eruption of Eyjafjallajökull in Iceland, planes were grounded all over the Europe for almost eight days. This inaction cost airlines an estimated £1 billion of losses.

Air traffic is suspended during a volcanic eruption, because the volcanic ash is extremely harmful to plane engines. If ash gets into the engines, it can cause them to stall and crash.

Eruption of Eyjafjallajökull volcano, Iceland, in 2010.

Research

Using library and internet resources, research the eruption of the Soufrière Hills volcano on Montserrat. Present your findings to your class either in the form of a poster or as a PowerPoint presentation.

Activity

Study the photographs on pages 142–145 showing the effects of volcanic eruptions. What damage can be seen from these photos? What impact to the climate do you think the photo on page 143 shows?

Exercise

4. What is the biggest cause of death during a volcanic eruption?

5. Name some of the deadliest volcanic eruptions in history.

6. What causes flights to be grounded during a volcanic eruption?

The positive effects of volcanoes

We are learning to:

- appreciate the socio-economic and environmental advantages of volcanoes.

Positive effects of volcanic eruptions ⟩⟩

Although the devastation caused by volcanic eruptions can be catastrophic, people continue to live near active volcanoes. This will be considered strange to some, but there are some advantages to living close to active volcanoes.

Tourism ⟩⟩

Volcanoes attract millions of visitors every year. People have an interest in visiting volcanoes because they have such unique features and landscapes, such as geysers and bubbling mudpools. They are also interested just to see the possibility of the volcano erupting.

The influx of tourists means that new businesses can be set up to cater for these visitors. Cafés, restaurants and shops can also be established in areas where tourist numbers are high. This then benefits the whole community.

Mount Vesuvius is one of the deadliest volcanoes, but it is also one of the most popular tourist attractions in Italy. Mount Etna is another famous volcano in Italy. Volcanic areas in Iceland are also popular tourist destinations, as well as the Kamchatka region in Russia, which has the well-known Mutnovsky volcano. Finally, Hawaii is one of the most popular attractions – in particular the Kilauea volcano.

The Blue Lagoon, Iceland, is one of the best known volcanic spas in the world.

Spas/mineral springs ⟩⟩⟩

One of the most well-known volcanic **spas** in the world is the Blue Lagoon in Iceland. This is a man-made pool that is heated by the lava flow to temperatures of 37 °C. It is rich in minerals, such as silica, that have medicinal properties.

Exercise

1. What attracts tourists to volcanic regions?

2. What are the benefits of tourism in these areas?

3. How is the Blue Lagoon heated?

Geothermal energy

In volcanic regions, there is the opportunity to use the heat from underground to help to generate electricity.

Underground rocks are able to heat water that produces steam. This then drives the turbines and generates electricity.

Geothermal energy is a clean and sustainable renewable energy source. The energy is natural, forming in the earth, causes no pollution and is completely free to use. Geothermal energy can be used to heat homes and offices, and to generate electricity.

Fertile soils

Many farmers choose to live close to volcanoes. This is because the land near volcanoes can be very **fertile**. This means that the soils are very rich in nutrients, so plants grow very well here.

The ash from volcanic eruptions makes the soils very fertile, which means that these areas can be very productive farming areas.

The land beside Mount Vesuvius is particularly fertile, and farmers are able to grow vines, plant and crops there.

New land

There are many countries in the world that would not exist if there had not been volcanic eruptions.

Countries and states such as Iceland, Hawaii and Bermuda only exist because of a series of volcanic eruptions. These three volcanic islands all have people living on them. However, there are many more islands that are uninhabited.

A vineyard at the base of Mount Vesuvius, Italy.

The Hellisheidi Geothermal Power Station, Iceland.

Activity

Imagine you live near the Soufrière Hills volcano and your family has been forced to relocate to the north of the island. Write a letter to a friend describing how you feel about the challenges you are facing.

Exercise

4. What is geothermal energy? What can it be used for?

5. Why is farming so good near volcanoes?

6. Give examples of countries/states formed from volcanic eruptions.

7. Create a photo montage showing at least three negative and three positive effects of volcanic eruptions in the Caribbean.

Key vocabulary

....

spa

geothermal energy

fertile

Weather and climate

We are learning to:

- differentiate between weather and climate
- state the elements of the weather and climate.

Weather and climate

Weather is a set of conditions in the atmosphere at a particular time and place. It changes all the time, and the weather in one place is different from the conditions elsewhere. For example, it may be dry in the morning, then rainy in the afternoon, or it may be calm at your home but windy at your school.

Climate is pattern of weather in a place over a longer period. The climate of a place controls the weather. For example, it would be very unusual to have a snowstorm in the Caribbean, because our climate is generally warm and mild.

The weather is a set of conditions at a certain time and place – for example, it may be windy and rainy one day, and sunny and hot the next day.

The weather

Most people watch, talk about and look up the weather daily. This is because the weather is so important to our everyday lives. We might only check the weather so that we can decide what to wear that day or see whether we should take an umbrella out with us.

For other people, the weather is more important, however. For example, it is vital that a farmer knows what is going on with the weather, so that he knows when to plough his fields or harvest his crops.

He might also need to keep up to date with the weather in case there is a risk of flooding, which might drown his crops or endanger his animals. Regardless of the reason we need to know the weather, the fact is, we check it on an ever-increasing basis.

Research

Using the internet, research which countries have the following:

a) highest and lowest recorded temperatures

b) wettest and driest rainfall figures

c) windiest conditions.

Exercise

1. What is the difference between weather and climate?
2. Look outside. What is the weather like today?
3. Is today's weather usual or unusual for this time of year? Give reasons for your answer.
4. Look at the photo above. Describe the weather in the photo.
5. Why might farmers need to know what the weather is going to be like?

Elements of weather and climate >>>

When we discuss weather, we usually start with how hot or cold it feels, and how wet or dry the conditions are. There are many other **elements of weather** we can measure to determine the weather conditions. The main weather elements are:

- **Temperature** – the measure of heat energy in the atmosphere around the Earth. When air has less heat energy, it feels cooler. Air temperature changes all the time, and it varies from place to place. We use a thermometer for measuring temperature. We measure temperature in degrees Celsius (°C) or degrees Fahrenheit (°F).

- **Precipitation** – usually refers to rainfall. However, precipitation is any kind of moisture that falls onto the Earth's surface, including rain, snow and sleet.

- Wind – air moving over the Earth's surface.

- Cloudiness – as warm air rises, it expands and cools. Cool air cannot hold as much water vapour as warm air can. As the water vapour cools, it condenses, forming tiny droplets around dust particles in the atmosphere. These droplets gather together to form clouds.

- Sunshine – light and heat that come from the sun.

- **Humidity** – the measure of how much water vapour is in the air at a given time. The warmer the air is, the more water vapour it holds. When air holds the maximum amount of water vapour possible, we say it is **saturated**.

- **Air pressure** – the weight of the Earth's atmosphere on its surface. Air pressure changes with the weather. It also varies from one place to another. Cold air is heavier and denser than warm air.

One of the elements of the weather that people often talk about is the temperature and how sunny it is.

Discussion

Working in groups, brainstorm two differences between weather and climate.

Exercise

6. What are the main weather elements?

7. How many of these weather elements have you seen today?

8. Observe and record the elements of weather for two weeks. Use a table like this:

	Monday	Tuesday	Wednesday	Thursday	Friday
Element					

Key vocabulary

weather

climate

elements of weather

temperature

precipitation

humidity

saturated

air pressure

Seasons and the climatic zones

We are learning to:

- describe the seasonal types experienced in the five climatic zones.

What are seasons? »

Seasons are how a year is divided and they generally have specific weather patterns associated with each season.

What are climate zones? »»

Climate zones are horizontal belts found at different **latitudes** and have varying average weather conditions. Each climate zone has different weather conditions and different seasons. There are five main climate zones.

- ● POLAR
- ● TEMPERATE
- ● ARID
- ● TROPICAL
- ● MEDITERRANEAN

DOTTED CLIMATE CLASSIFICATION WORLD MAP

A world map showing the five climate zones – equatorial (tropical), hot desert, Mediterranean, temperate and tundra (polar).

EQUATORIAL (TROPICAL) CLIMATES

Location: 10° north and south of the Equator; referred to as tropical climates as they are found between the Tropic of Cancer and the Tropic of Capricorn.

Countries:
Brazil, Venezuela, Guyana

Temperatures:
average about 27 °C

Rainfall:
around 1 500 mm per year

Seasons:
only one season throughout the year

HOT DESERT CLIMATES

Location:
20° and 35° north and south of the Equator

Countries:
Egypt, Saudi Arabia, United Arab Emirates

Temperatures:
can be as high as 50 °C but will fall at night; temperatures are hottest between April and October

Rainfall:
very little rainfall in hot desert regions; in order to be classed as a desert, there must be less than 250 mm of rain every year

Seasons:
two seasons – summer and winter

MEDITERRANEAN CLIMATES

Location:
30° and 45° north and south of the Equator

Countries:
Italy, Spain, southern Australia

Temperatures:
hot in summer months (up to 40 °C); winter temperatures average 10–15 °C

Rainfall:
there is rainfall in most months of the year other than June, July and August

Seasons:
two main seasons – summer and winter

TEMPERATE CLIMATES

Location:
40° and 60° north and south of the Equator

Countries:
UK and western states in the USA

Temperatures:
summer months average 20 °C; winter months can be cold, often falling below 0 °C

Rainfall:
rainfall all year round, including the summer months, although autumn and winter have the most rainfall

Seasons:
four seasons – spring, summer, autumn, winter

TUNDRA (COLD DESERT) CLIMATES

Location:
60° and 75° north and south of the Equator

Countries:
Greenland, northern Canada, northern Russia

Temperatures:
summer months reach 10 °C; coldest during the winter, when temperatures can go down to –50 °C

Rainfall:
very low in cold desert regions – less than 250 mm of rainfall; precipitation is most likely to fall as snow rather than rain in these regions

Seasons:
two seasons – summer and winter

Exercise

1. For each of the five climate zones, answer the following questions:

   a) On what latitude are they found?

   b) Give examples of countries that are found there.

   c) How many seasons do they have?

   d) What are temperatures like throughout the year?

   e) What is rainfall like throughout the year?

Key vocabulary
....

seasons

climate zones

latitudes

How the climate affects how we live

We are learning to:

- examine the ways climate influences ways of life.

How do the weather and climate affect us day to day?

What the weather is like affects us in our everyday lives. It influences our decisions about what we wear and what we do each day. Weather and climate affect people, industries and the environment all over the world.

Clothes worn

If you live in a very warm country, you will want to wear loose clothes made from cotton or linen, as these are cooling in warm temperatures. You will most likely wear shorts and T-shirts in warm countries, to try to stay as cool as possible.

In contrast, if you live in cold countries you will want to wrap up really warm and wear as many layers as possible. In some of the coldest countries in the world, such as northern Russia, people wear **animal hides** (skin) to keep warm. The hides of animals such as caribou and hares can be worn to protect people from the very cold air, because if you wore short sleeves in these countries you could very easily get **frostbite**. There is a phrase used in Iceland that says, 'There is no such thing as bad weather, just bad clothing.'

The sunny climate in the Caribbean means that the cricket season takes place between November and May.

Health problems

Climate affects what diseases are found, and spread, in different countries. Most diseases are very heavily influenced by the weather, and many diseases need specific weather conditions. For example, malaria is a very dangerous disease spread by mosquitoes. Mosquitoes are found all over the world and they are not all harmful. However, tropical areas, where temperatures are warm and the air is **humid** (moist), make excellent breeding conditions for mosquitoes and for this reason malaria is a problem in these areas.

Not only does warm weather cause disease, but it can also lead to other serious medical conditions such as sunburn, heatstroke and even skin cancer. Colder temperatures can cause illnesses such as frostbite, pneumonia and hypothermia.

Sporting activities

The climate affects the different sporting activities that are possible in a country.

For example, countries that have snow in the winter months can be very popular ski and snowboarding destinations. Countries such as New Zealand, France and the USA (for example, in Colorado) are all very popular ski areas. Many people visit these countries from all over the world.

Sports such as cricket are heavily influenced by the climate. In the Caribbean, where the cricket season takes place between November and May, whereas in the UK – which has far less reliable sunshine – the season can only be played in the warmer months, between April and September.

Farming is an important industry and highly dependent on climate.

Crops planted

Farming is a very important industry around the world. It is not necessarily a big industry in many countries now, but it is still a very important industry and one that is highly dependent on the climate. Not all crops need the same weather conditions.

While it is true that most crops need sunshine and rain to grow, too much sunshine or too much rainfall will not produce many crops.

Countries that are very hot, such as Ethiopia, struggle to grow crops because the temperatures are so high and there is very little rainfall.

Some regions, such as certain states in the USA (for instance, Alaska), cannot grow crops easily because there are very low temperatures and very little rainfall.

Some of the best regions to farm are in temperate areas, where there are no extreme weather conditions.

Exercise

1. How do the weather and climate affect our decisions about what to wear?
2. What health problems are caused by the weather?
3. Give examples of sports that need specific weather conditions.
4. How is farming affected by the weather?

Key vocabulary

animal hide

frostbite

humid

Climate graphs

We are learning to:

- interpret line and bar graphs with temperatures and rainfall statistics
- interpret isohyet maps showing rainfall.

Climate graphs 》

Climate information is shown using **climate graphs**. These are graphs that show temperature and rainfall statistics for a country or area over a period of time. The most common type of climate graph shows the annual temperature and rainfall over a one-year period. Temperatures are shown as a line graph and rainfall is shown as a bar graph.

Interpreting climate graphs 》》

When studying climate graphs, there are a few things that you must take into consideration:

- What is the **range** of temperatures across the year? (To find this out, you subtract the minimum temperature from the maximum temperature.)
- What month(s) of the year are the hottest? What is the temperature?
- What month(s) of the year are the coldest? What is the temperature?
- Is there rainfall in every month of the year?

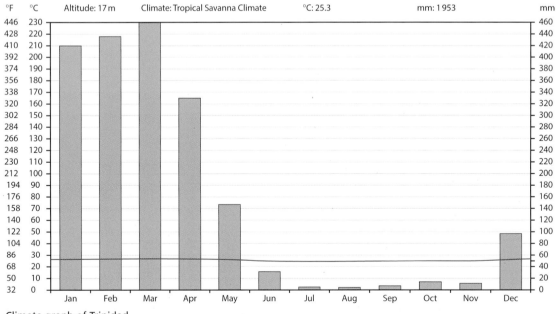

Climate graph of Trinidad.

- If a month is dry, what month of the year is it?
- Is there a lot of rain?
- What is the total annual rainfall? (To find this out, you add up all the rainfall in every month of the year.)

Interpreting isohyet maps >>>>

Isohyet maps are maps that are used to show rainfall figures. They connect different places on a map that have the same amounts of rainfall at a specific time.

When studying isohyet maps, there are a couple of things that need to be considered:

- What is the overall pattern of rainfall like? Are some areas much wetter than others? What are the figures?
- Are there any extremes – for example, some areas that have a lot of rainfall, compared to others that have none? What are the figures?

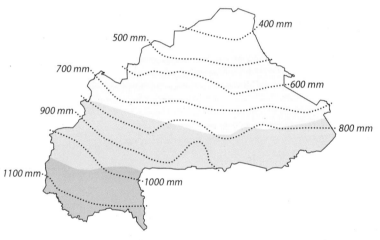

Climate graph.

Activity

Using an atlas and other sources, gather and interpret information on temperature and rainfall in your country. Create a PowerPoint presentation to show what you have found.

Activity

Your teacher will arrange a field trip to the Meteorological Office in your country. Write up what you observed. Use around 250 words, and include sketches.

Activity

Your teacher will arrange a visit to your class from a meteorologist. They will discuss why it is important to be able to provide climate data to citizens.

Exercise

1. What do climate graphs show?

2. Look at the climate graph above.

   a) Which months have the least and most rainfall?

   b) Which six months form the 'wet season'?

3. What do isohyet maps show?

4. From the isohyet map, can you give reasons as to why some areas are wetter or drier than others?

5. What should you consider when interpreting climate and isohyet maps?

6. In your own words, explain how graphs are used to show temperature and rainfall.

Key vocabulary

climate graphs

range

isohyet maps

Hurricanes

We are learning to:

- define the weather system hurricanes
- classify hurricanes according to the Saffir-Simpson Scale.

Tropical storms >>

Tropical storms – also known as **hurricanes**, **cyclones**, **typhoons** and **willy-willies** – are areas of extreme low pressure.

Hurricane	North America, such as USA and Honduras
Cyclone	Southeast Asia, such as India and Bangladesh
Typhoon	East Asia, such as Japan
Willy-willy	Australia

They are found in areas between the Tropic of Cancer and the Tropic of Capricorn. Tropical storms need very specific conditions in order to form.

Hurricane Matthew approaching Florida coastline.

Formation of a tropical storm >>>

- All tropical storms start over warm tropical seas with temperatures over 27 °C.
- Warm air rises and water is **evaporated**.
- The warm air and evaporated water rise, cool and **condense** to form thick clouds.
- More air is sucked in to fill the gap caused by the rising air, which is also heated.
- This sucking and rising movement causes the clouds to start spinning.
- The Earth's rotation also helps to spin the storm clouds.
- These storms are now able to move at great speeds across the ocean.

Structure of a tropical storm >>>>

- Tropical storms can be over 200 km wide.
- The centre of the storm is called the **eye**.
- The eye is usually 30–50 km across.
- Large, thick rain clouds (cumulonimbi) surround the eye.

The Saffir-Simpson Scale is used to categorise hurricanes. The categories range from 1 to 5, with 5 having the strongest winds.

Saffir-Simpson Hurricane Scale

Category	Wind speed (mph)	Type of damage	
1	74–95	Some damage	• damage mainly to trees • no substantial damage to buildings, some damage to poorly constructed signs
2	96–110	Extensive damage	• some trees blown down • some damage to windows, doors and roofing, but no major destruction to buildings • coastal roads cut off
3	111–129	Devastating damage	• large trees blown down • some damage to roofing, windows and doors • some structural damage to small buildings • serious flooding along the coast
4	130–156	Extreme damage	• shrubs, trees and all signs blown down; • extensive damage to roofs, windows and doors • flooding and floating debris cause major damage to houses
5	157 and above	Catastrophic damage	• considerable damage to roofs of buildings • very severe and extensive damage to windows and doors • complete buildings destroyed • major damage to homes

Exercise

1. What are the four names for tropical storms?
2. Why are hurricanes only found in tropical regions?
3. What is the centre of a hurricane called?
4. What is the system for measuring hurricanes called?
5. What damage might occur during a category 1 hurricane?
6. What damage might occur during a category 3 hurricane?
7. What damage might occur during a category 5 hurricane?

Key vocabulary

hurricane

cyclone

typhoon

willy-willy

evaporation

condenses

eye

Hurricanes in the Caribbean

We are learning to:

- explain the system used to name hurricanes
- name hurricanes which have had significant impacts in the Caribbean.

The system used to name hurricanes

Originally, tropical storms in the Caribbean were named after the saint's day on which the hurricane happened – for example, Santa Ana in 1825. From 1953, the United States began to use female names, and in 1979 the practice of using both male and female names began.

Naming tropical storms and hurricanes makes it easier to communicate their details, rather than having to use the longitude and latitude method. It also makes it easier for storms and hurricanes to be identified if there is more than one hurricane at the same time.

Meteorologists start with the letter A and work alphabetically, alternating men's and women's names. For example, if the first storm of the season is Adam, the next could be Barbara, and so on. The only letters that are not used are Q, U, X, Y and Z. If a storm has been particularly deadly, costly or devastating, then the name will not be used again. For example, Harvey and Katrina will not be reused.

Each storm is given a name once it reaches the level of tropical storm (wind speed of 65 km per hour). If the wind speed increases to 120 km, it is declared a hurricane.

Below is a list of some of the retired names in the Caribbean.

Name	Year	Areas affected
Harvey	2017	Barbados, St Vincent and the Grenadines, Suriname, Guyana, USA
Irma	2017	Anguilla, the Bahamas, Barbados, St Kitts and Nevis, USA
Tomas	2010	Barbados, St Vincent and the Grenadines, St Lucia, Haiti, Turks and Caicos
Igor	2010	Newfoundland, Bermuda
Paloma	2008	Cayman Islands, Cuba
Ike	2008	Turks and Caicos, Cuba, Texas (USA)

Did you know...?

In 2017, the named tropical storms (TS) and hurricanes (H) for the Atlantic were:

Arlene (TS)

Bret (TS)

Cindy (TS)

Don (TS)

Emily (TS)

Franklin (H)

Gert (H)

Harvey (H)

Irma (H)

Jose (H)

Katia (H)

Lee (H)

Maria (H)

Nate (H)

Ophelia (H)

Philippe (TS)

Rina (TS)

Exercise

1. In your own words, explain why hurricanes are given names.
2. At what wind speed does a tropical storm become a hurricane?
3. Why does a name become retired?

Tropical storms in the Caribbean

Hurricane Ivan

Hurricane Ivan was a category 5 hurricane that affected the Caribbean in September 2004. It caused a huge amount of damage to the Caribbean and USA as it tore across the Atlantic Ocean.

When the storm hit Grenada, it was only a category 3 hurricane, but it caused widespread damage there. Hurricane Ivan killed 39 people in Grenada and caused serious damage to hospitals, schools, roads and farmland.

By the time the hurricane reached Jamaica, it had increased to a category 4 hurricane, and caused widespread flooding.

Hurricane Sandy

Hurricane Sandy was a category 3 hurricane that caused extensive damage to the Caribbean and USA in November 2012.

The storm formed in the Atlantic Ocean and ripped through the Caribbean region, killing 80 people – 60 in Haiti, 11 in Cuba, 2 in the Bahamas, 2 in the Dominican Republic and 1 in Jamaica.

Hurricane Sandy caused millions of dollars' worth of damage in the Caribbean. Roads, schools and hospitals were destroyed, as well as 18 000 homes.

Hurricane Irma

Hurricane Irma (2017) was a category 5 hurricane with landfalls in Antigua and Barbuda, St Martin, Anguilla, Turks and Caicos, the Bahamas, Cuba and the United States in August/September 2017. When the hurricane made landfall in Barbuda it had a catastrophic effect, destroying 95% of its buildings including hospitals, schools and residential homes. Hurricane Irma caused billions of dollars' worth of damage across the Caribbean, as well as widespread flooding and destruction of wildlife and their habitats.

Questions

1. Which of the three hurricanes mentioned has the lowest category?

2. Which country suffered the most from Hurricane Sandy?

3. In your own words, describe the impact that a hurricane of these strengths can have on a country.

Damage caused by Hurricane Sandy in Queens, New York, 2012.

Discussion

In groups, discuss the names of hurricanes and the system used to name them – that is, male and female names.

Activity

Write a two-verse poem about a name you have given to a hurricane.

Research

Using the internet, go to the National Hurricane Centre website. Research one of the 2017 hurricanes (Harvey, Irma) and write a report detailing its route and the damage it caused. Add any photographs to your report.

Passage of a hurricane

We are learning to:

- describe the weather conditions associated with the passage of a hurricane (before, during and after).

Weather and hurricanes

Hurricanes are areas of very low pressure. Low pressure tends to bring wind and rain. However, the extreme low pressure that hurricanes experience brings far more severe weather conditions than a normal **depression**.

As a hurricane passes over an area, it will experience different weather conditions depending on what 'stage' of the storm it is in.

Before

Before a hurricane approaches, the weather starts to change noticeably:

- air pressure starts to fall
- temperatures start to fall
- winds increase
- clouds start to develop
- rain begins.

During

The eye wall

This is the first wall of thick cloud that approaches. At the eye wall:

- air pressure falls very quickly
- temperatures fall
- winds pick up
- huge storm clouds form
- torrential rain falls.

The eye

This is the centre of the hurricane. In the 'eye':

- air pressure is very low
- temperatures are higher
- it is calm with very little wind
- it is sunny
- there is no rain.

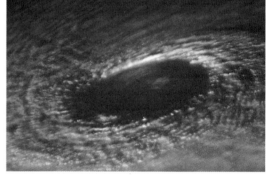

The eye of Hurricane Ivan, photographed in 2004 from above the Earth.

The second eye wall

This is the second wall of thick cloud that approaches. At this eye wall:

- air pressure rises
- temperatures fall again
- winds reach their strongest force
- huge, thick clouds form
- torrential rain falls.

Discussion

In groups, discuss what weather to expect during the passage of a hurricane.

After

After a hurricane passes, all these weather conditions dissipate:

- air pressure continues to rise
- temperatures increase
- winds die down
- the thick cloud breaks up
- rain turns to showers.

Damage from Hurricane Ivan on Grand Cayman Island, 2004.

Exercise

1. What is the weather like before a hurricane?

2. Describe the weather conditions in the 'eye' of a hurricane.

3. What is the worst part of a hurricane, and what is the weather like there?

4. What is the weather like after a hurricane passes over?

Key vocabulary
....
depression

The effects of hurricanes

We are learning to:

• examine the effects of hurricanes.

The effects of hurricanes 〉〉

Hurricanes are often devastating for a country. Billions of dollars of damage can be caused and many people may get killed. These two pages discuss the most serious effects of hurricanes.

A storm surge is one effect of a hurricane.

Storm surge 〉〉〉

Storm surges are one common side effect of a hurricane. A storm surge is a rise in sea level that occurs during hurricanes. They are very dangerous, because they can lead to widespread coastal flooding.

Storm surges occur when strong winds push the surface water towards the coast. They generate large waves that can be very destructive.

Hurricane Katrina, which affected the USA in 2005, produced an 8.5 m storm surge. This was the highest recorded storm surge ever to affect the country.

Flooding 〉〉〉〉

Flooding is a major consequence of hurricanes. Because so much rain falls in such a short space of time during a hurricane, the water can completely cover the land.

Floodwater is very destructive as it can be very powerful; it has the ability to destroy buildings, vegetation and farmland. Flooding can be responsible for the most deaths and most economic damage that a hurricane can cause. Following Hurricane Katrina in 2005, approximately 80% of New Orleans was under water that, in some places, was 6 m deep.

Exercise

1. What is a storm surge and what causes it?

2. Why is floodwater so damaging?

3. Using library and internet resources, research the effects of a hurricane that has affected the Caribbean. Create a presentation and include the following: the name of the hurricane, the island that was affected and at least three effects of the hurricane.

Damage to vegetation >>

Floodwater can drown plants and vegetation and the strong winds can uproot trees. Many acres of farmland can be destroyed during hurricanes, killing all crops.

Following Hurricane Ivan in 2005, Grenada suffered a tremendous amount of damage. In total, it is thought that 900 million dollars' worth of damage was made to Grenada – 80% of its buildings were destroyed, 90% of its homes were ruined, 73 of the 75 schools were damaged and 80% of its power was lost. Farmland was also destroyed, and all the year's crops were lost.

Floodwater following a hurricane can cause widespread damage to agricultural land, villages, towns and cities, and can cause loss of life.

Loss of life and property >>>

Hurricanes can cause widespread loss of life. The winds, rain, floodwater and storm surges can all be deadly for people living in areas affected by hurricanes.

Buildings, roads, houses and bridges can be completely destroyed during a hurricane and people can be killed from the winds, falling trees or buildings, or the floodwater.

The table shows a selection of hurricanes that have affected Caribbean regions over the last 100 years. It is clear from the table that there is no relationship between strength of hurricane and damage and deaths caused.

Name (date)	Category	Cost of damage ($)	Number of deaths
Galveston (1900)	4	21 million	6 000–12 000
Jérémie (1935)	1	16 million	2 150
Flora (1963)	4	529 million	7 193
David (1979)	5	1.5 billion	2 068
Jeanne (2004)	3	7.94 billion	3 035
Harvey (2017)	4	125 billion	69 direct, 39 indirect
Irma (2017)	5	64.2 billion	477–1 492

Exercise

4. Look at the table:

   a) Which hurricane caused the most damage?

   b) Which hurricane caused the most deaths?

   c) Following Hurricane Ivan in 2005, what damage was caused to Grenada?

Key vocabulary

storm surge

flooding

Preparing for a hurricane

We are learning to:

- outline precautions used to minimise the effects of hurricanes
- practise responsible behaviour in times of disaster.

How can Caribbean countries, and people who live in those countries, prepare themselves to minimise the impact of a hurricane?

Disaster supply kit

Disaster supply kits are backpacks filled with essential items that people can take to a hurricane shelter. As space is restricted, people should only take a limited number of items with them – for example, food, such as tinned food, bottles of water, first-aid kits, torch, copies of personal documents and emergency telephone numbers. Clothing and bedding should also be included.

A hurricane shelter on a beach.

Hurricane shelter

Hurricane shelters are safe buildings built specifically to protect the public from the devastating effects of a hurricane. Their special features include the following:

- They are built on high ground and made of solid concrete.
- They are built in the shape of a triangle, with the point of the triangle (the strongest part) facing the direction the storm will come from.
- There is a set of stairs at the back, to shelter people from the wind.
- The building is raised on **stilts**, so the storm surge waters will flow under the building, not through it. To keep it stable, the **foundations** are 4 m deep.
- There are often two rooms inside – one for men and one for women and children. Each shelter can house 1000 people.
- There are bars and metal shutters on the windows, and no glass, as that could be shattered by the storm.

Key vocabulary

hurricane shelter

stilts

foundations

Exercise

1. What items would you typically include in a disaster supply kit?
2. What are hurricane shelters?
3. List some of the special features of a hurricane shelter.

Building design

Although hurricanes occur every year, people continue to live in hurricane-prone areas. However, they do take extra precautions wherever they can. One of the things people do is build their houses to withstand hurricanes. Building design is very important, and some of the building features include:

- deep foundations to make the building stronger
- building houses/buildings on pillars/stilts to raise them above the ground, so floodwater flows underneath the building
- using materials that can survive getting wet
- using shatterproof or plastic windows
- using metal shutters on the windows.

Insurance

As with earthquakes, insurance can be taken out on homes, property and possessions. This is a policy where the insurance company will pay out to replace anything that is damaged in a hurricane.

This can be great for replacing possessions, but it will not make up for sentimental items lost or damaged during a hurricane.

Early warning and detection

Nowadays, it is easy to track hurricanes by using satellites, although they can be quite unpredictable in their movements.

Satellites allow us to take photographs of the hurricane so we can track its speed and direction. From there, warnings can be given out to the public – via radio, television or over the internet. This keeps people informed and ensures that they make arrangements to stay safe during the hurricane.

Satellites such as GLONASS (Global Navigation Satellite System) can help to track hurricanes.

Research

Using the internet, and working in groups, go to the United Caribbean Trust's website (http://unitedcaribbean.com/femadisastersupplykit.html). Research the items they list as necessary in an emergency kit – water, food, clothing and bedding, first aid and toolkit. Then, create your own disaster kit. Create an emergency contact list of at least three people. When you have finished, share your kit and list with the rest of the class. Explain why the items in the kit are essential and why you chose the three emergency contacts.

Exercise

4. What design features are important when building houses in hurricane-prone areas?

5. What will insurance not cover?

6. How are people warned about approaching hurricanes?

Activity

Design an action plan to assist a neighbouring country that has been affected by a hurricane.

Questions

See how well you have understood the topics in this unit.

1. Match the key vocabulary word (i–viii) with its definition (a–h).

   i) crust   **a)** sections of the Earth's core

   ii) mantle   **b)** part of the crust that the oceans are on

   iii) core   **c)** outside layer of the Earth

   iv) continental crust   **d)** section of the Earth's crust

   v) oceanic crust   **e)** centre of the Earth

   vi) tectonic plates   **f)** liquid rock found inside the mantle

   vii) magma   **g)** part of the crust that the continents are on

   viii) inner/outer   **h)** middle layer of the Earth

2. True or false?

   a) Constructive plate margins are when two plates move towards each other.

   b) Destructive plate margins are when an ocean plate and continental plate move towards each other.

   c) Conservative plate margins are when two continental plates move towards each other.

   d) Collision plate margins are when two continental plates move away from each other.

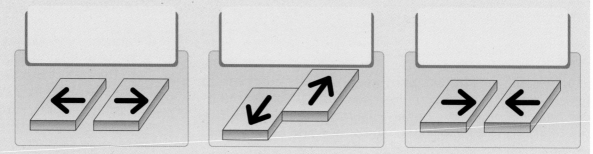

3. Name the types of plate margins shown above.

4. Write two paragraphs explaining why earthquakes and volcanoes tend to occur at plate boundaries.

5. In your own words, define the terms earthquake, seismic, focus, epicentre and magnitude.

6. Explain why early warning systems are helpful in minimising damage.

7. How do volcanic eruptions cause temperatures to decrease?

8. Draw a mind map to show the effects of an earthquake on the human and physical environment.

9. Explain the difference between an active, dormant and extinct volcano.

10. Name the materials that are ejected by volcanoes during an eruption.

11. Write 250 words on the positive and negative effects of volcanoes.

12. Name five of the main weather elements.

13. Match the climate zone (i–v) with the description (a–e).

i) equatorial	**a)** temperatures in the summer up to 40 °C
ii) hot desert	**b)** temperatures average about 27 °C
iii) Mediterranean	**c)** temperatures can go down to −50 °C
iv) temperate	**d)** temperatures as high as 50 °C
v) tundra	**e)** temperatures average 20 °C in summer

14. Label the diagram of the structure of a volcano with terms from the word box below.

crater	layers of lava and ash	ash cloud	lava flow
rock	conduit	magma chamber	

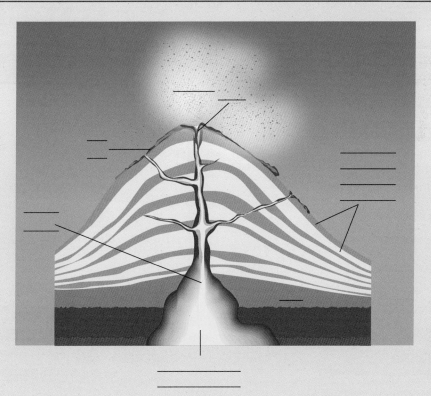

Checking your progress

To make good progress in understanding different aspects of the physical Earth and human interactions, check to make sure you understand these ideas.

Understand the structure of the Earth.

Discuss where earthquakes and volcanoes are found and the relationship between the movement of plates and the features found there.

Explain the formation of the three types of rock and give examples.

Examine the effects of earthquakes on the physical and human environment.

Outline strategies to reduce the amount of damage caused during an earthquake.

Create an action plan for an earthquake.

Examine the effects of volcanoes on the physical and human environment.

Examine the positive and negative effects of volcanoes.

Create a photo montage showing at least three positive and three negative effects of volcanic eruptions in the Caribbean.

State the elements of the weather and climate.

Describe the seasonal types experienced in the five climatic zones.

Examine the effects of hurricanes and precautions used to minimise the effects of hurricanes.

End-of-term questions

See how well you have understood the ideas in Unit 4.

1. You have created a portfolio giving information about elections in your country. Go to www.caribbeanelections.com, use 'Country Browser', find your country, click 'Elections'. Find out information about the last general election in your country and write a report about the outcome of that election. Add the report to the information you have already gathered in your portfolio.

2. Write an information leaflet in which you explain why elections should be free and fair, and why general elections need to be transparent. Write about 150 words.

3. Work in groups. Read and listen to the news, then find a current conflict in which you think there have been humanitarian law violations.

   Identify the violations, then role-play a presentation in which you argue that the International Criminal Court should investigate the matter. Some members of the group can make arguments to the ICC. Others can be judges at the ICC who listen to the arguments and ask questions.

4. Match the key vocabulary word (i–vii) with its definition (a–g).

i) conflict	**a)** administering the law in a fair way
ii) amnesty	**b)** an act relating to a crime, such as robbery or murder
iii) humanitarian aid	**c)** an act relating to relationships between members of a society, such as trespassing on someone else's property
iv) justice	**d)** a serious disagreement which can often become violent or involve an armed struggle
v) violate	**e)** official pardon
vi) criminal offence	**f)** break (the law)
vii) civil offence	**g)** help for people who are suffering, such as medical care, food and water

See how well you have understood the ideas in Unit 5.

5. Write a newspaper report outlining the technological developments in farming in recent years. Write about 150 words.

6. Name the ways in which society is becoming better connected through the use of technology.

7. Write a report outlining the effects that human activities and technology can have on the environment. Use about 200 words.

8. Match the key vocabulary word (i–vii) with its definition (a–g).

i) urbanisation	**a)** a method of farming where only enough food is produced for the farmer and his family
ii) urban	**b)** places which are located in the countryside, away from towns and cities
iii) rural	**c)** when a country has many industries that allow them to become richer
iv) industrialise	**d)** belonging to a town or a city
v) standard of living	**e)** to have moved from one place to another
vi) subsistence	**f)** increasing numbers of people living in the cities
vii) migrated	**g)** the level of comfort and wealth that a person or family may have

Questions 9–12 ▶▶

See how well you have understood the ideas in Unit 6.

9. Create sentences:

i) A constructive (or divergent) boundary …

ii) A conservative (or transform) boundary …

iii) A destructive (or convergent) boundary …

a) occurs where two plates slide past each other.

b) occurs where two plates made up of continental and oceanic crust are pushing towards each other.

c) marks two plates that are moving apart from each other.

10. Write an essay of about 200 words explaining some of the mitigation strategies that can be used against earthquakes.

11. Write a report of about 200 words explaining the negative and positive effects of volcanoes.

12. Match each description to the climate zone.

hot desert	temperate	tundra	Mediterranean	equatorial (tropical)

a) This climate has around 1 500 mm per year and only one season throughout the year. _____

b) This climate has very little rainfall and has two seasons – summer and winter. _____

c) This climate has rainfall in most months of the year other than June, July and August, and has two main seasons – summer and winter. _____

d) This climate has rainfall all year round and has four seasons – spring, summer, autumn, winter. _____

e) This climate has very low rainfall (precipitation is most likely to fall as snow) and has two seasons – summer and winter. _____

Unit 7: Caribbean integration and global links

Regional integration

- Define relevant terms and concepts
  - regional integration
  - bilateral agreement
  - cooperation
  - dependence
  - economy
  - interdependence
  - region
  - multilateral agreement
  - multinational corporation
- Describe the Caribbean integration process from the 1950s to the present
- Outline the objectives and membership of institutions/bodies which form part of the integration process:
  - West Indian Federation
  - CARIFTA
  - CARICOM and CSME
  - OECS
  - Association of Caribbean States
  - sport, education, medicine, culture, disaster preparedness
- How the individual, businesses and countries benefit from regional integration
- Examine issues that affect the Caribbean and the world and develop action plans to solve these issues:
  - drugs, crime, HIV
  - poverty, unemployment
  - pollution, terrorism

Regional integration

We are learning to:

- define relevant terms and concepts: regional integration, bilateral agreement, cooperation, dependence, economy, interdependence, region.

Regional integration is when countries in a region cooperate and work together towards common goals. This has been a priority since the 1950s, when the first attempts were made by Caribbean states to work cooperatively towards common goals. This came about because states wanted to be less dependent on former colonial powers.

Carnival is an event where people from different cultural backgrounds can come together.

Integration

To **integrate** means to bring together ideas and people so that they work together or become part of the same group. The aim of integration is to give members equal status in a group and to share the advantages and strengths that the group brings. There are several types of integration:

- **Social integration** happens when people of different cultural backgrounds learn tolerance and respect for each other.
- **Racial integration** is when people of different races are treated equally so they can live and work together.
- **Economic integration** is achieved when two or more states in a geographic area set common economic goals and reduce the barriers to trade between them. This complements a country's own economy, which is made up of businesses that provide goods and services to meet people's needs.

Cooperation

Cooperation means working together and helping each other to achieve common goals. For example, we need to cooperate with our neighbours and other members of our community. If there is a problem in a community and everyone cooperates fully, the problem can be solved.

Discussion

Work in groups and discuss how interdependence can help the states in the Caribbean to develop.

Project

Do your own research in groups. Take one of the terms explained on these pages, and find out more about the term. Then look in newspapers and find examples of events that illustrate what it means. For example, a community event could illustrate integration in an area. Some news about trade between different Caribbean states could illustrate interdependence in the Caribbean region.

Exercise

1. In your own words, define regional integration.

2. How many different types of integration are there? Write your own definition of each.

3. Why do you think social integration is important in Caribbean countries?

Dependence ▶▶▶

To depend on something is to rely on or be controlled by it. **Dependence** on other people has many disadvantages, because it means you are not free to do as you wish.

During colonial times, Caribbean colonies were dependent on their colonial masters (for example, the United Kingdom) and were forced to live by the social and economic laws and rules of their colonisers.

Colonies had little or no control over their own laws or the economic and social development of their own countries.

In the 1960s, when many Caribbean states gained independence, foreigners still owned much of the good farming land and also many of the businesses. The profits from these economic activities were not used to develop the Caribbean countries.

From the 1950s onwards, Caribbean states tried to lessen their dependence on their former colonial rulers in order to strengthen their economies.

Countries began to establish **bilateral agreements** – agreements where two countries help each other – and **treaties** to help develop the **region** as a whole.

US President Barack Obama (centre, third from the left) takes part in a meeting with Caribbean Community (CARICOM) leaders at the University of the West Indies (Kingston) on 9 April 2015.

Interdependence ▶▶

Countries that help each other or rely on each other are **interdependent**. The leaders of states in the Caribbean saw **interdependence** as the way forward and as a means of strengthening the development of states in the region.

This interdependence started in the 1950s with the West Indian Federation and continues today through organisations like CARICOM and the Association of Caribbean States (ACS).

Key vocabulary

regional integration

integrate

social integration

racial integration

economic integration

cooperation

dependence

bilateral agreement

interdependent/ interdependence

treaty

region

Exercise

4. In your own words, define the terms dependence and interdependence.

5. Did the Caribbean colonies have control of their own laws when they were a Crown Colony?

6. In what way were the Caribbean colonies once dependent on the United Kingdom?

The West Indian Federation

We are learning to:

- define relevant terms and concepts: multilateral agreement, multinational corporation
- describe the Caribbean integration process from the 1950s to the present: West Indian Federation
- outline the objectives and membership of institutions/bodies which form part of the integration process: West Indian Federation.

West Indian Federation

The first significant attempt at integration by Caribbean states took place in 1958, when 10 Caribbean countries, who were all still British colonies at the time, formed the **West Indian Federation** as an attempt at a political union.

The West Indian Federation was the first example in the region of an organisation that was based on **multilateral agreement**. A multilateral agreement usually refers to agreements between more than one country or **multinational corporation** (a large organisation that has business interests in more than one country). The West Indian Federation is an example of a multilateral agreement.

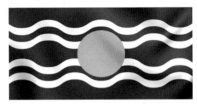

The flag of the West Indies.

Objectives and membership of the West Indian Federation

At the time of its formation in 1958, the membership of the West Indian Federation was:

- Antigua and Barbuda
- Barbados
- Dominica
- Jamaica
- Grenada
- St Kitts-Nevis-Anguilla
- Montserrat
- St Lucia
- St Vincent and the Grenadines
- Trinidad and Tobago.

The main aim of the Federation was to reduce dependence on (and ultimately to achieve independence from) Britain.

Exercise

1. When was the West Indian Federation set up?
2. Name the members of the West Indian Federation.
3. What were the main advantages of creating a Federation?

Did you know...?

The following states were members of the Federation:

- Antigua and Barbuda
- Barbados
- Dominica
- Grenada
- Jamaica
- Montserrat
- St Kitts-Nevis-Anguilla
- St Vincent and the Grenadines
- St Lucia
- Trinidad and Tobago

The Federation is disbanded ▶▶▶

The West Indian Federation lasted until 1962. The Federation was **disbanded** when Jamaica and Trinidad and Tobago decided to leave it. There were a number of reasons for this:

- Trinidad and Tobago and Jamaica were the biggest countries in the Federation and they were expected to bear most of its costs. This was considered to be unfair.
- The smaller countries feared that the more powerful countries would dominate the Federation.
- There was disagreement as to where the capital of the Federation should be.
- Jamaica objected to the colonial status of the Federation and felt that it was holding back independence from Britain.
- The most respected leaders of the time preferred to stay on as leaders in their own country, rather than lead the Federation,
- In September 1961, Jamaica held a **referendum** in which the people of Jamaica elected to pull out of the Federation. This led to the withdrawal of Trinidad and Tobago as well, after Dr Eric Williams famously said in a speech that 'One from ten leaves zero.'

Activity

Do you think countries can get cheaper imports by working together? How would this work?

Exercise

4. Outline the reasons why the West Indian Federation disbanded.

5. Your teacher will play you the calypso 'Federation', by Mighty Sparrow. Listen carefully to the lyrics and then discuss these questions.

   a) Why, in the opinion of Mighty Sparrow, did Jamaica want to pull out of the Federation?

   b) What reasons did Mighty Sparrow give for the collapse of the Federation?

   c) What is Mighty Sparrow's opinion of the Federation? Was it a good thing or not?

   d) Do you think Trinidad and Tobago was to blame in any way?

6. Compile a timeline of the key dates of the history of the West Indian Federation.

Key vocabulary

West Indian Federation

multilateral agreement

multinational corporation

disbanded

referendum

CARIFTA

We are learning to:

- define relevant terms and concepts: free trade, liberalisation
- describe the Caribbean integration process from the 1950s to the present: CARIFTA
- outline the objectives and membership of institutions/bodies which form part of the integration process: CARIFTA.

CARIFTA ⟫

The next attempt at integration occurred when the **Caribbean Free Trade Association (CARIFTA)** was formed in 1965 with the signing of the Dickenson Bay Agreement. This was a much more successful attempt, which later led to the formation of CARICOM – an organisation that is still very active today.

Membership of CARIFTA ⟫⟫

The idea of a **free trade** region was first discussed at meetings between the leaders of Trinidad and Tobago, Guyana (then called British Guiana), Antigua and Barbuda and Barbados – the original members of CARIFTA.

The Prime Minister of Trinidad and Tobago convened this meeting in 1963 after announcing that the country intended to pull out of the West Indian Federation. As a result of these discussions a formal agreement was drawn up, and the Caribbean Free Trade Association (CARIFTA) was formed in 1965 with the signing of the Dickenson Bay Agreement.

On 1 July 1968, Dominica, Grenada, St Kitts and Nevis, Anguilla, St Lucia and St Vincent and the Grenadines joined CARIFTA. A few years later in 1971, Belize (then called British Honduras) joined as well. By this time, several of the states had achieved independence.

Cargo is loaded onto a boat in Kingstown harbour in St Vincent and the Grenadines.

> **Did you know...?**
>
> The members of CARIFTA were:
>
> - Antigua and Barbuda
> - Barbados
> - Belize
> - Dominica
> - Grenada
> - Guyana
> - Jamaica
> - Montserrat
> - St Kitts and Nevis
> - Anguilla
> - St Lucia
> - St Vincent and the Grenadines
> - Trinidad and Tobago

Exercise

1. What do the initials CARIFTA stand for?
2. Which countries first discussed the idea of a new trade association?
3. Name the countries that became members of CARIFTA.
4. What role did Trinidad and Tobago have in the formation of CARIFTA?

Objectives of CARIFTA ⟫⟫⟫

The main objective of CARIFTA was to unite the economies of the member countries, improve relationships between the states and, as a result of this, give them a powerful joint international presence.

The best way of doing this was to increase trade between members of the organisation. It was thought that this would also encourage development in the region.

The agreement encouraged member states to:

- buy and sell more goods between themselves
- diversify and expand the variety of goods and services available in the region
- make sure there was fair competition, especially for smaller businesses
- make sure that the benefits of free trade were equitably distributed among member states.

Trade between member states was **liberalised**. There was to be free trade between the member states. This meant that states did not charge each other tariffs (taxes or customs duties) on goods imported from other member states.

There were also no quotas on goods traded between member states, so states could trade as much as they liked.

Over and above this, CARIFTA also promoted industrial development of less developed states, the development of the coconut industry and an improved way to market agricultural goods.

Bananas being packed in Dominica for sale in the UK, as part of a special agreement between Caribbean islands and the UK.

Discussion

Do some research and then discuss whether CARIFTA was successful. Why/why not?

Exercise

5. What were the main objectives of CARIFTA?

6. Explain in your own words what free trade means.

7. What are the advantages of free trade?

8. Why do you think it was so important for newly independent states in the Caribbean to form strong ties?

9. Which countries played leading roles in the development of CARIFTA? Why?

10. Compare the West Indian Federation and CARIFTA. What were the similarities and differences between them?

11. Compile a timeline of the key dates of the history of CARIFTA.

Key vocabulary

CARIFTA

free trade

liberalised

CARICOM and CSME

We are learning to:

- define relevant terms and concepts: globalisation
- describe the Caribbean integration process from the 1950s to the present: CARICOM, CSME
- outline the objectives and membership of institutions/bodies which form part of the integration process: CARICOM, CSME.

CARICOM and CSME 》》

The success of CARIFTA encouraged member states to broaden cooperation in the Caribbean. The CARIFTA agreements did not allow for the free movement of workers or of capital between the member states, nor did it allow for the coordination of agricultural, industrial and foreign policies.

The result was an improved association called the Caribbean Community or **CARICOM**. This came into being in 1973 and replaced CARIFTA, although the CARIFTA Games and sporting events continued.

A meeting of CARICOM leaders.

Membership of CARICOM 》》

CARICOM is an organisation of Caribbean states that promotes cooperation and integration between member states, especially in areas like trade and transportation. It also coordinates foreign policy. This has resulted in many benefits for the citizens of Caribbean states. People can move around freely to study and to look for work, and goods and services can be traded easily between these countries.

CARICOM was formed with the signing of an agreement at Chaguaramas in Trinidad and Tobago, between Trinidad and Tobago, Barbados, Jamaica and Guyana. The organisation grew quickly and now includes 15 member states:

- Antigua and Barbuda
- the Bahamas
- Barbados
- Belize
- Dominica
- Grenada
- Guyana
- Haiti
- Jamaica
- Montserrat
- St Lucia
- St Kitts and Nevis
- St Vincent and the Grenadines
- Suriname
- Trinidad and Tobago

> **Did you know...?**
>
> The CCs on the CARICOM flag are like the links on a chain. A linked chain represents unity. The fact that the links are not complete represents a break with the colonial past. What do you think the colours of the flag represent?

In 1989, the CARICOM heads of government agreed to advance the process of economic integration and to increase their ability to respond as a group to the challenges and opportunities of globalisation. This led to the creation of the CARICOM Single Market and Economy (**CSME**).

Globalisation is a process of making the world more connected, with goods, services and people moving and communicating easily and quickly all around the world.

The main economic objectives of the CSME are:

- improved standards of living and work
- full employment of labour and other factors of production
- coordinated and sustained economic development and convergence
- expansion of trade and economic relations with other states
- increased levels of international competitiveness
- increased production and productivity
- greater economic leverage in dealing with other states
- coordination of members' economic policies
- increased cooperation of common services and activities.

The CSME also allows for the free movement of money and skilled labour between member states, the right to set up a business in another member state, free movement of goods and a common trade policy.

Several other states have associate member states, including the British Virgin Islands, Turks and Caicos, Anguilla, the Cayman Islands and Bermuda.

The CARICOM flag.

Activity

Work in pairs and look online and in newspapers for interesting reports about CARICOM activities. Select a report, then describe what you have discovered to the class.

Exercise

1. What are the main objectives of CARICOM?

2. Why was the CSME agreement signed?

3. If they want to set up a new business, what advantages do businesspeople from CARICOM member states have?

4. Compile a timeline of the key dates in both CARICOM and the CSME's history.

Key vocabulary
....

CARICOM

CSME

Organisation of Eastern Caribbean States

We are learning to:

- describe the Caribbean integration process from the 1950s to the present: OECS
- outline the objectives and membership of institutions/bodies which form part of the integration process: OECS.

OECS

The Organisation of Eastern Caribbean States (OECS) is an **inter-governmental** organisation formed in 1981 to promote unity and solidarity amongst its members.

OECS logo

The origins of the OECS lie in the West Indian Federation, which was disbanded in 1962. When Trinidad and Tobago and Jamaica became independent of Britain in 1962, the remaining countries – Barbados, Dominica, Grenada, St Lucia and St Vincent and the Grenadines, Antigua and Barbuda, St Kitts and Nevis, Anguilla and Montserrat – formed a new organisation to continue dealings with Britain.

This eventually led to the 1981 Treaty of Basseterre, in which Antigua and Barbuda, Dominica, Grenada, Montserrat, St Kitts and Nevis, St Lucia and St Vincent and the Grenadines signed a formal agreement.

Membership of OECS

Today, the OECS has 10 members, made up of islands from the Leeward Islands and the Windward Islands: Anguilla, Antigua and Barbuda, British Virgin Islands, Dominica, Grenada, Martinique, Montserrat, St Kitts and Nevis, St Lucia and St Vincent and the Grenadines.

Anguilla, the British Virgin Islands and Montserrat are Associate members of the OECS, although they enjoy full membership status for many of the organisation's activities.

Exercise

1. When was the idea of an OECS-type organisation first considered?
2. When was the OECS finally formed?
3. Which countries were in the OECS originally?
4. Name the countries that are in the OECS today.

Structure of the OECS

The OECS has five sections:

- Authority of Heads of Government of the Member States – leads on policy and makes decisions on all matters related to the OECS; made up of the heads of government from each country
- Council of Ministers – implements the policies made by the Authority
- OECS Assembly – reviews legislation passed by the Authority
- Economic Affairs Council – helps to develop close working relationships with all member countries
- OECS Commission – the administrative part of the organisation.

The headquarters of OECS.

Objectives of the OECS

The broad aim of the OECS is to promote economic growth, social inclusion and protection of the environment amongst its members.

Today, the main objectives of the OECS are to promote:

- regional integration
- the free movement, growth and development of people, goods, services and capital
- the security and well-being of citizens
- key economic priorities – including climate change, jobs, transportation, trade, energy, food security and production
- a high-performing organisation capable of delivering the strategic priorities.

The OECS also works to end poverty, build economic growth and address a range of social issues, such as education, health and social protection.

Research

Using the internet, go the OECS website (www.oecs.org), look under 'Topics' and select three of the areas the OECS works in to help regional integration. Write a short report of about 200 words, using illustrations. Try to choose three topics that are similar – for example, economic development, business development and trade.

Exercise

5. Draw a flow diagram of the structure of the OECS.

6. Outline the objectives of the OECS.

7. Explain in your own words what you think is meant by the objective 'Consolidating the architecture of regional integration'.

Key vocabulary

inter-governmental

Association of Caribbean States

We are learning to:

- describe the Caribbean integration process from the 1950s to the present: Association of Caribbean States
- outline the objectives and membership of institutions/bodies which form part of the integration process: Association of Caribbean States.

Association of Caribbean States

In 1994, the Association of Caribbean States (ACS) was set up to build on existing links in the Caribbean and to integrate the area further. The organisation was formed with the aim of promoting the interests of the Caribbean region within its member states.

The ACS was formed when US President Clinton put forward an idea for an organisation for Free Trade of the Americas (FTAA). The FTAA would encourage the movement of goods without any involvement by customs for North and South American and Caribbean countries.

Countries could not agree on the terms of the FTAA, so it was never formed. The ACS was formed in response to the proposed FTAA.

The agreement to form the Association of Caribbean States (ACS) was signed in Colombia in 1994. The **Secretariat** of the ACS is in Port of Spain.

The chairman of the Association of Caribbean States, John Williams (centre), speaks during the 3rd meeting of the Caribbean Sea Commission in 2007.

Membership

In addition to the main member states, there are also **associate members** such as Aruba and Guadeloupe. Countries like Norway and the UK also have **observer status**, which means they can attend certain meetings. Currently there are 25 member states and 7 associate member states:

Antigua and Barbuda, the Bahamas, Barbados, Belize, Colombia, Costa Rica, Cuba, Dominica, Dominican Republic, El Salvador, Grenada, Guatemala, Guyana, Haiti, Honduras, Jamaica, Mexico, Nicaragua, Panama, St Kitts and Nevis, St Lucia, St Vincent and the Grenadines, Suriname, Trinidad and Tobago and Venezuela.

> **Did you know...?**
>
> The associate members of the ACS are as follows:
>
> Aruba, Bonaire, Curaçao, French Guiana, Guadeloupe, Martinique, Saba, St Barthélemy, St Martin, St Eustatius, and St Maarten.

Objectives ▶▶▶

The ACS membership has identified five objectives for their organisation:

- the preservation and conservation of the Caribbean Sea – to ensure that the Caribbean region as a natural resource is protected for future generations
- **sustainable tourism** – protecting the environment, while developing long-term economic opportunities, which in turn creates job opportunities for the local community
- to develop greater trade between the nations
- natural disasters – to develop and put measures in place that will help protect countries and their economies in the event of a natural disaster (such as a hurricane), and to coordinate responses to natural disasters in the Caribbean
- transport – better air and sea routes between the member states and a focus on the safety of travellers in the region.

The ACS has Special Committees, each of which meet twice a year to discuss the organisation's objectives in relation to current regional issues. The Special Committees include:

- Trade Development and External Economic Relations
- Sustainable Tourism
- Transport
- Disaster Risk Reduction
- Budget and Administration.

Opening meeting of the 22nd meeting of the Association of Caribbean States in Havana, Cuba, 2017.

Project

Compile a report summarising what you have learned about the different organisations helping to foster integration in the Caribbean. Using the internet and what you have learned so far, name the member states involved in each organisation and list two main objectives for each organisation. Create a poster showing your findings, and present them to the class.

Exercise

1. What is the main aim of the ACS?

2. Name two countries that are part of the ACS but not part of CARICOM.

3. Why do you think the preservation of the Caribbean Sea is a focus?

4. Discuss how transport within the region can strengthen economic development and cooperation.

5. What is sustainable tourism, and why is it important?

6. Write an essay with the title 'The role of regional agencies in facilitating regional integration'. Write 250–300 words.

Key vocabulary
....

secretariat

associate member

observer status

sustainable tourism

Sport

We are learning to:

- identify non-political areas of cooperation within the Caribbean region: sports
- assess the role of regional agencies in facilitating the integration process.

Economic affairs were not the only concern of Caribbean leaders. In order to promote **unity** amongst people in the Caribbean, **integrated** sporting events were also set up. These have proved to be most successful.

CARIFTA Games

The CARIFTA Games were held for the first time in 1972. They consist of athletic field and track events, including sprints, middle-distance running races, hurdles, jumping events, throwing events and relay races between teams.

The Games are held annually. There are two categories: one for athletes under 17 years old, and the other for athletes under 20. Athletes are only allowed to compete if they are from countries that are members or associate members of CARICOM.

Purpose of the CARIFTA Games

The CARIFTA Games were founded to improve relations between people of the English-speaking countries of the Caribbean. Since then, athletes from French- and Dutch-speaking countries have also been encouraged to take part.

Location of the Games

The CARIFTA Games have been held in many different countries, including Trinidad and Tobago, Jamaica, Barbados, the Bahamas, Martinique, Guadeloupe, Bermuda, Grenada, Turks and Caicos, St Kitts and Nevis and St Lucia. New sports facilities have been built in many places in order to host the Games.

Sport can bring communities together.

> **Did you know...?**
>
> Cricket West Indies (CWI) is one of the oldest examples of regional cooperation. It was founded in the early 1920s, when it was called the West Indies Cricket Board.

Research

Work in pairs. Visit the Cricket West Indies website (cricketwestindies.org) and research the mission, values and vision of this organisation. What do they aim to achieve?

Exercise

1. When were the CARIFTA Games first held?
2. Which sporting events feature in the CARIFTA Games?
3. What was the purpose of founding the CARIFTA Games?
4. In which countries have the Games been held?

Successful athletes

The CARIFTA Games have been a starting point for many athletes who have gone on to become world record holders, and world and Olympic champions. These include:

Usain Bolt (sprinter from Jamaica), Darrel Brown (sprinter from Trinidad and Tobago), Veronica Campbell-Brown (track and field athlete from Jamaica), Kim Collins (track and field athlete from St Kitts and Nevis), Pauline Davis-Thompson (sprinter from the Bahamas), Alleyne Francique (track athlete from Grenada) and Obadele Thompson (sprinter from Barbados).

West Indies cricket team

The West Indies cricket team is made up of players from CARICOM countries.

The West Indian cricket team, commonly known as the Windies, is one of the most successful cricket teams in the world.

The team is made up of players from CARICOM countries. It competes successfully in international tournaments and is an example of the benefits of regional cooperation between CARICOM countries. Cricket West Indies encourages regional development as part of the International Cricket Council's development programme.

Some of the best cricketers in the world come from the West Indies. Over the years, players like Sir Garfield Sobers, Gordon Greenidge, Brian Lara, Clive Lloyd, Malcolm Marshall, Sir Andy Roberts, Sir Frank Worrell, Sir Clyde Walcott, Sir Everton Weekes, Sir Curtly Ambrose, Michael Holding, Courtney Walsh, Joel Garner and Sir Viv Richards have made the Windies a force to be reckoned with.

Many players have been rewarded for their great contributions to the game of cricket.

The Windies have won the ICC Cricket World Cup, the ICC World Twenty20 and the ICC Champions Trophy. The Under 19 teams have also been successful.

Discussion

Your teacher will help you to arrange a class debate. You will discuss whether or not West Indies cricket benefits the Caribbean. Some of the class should argue that it does have benefits for the region, while others should suggest that is does not. Prepare your case and think of good reasons to back up your arguments.

Exercise

5. Which countries form the West Indies cricket team?

6. Work in pairs. Find out about the medals (gold, silver and bronze) that have been won by athletes from your country in the CARIFTA Games. Find pictures of the athletes and report back to the class.

Key vocabulary

unity

integrated

Education and medicine

We are learning to:

- identify non-political areas of cooperation within the Caribbean region: education, medicine
- assess the role of regional agencies in facilitating the integration process

Education (University of the West Indies) 》

This University of the West Indies (UWI) developed from the University College of the West Indies, which had been established in 1948 as an independent external college of the University of London. The UWI became completely independent in 1962, at a time when many countries in the Caribbean achieved independence. This helped in efforts to make the region more autonomous and less dependent on former colonial rulers. The UWI aids in regional development by providing tertiary education and research facilities.

Students and their lecturer at the university campus in Kingston, Jamaica.

UWI is internationally recognised for its excellence. Graduates of the university have helped to provide leadership in Caribbean states and to promote economic and cultural growth. Graduates of the university include many current and former prime ministers as well as Nobel laureates and Rhodes Scholars.

The university has three main campuses:

- Mona – in Jamaica
- St Augustine – in Trinidad and Tobago
- Cave Hill – in Barbados.

There are several smaller campuses in other states, as well. The Open Campus of the university provides for online learning.

The university offers diplomas and degrees in Engineering, Humanities, Education, Law, Medicine, Science, Agriculture and Social Sciences.

> **Did you know...?**
>
> Sir Derek Walcott, the Caribbean poet and playwright who won the Nobel Prize for Literature in 1992, was a graduate of the University College of the West Indies. He studied in Jamaica.

Exercise

1. How long has UWI been a fully independent Caribbean university?

2. What courses can you study at this university?

3. Analyse the role that UWI plays in the development of the Caribbean.

Promoting good health is essential to the development of the Caribbean. There is widespread **cooperation** between healthcare providers across the Caribbean.

One example is the Caribbean Environmental Health Institute (CEHI). This was set up in 1989 by CARICOM to respond to the environmental health concerns of its members.

The CEHI provides advice to members in all areas of environmental management, including:

- water supplies, liquid waste and excrement disposal
- solid waste management – for example, from shelters and health facilities
- water resources management – for example, collecting and distributing treated rainwater
- coastal management, including beach pollution
- air pollution, occupational health
- disaster prevention and preparedness, such as planning for floods
- natural resources conservation
- environmental institution development
- social and economic aspects of environmental management.

Promoting good health is essential to the development of the Caribbean.

Currently, members of the CEHI include Anguilla, Antigua and Barbuda, the Bahamas, Barbados, Belize, British Virgin Islands, Dominica, Grenada, Guyana, Jamaica, Montserrat, St Kitts and Nevis, St Lucia, St Vincent and the Grenadines, Trinidad and Tobago, Turks and Caicos Islands.

Exercise

4. How and why is medical expertise shared across the Caribbean?

5. Why do you think it is important to share such expertise?

6. In your own words, explain the services that CEHI provides and why it is important to the well-being of the people of the Caribbean.

7. How is awareness about diseases created? Give an example of something you have seen or heard in your community.

Key vocabulary

cooperation

Culture and disaster preparedness

We are learning to:

- identify non-political areas of cooperation within the Caribbean region: culture, disaster preparedness
- assess the role of regional agencies in facilitating the integration process.

Other forms of cooperation between Caribbean states include **cultural festivals** like **CARIFESTA** and a combined disaster management agency called CDEMA.

Culture (CARIFESTA) 〉〉

Since this first festival in 1972 in Guyana, CARIFESTA has been strengthening the **cultural bonds** between the people of the Caribbean. The aims of CARIFESTA are as follows:

- to depict the life of the people of the region – their heroes, morale, myths, traditions, beliefs, creativeness and ways of expression
- to show the similarities and the differences between the people of the Caribbean and Latin America
- to create a climate in which art can flourish so that artists are encouraged to return to their homeland
- to awaken a regional identity in literature
- to stimulate and unite the cultural movement throughout the region.

The festival has achieved its aims and created numerous benefits for the people of the Caribbean. It has become a major tourist attraction that unifies Caribbean nations and expresses their diversity at the same time.

The festival has helped to create a unique **identity** for people from the Caribbean. The festival has also promoted cultural activities as a form of entertainment as well as creating opportunities for many artists to forge good careers.

Research

Work in pairs and find newspaper articles about CARIFESTA. Find out how the celebrations help to bring people of the region together. Report back to the class with a summary of what you have discovered.

Discussion

a) In a class discussion, express your opinions about the benefits of CDEMA to Caribbean unity. Has CDEMA really been effective? What more could be done to improve regional cooperation in this regard?

b) Work as a class and express your opinions about the benefits of CARIFESTA and its contribution to regional unity.

Exercise

1. What would you expect to see and do at CARIFESTA? Make a list of 10 items or activities.

2. What is a regional identity and how does CARIFESTA promote this?

3. How do you think the people of the Caribbean region have benefited the most from CARIFESTA?

CDEMA (the Caribbean Disaster Emergency Management Agency) was set up to coordinate responses to **natural disasters** such as hurricanes, volcanoes, earthquakes and tsunamis in CARICOM member states and associate member states. The responsibilities of CDEMA include:

* managing and coordinating disaster relief
* getting reliable information on disasters
* reducing or eliminating the impact of disasters
* setting up and maintaining adequate disaster response.

Case study

Read this press release issued by CARICOM after the 2010 earthquake in Haiti and answer the questions.

'More than 300 persons from 11 Caribbean Community (CARICOM) Member States and Associate Members have so far been involved in the response to the devastating earthquake which struck Haiti on 12 January. The Region's initial response was spearheaded by Jamaica, the sub-regional focal point with responsibility for the northern geographic zone of CDEMA which includes Haiti.

Personnel from Antigua and Barbuda, Barbados, Belize, the Bahamas, Dominica, Guyana, Grenada, St Lucia, St Vincent and the Grenadines and the British Virgin Islands provided support after the initial search and rescue, medical, security and engineering teams had been supplied by Jamaica within 48 hours of the earthquake.

CARICOM's continuing interventions in Haiti include: Emergency Response Coordination; Medical Assistance; Logistics, inclusive of the distribution of relief supplies and engineers assessments; Security; CARICOM Civilian Evacuation and Resource Mobilisation.'

Questions

1. How did CARICOM respond to the 2010 earthquake in Haiti?
2. Which members of CARICOM were involved in the response?
3. Which country led the response team? Why do you think they led it?

Activity

Write a report about the benefits of belonging to regional integration organisations. Outline the advantages and any disadvantages.

Did you know...?

Members of CDEMA include:

* Anguilla
* Antigua and Barbuda
* the Bahamas
* Barbados
* Belize
* British Virgin Islands
* Dominica
* Grenada
* Guyana
* Haiti
* Jamaica
* Montserrat
* St Kitts and Nevis
* St Lucia
* St Vincent and the Grenadines
* Suriname
* Trinidad and Tobago
* Turks and Caicos.

Key vocabulary

cultural festivals

CARIFESTA

cultural bonds

identity

CDEMA

natural disasters

Regional integration and cooperation

We are learning to:

- analyse ways in which the individual, businesses and countries benefit from regional integration.

The benefits and achievements of regional integration and cooperation

Integration in the Caribbean has brought many benefits to the region.

Free movement of goods, labour and capital

Regional integration has improved the ability to move goods, **labour** and **capital** freely across the region, increasing opportunities to grow regional economies and to improve levels of employment.

Unemployment is a big problem within the Caribbean region, but access to greater resources can lead to better job opportunities, a larger population can offer more skills and a larger regional economy is more attractive for investment.

Regional integration has given businesses and industries in the Caribbean access to a larger market.

Expansion of trade

Regional integration has given businesses and industries in the Caribbean access to a larger market. Trade expansion means a diversification of products available to larger markets, which leads to greater economic growth. Regional integration assists trade expansion because:

- the entire region becomes a market of goods and services starting from within the region
- the region can trade more effectively on the world market.

Various **trade agreements** between member countries of organisations such as CARIFTA, the removal of trade barriers and a larger market to trade in have resulted in more goods being traded between Caribbean countries. There is also a greater awareness in the world about goods and services provided by the Caribbean.

Discussion

Have a class discussion about the ways young people and adults can help promote Caribbean integration and the development of a Caribbean identity.

Exercise

1. In your own words, explain the benefits of regional integration for trade. Write 100 words.

2. How can unemployment be reduced by greater regional integration?

Improvement in the quality of life ⟫

Regional integration, along with steady economic growth and prosperity, means that there is more money available for social programmes (better housing, health care, **sanitation**). It also creates jobs, which means people have more money. There is better access to education, as well – for example, the University of the West Indies. Member states also help each other to combat crime through the Regional Security Service.

Increased cooperation among member states ⟫⟫

Regional integration has increased cooperation among the member states. Participation in organisations such as CARIFTA (trade), CARICOM/CSME (economy), OECS (unity), ACS (heritage and sustainable tourism), CARIFESTA (culture) and CDEMA (disaster preparedness) contributes to increased cooperation between member states.

Closer cooperation between member states also helps to reduce the cost of government (CARICOM, for example, provides many services that individual countries could only provide for themselves at a much higher cost), reduces duplication of effort and increases bargaining power with markets outside the region. Member states that work closely together create a stronger community sense and a closer-knit region that already has a long shared history.

Better response to global environment ⟫⟫⟫

Regional integration offers greater opportunities for the region to compete on a global scale and to take part in globalisation. Working cooperatively to produce certain goods reduces the costs of production and offers economies of scale. This helps to make the Caribbean region more competitive on a global scale. However, retaining a strong regional market also means that the region does not need to rely on global markets in times of global economic difficulty.

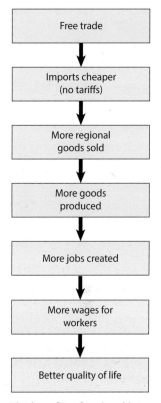

The benefits of regional integration.

Project

Students work in groups to create a jingle or advertisement that informs individuals and businesses about ways they can support regional integration.

Exercise

3. In your own words, explain how regional integration can improve the quality of life in the region. Write 100 words.

4. Name the organisations that help to improve regional integration and explain what they do.

5. Name three ways that quality of life can be improved through regional integration.

Key vocabulary

labour

capital

trade agreements

sanitation

Regional integration

We are learning to:

- discuss ways the individual, businesses and countries can deepen regional integration
- role of individual citizens and business organisations in the integration process.

Role of the individual >>

We have been discussing integration at a regional level, which involves countries working together to achieve common goals. Individual citizens also have a role to play, though – at local, national and regional level.

At an individual level, citizens share family duties, such as washing and cleaning, and looking after family members.

Citizens can also work and cooperate together at a community level, by taking part in community events (and regional events such as CARIFESTA), helping their neighbours, joining local community groups, such as youth groups or sport clubs, neighbourhood watch groups.

At a national level, citizens can help the local authorities with national initiatives such as looking after the environment.

The role of the citizens at a regional level can include:

- being informed – citizens should be aware of issues (social, political, economic, cultural) at local, national and regional level
- purchasing regional products – buying local goods and products helps local producers rather than producers in other parts of the world
- showing solidarity and mutual support towards regional fellow citizens – the Caribbean is a multicultural region and on each island there are people from different cultural backgrounds; it is important to respect people who come from different backgrounds.

One of the roles of being a citizen, is to show solidarity and support towards fellow citizens.

Discussion

In groups discuss this question: 'Do individuals benefit from regional integration or not?'

Exercise

1. Name three ways an individual can help with regional integration at an individual level and a regional level.

2. Give examples of things that citizens should stay informed about.

Role of business organisations >>>

The role of businesses in regional integration include:

- Increasing range of goods and services – businesses have an important role to play in creating a wide range of goods and services for the region. Increased goods and services means more jobs.

- Providing opportunities for investment and employment – companies often need **investment** to expand or bring in new equipment, and this attracts investors, which in turn can create employment. In return, the investors are looking to make more money themselves.

- Competition – increased competition can help to raise employment and boost sales outside the region, which in turn increases earnings and improves living standards.

- **Multinational companies** – large companies that are based in different countries in the region and that often produce a number of different products. They produce goods which are used in the region, are exported outside the region and employ large numbers of people within the region. Examples in the Caribbean include:

  - Massy Group – machinery, engineering, retail, real estate, insurance, finance, energy and gas

  - ANSA McAL – retail, car industry, manufacturing, media, finance

  - TCL Group – cement and ready-mixed cement products.

The role of countries >>>

The role of government includes making sure that:

- legislation works across the region
- policies across the region work for all members of the region in a similar, or same, way
- government agreements are followed, such as environmental protection agreements.
- citizens are aware of the objectives and benefits of integration.

Exercise

3. Explain the role of businesses in regional integration.

4. How can multinational companies help regional integration? Give an example of a multinational company.

5. Explain how governments can help regional integration.

MASSY

Massy Group is a multinational company which works in engineering, machinery, finance, retail, real estate, insurance, energy and gas.

Research

Research a multinational company that is present in the Caribbean. Identify the different types of industry they are involved in, and where. Write a short report of around 100 words and use photos if you can find them.

Project

Create a brochure that outlines the benefits of integration to individuals, businesses and countries. To illustrate your brochure, use images from magazines, the internet or newspapers.

Key vocabulary

investment

multinational company

Issues that affect the Caribbean

We are learning to:

- examine issues that affect the Caribbean and the world and develop action plans to solve these issues: drugs, crime, HIV.

Drugs and crime 〉〉

Drugs are medicines or other substances that can have serious effects on the body. Drugs prescribed by medical staff can be obtained legally. Other substances include illegal drugs, such as marijuana, heroin, cocaine, LSD and ecstasy.

Substance abuse can cause short- and long-term health problems, loss of work and money, broken families and underachievement at work, school and in the community.

In most communities, **crime** is a serious problem. It can take on many forms, ranging from minor offences like vandalism and stealing, to major offences such as murder, gang violence, armed robbery and rape. Gangs are often associated with drugs and crime in the Caribbean.

Gangs are often associated with drugs and crime in the Caribbean.

Action plan 〉〉〉

Some of the strategies to prevent drug abuse include:

- educating people about the effects of substance abuse
- offering guidance for parents to help their children avoid drug abuse
- counselling services for those directly or indirectly affected by drug abuse.

Some of the strategies to combat crime can include:

- making sure that crimes are punished fairly
- crime prevention programmes, such as community policing, presentations at schools, anti-crime campaigns
- awareness campaigns showing the effect that crime has on individuals and society.

Exercise

1. In your own words, outline why drugs and crime are an issue in the Caribbean.

2. What are some of the strategies used to combat drug and crime issues?

3. Create a poster highlighting one of these problems, along with ways to solve it.

Activity

Work in groups. Write a song about the activities of gangs and perform it for the rest of the class. Discuss the song in class.

HIV and AIDS ▶▶▶

HIV is a virus that causes the disease of **AIDS**. There is no cure for HIV/AIDS at present, although the effects of the disease can be treated. HIV/AIDS can be transmitted through:

- unprotected sex
- untested blood transfusions
- by sharing razors and syringes
- through any contact with infected blood or other body fluids
- mothers with HIV or AIDS can also pass the infection onto their babies.

Poverty, gender inequality, sex tourism and stigma are all factors associated with HIV/AIDS. AIDS is a serious threat to the development of a country. Workers with AIDS may not be able to work as they did before and will need expensive medical treatment in order to be able to lead productive lives. Parents who die of AIDS leave orphaned children, who need to be cared for.

Activity

Write a story about someone who becomes infected with HIV. Describe how other people react to this person and what he or she does in order to live with the disease.

Action plan ▶▶

Some of the strategies to help prevent HIV/AIDS include:

- abstaining from sexual activity
- using condoms during sexual activity, which reduces the risk of infection
- distribution of free condoms
- staying faithful to one partner
- taking regular tests to check for infection
- avoiding touching other people's blood and dirty syringes
- government campaigns on prevention by providing information and advice
- campaigns in schools.

AIDS is no longer considered a death penalty should anyone become infected, but ongoing treatment can be very costly to governments. In addition to this the loss of days at work and other social costs, such as the state looking after AIDS orphans, can increase the economic cost to the state.

Exercise

4. Have HIV/AIDS awareness campaigns been successful in your community?

5. Do some people still prefer not to reveal their HIV status because of the perceived stigma involved?

6. What further action is needed in your community?

Key vocabulary

drugs

crime

HIV

AIDS

Poverty and unemployment

We are learning to:

- examine issues that affect the Caribbean and the world and develop action plans to solve these issues: poverty, unemployment.

Unemployment ⟩⟩

UNICEF estimates that about 10 million young people in Latin America and the Caribbean are **unemployed**. Many of these young people have also dropped out of school. The rate of unemployment varies from country to country. Here are some of the general reasons for unemployment across the region:

- general economic decline and job losses
- young people lack the practical experience and skills needed to compete against older, more experienced workers
- younger workers are likely to be fired first if a business needs to reduce staff, because it is assumed that they have fewer dependants
- cuts in government spending
- loss of markets and industries (such as the sugar industry).

Some of the consequences of youth unemployment are:

- Young people turn to illegal activities to get money.
- The country does not gain from new ideas and skills.
- Young people become disillusioned and unhappy.

Action plan ⟩⟩⟩

What can be done? Caribbean governments have put a lot of effort into teaching young people skills so they can find work. Many efforts have also been aimed at helping young people to start their own businesses and become self-employed. Young people can also gain experience by: working as volunteers, joining government-sponsored work schemes or taking courses that include practical work experience.

Activity

Work in groups and conduct a survey in your own community. Your teacher will help you. Different groups can focus on different issues. For example:

- How many people are currently unemployed?
- How many people have lost their jobs in the last year?
- Are there more men or more women who are unemployed?
- What have people done to earn money?
- Have people received any aid from the government, charities or NGOs?

Exercise

1. How many unemployed young people does UNICEF estimate are in Latin America and the Caribbean?

2. Name three reasons for unemployment across the Caribbean and two consequences of youth unemployment.

3. How can governments help with unemployment amongst the young?

Poverty is the state of being poor and not having enough money to live a comfortable life. Poverty in the Caribbean is caused by:

- unemployment and low levels of income
- regional inequality of income and wealth
- global inequality of income and access to resources
- lack of access to education
- volatile economies (that is, prone to change)
- the absence of government-funded social care programmes for poorer families
- an income ceiling, as a result of the level of education or skills training received
- gender inequality and exclusion from parts of society.

Poverty is also often closely linked to crime and violence, although of course some families living in poverty are also strong, happy and stay away from crime. Some researchers have suggested that there are three main types of poverty in the Caribbean:

- families who have been poor for many generations
- families who are poor because people in the family have lost their jobs due to economic conditions
- families who are poor for part of the year, because the work they do is seasonal – for example, some families only work during Carnival.

Would you say that this family in the Dominican Republic lives in poverty? Do people have different ideas about what poverty means?

Action plan >>

Some strategies to combat poverty include:

- increasing economic growth, which leads to higher employment and income
- higher levels of investment, improvements in productivity
- better education and training
- improving social services, to support families that are less well off
- improving opportunities for poorer countries to trade with the more well-off countries
- greater foreign investment.

Discussion

Work in groups. Brainstorm ideas that you think could be used to help stop poverty in your country. Write down all your ideas, then focus on two that you think are practical and workable. Present your ideas to the rest of the class.

Exercise

4. In your own words, outline the main types of poverty in the Caribbean, and their causes.
5. What strategies are there to combat poverty?

Key vocabulary

unemployed

poverty

Pollution and terrorism

We are learning to:

- examine issues that affect the Caribbean and the world and develop action plans to solve these issues: pollution, terrorism.

Pollution

There are a number of pollution problems in our region.

- Air pollution – dust from local industries can be a problem, creating **smog** in large towns and cities and causing asthma and respiratory issues, while weakening sunlight can affect plant growth. Carbon dioxide released into the atmosphere contributes to climate change.

- Water pollution – releasing untreated sewage into the sea or rivers can affect humans and marine life. Chemicals such as mercury can cause health risks to humans and carbon dioxide makes the sea more acidic, damaging coral reefs. Caribbean coral reefs are vital for marine life and the tourist industry.

- Land pollution – household and industrial waste is often disposed of incorrectly. The amount of waste is a problem for all countries. Landfill is no longer a solution, as chemicals can leak into rivers, then public supplies.

- Noise pollution – this is an increasing problem, caused by a large amount of traffic, airports and aeroplanes, industrial machines and construction, but also music.

Low visibility caused by pollution in an urban area.

Research

Revise the terms reduce, reuse and recycle, which were studied in Form 1. Research what individuals can do to reduce, reuse and recycle.

Action plan

Some of the strategies that governments can employ include:

- regulations setting out the correct disposal of waste
- building and maintaining more sewage plants
- educating citizens about pollution and waste disposal
- providing facilities for **recycling**.

Some of the strategies that businesses can employ include:

- disposing of and recycling waste correctly and safely
- **reducing** the amount of packaging on materials
- **reusing** packaging materials.

Some of the strategies that individuals can employ include:

- disposing of and recycling household waste correctly and safely – for example, paper, plastics and glass
- composting organic house waste and refuse.

Did you know...?

There are three principles that governments, businesses and individuals should follow to reduce the impact on our environment: the '3 Rs' – reduce, reuse and recycle.

Terrorism 〉〉〉

A particular challenge in the modern world is the increase of **terrorism**. This is the use of violence, such as bombing, to achieve political aims or to force a government to do something.

Case study

Terrorism

In general, the Caribbean is seen as a low risk for terrorist attacks. However, there are still threats in the region, such as Trinidad and Tobago nationals who have recently travelled to Syria and Iraq to fight along with Daesh (formerly referred to as ISIL). They may pose a security threat on their return.

There is also a threat from individuals who may have been inspired by **terrorist** groups, including Daesh and al Qaeda, to carry out so-called 'lone actor' attacks targeting public events or places.

Countries in the Caribbean work closely with international partners in strategic areas such as intelligence and information sharing on people who are found to be associated with any terrorist group, whether locally or internationally.

St Ann's Square in Manchester is filled with flowers and teddies in the wake of the Manchester Arena bombing that killed 22 people, 2017.

Action plan 〉〉

Measures set up by Caribbean countries to combat terrorism include:

- making it an offence to finance someone to travel overseas to train for and take part in terrorist acts
- having security checks on aircraft and cruise ships
- strict immigration controls
- financial controls on money laundering and the financing of terrorists through Caribbean banks.

Exercise

1. Give three examples of pollution affecting the Caribbean region.

2. Name one way that governments, businesses and individuals can each reduce pollution.

3. What measures have Caribbean countries put in place to combat terrorist threats?

Key vocabulary

smog

recycling

reducing

reusing

terrorism

terrorist

Questions

See how well you have understood the topics in this unit.

1. Match the key vocabulary word (i–vii) with its definition (a–g).

    i) regional integration

    ii) integrate

    iii) social integration

    iv) racial integration

    v) economic integration

    vi) interdependence

    vii) region

    a) when people of all cultural groups, sexes and ages live and work together in an area

    b) an area of the world – for example, the Caribbean

    c) the joining or working together of countries that are near to each other, in order to make them economically and politically more powerful

    d) when two or more things or people rely on each other or help each other

    e) bring together ideas and people so that they work together or become part of the same group

    f) when people from different cultural groups live and work together on an equal basis

    g) cooperation in business, such as trading and finance

2. Which organisation was the first attempt at integration by Caribbean states?

3. Match the dates (i–vi) to the events (a–f):

    i) 1958

    ii) 1962

    iii) 1965

    iv) 1973

    v) 1981

    vi) 1989

    a) CARIFTA formed

    b) CSME formed

    c) West Indian Federation formed

    d) Treaty of Basseterre/OECS formed

    e) West Indian Federation disbanded

    f) CARICOM formed

4. Complete this table with ticks (✓) to show which groups the Caribbean countries have belonged/belong to.

	West Indian Federation	CARIFTA	CARICOM	ACS	OECS	CDEMA	CEHI
Anguilla							
Antigua and Barbuda							
the Bahamas							
Barbados							
Belize							
British Virgin Islands							
Colombia							
Costa Rica							
Cuba							
Dominica							
Dominican Republic							
El Salvador							
Grenada							
Guatemala							
Guyana							
Haiti							
Honduras							
Jamaica							
Mexico							
Montserrat							
Nicaragua							
Panama							
St Kitts and Nevis							
St Lucia							
St Vincent and the Grenadines							
Suriname							
Trinidad and Tobago							
Turks and Caicos							
Venezeula							

Checking your progress

To make good progress in understanding different aspects of Caribbean integration and global links, check to make sure you understand these ideas.

Understand the term regional integration and the history of the integration process in the Caribbean.

Understand objectives and membership of institutions/bodies which form part of the integration.

Write an essay about the role of regional agencies in facilitating regional integration.

Identify non-political areas of cooperation within the Caribbean region.

Analyse ways in which the individual, businesses and countries benefit from regional integration.

Discuss the ways young people and adults can help promote Caribbean integration and the development of a Caribbean identity.

Discuss ways the individual, businesses and countries can deepen regional integration.

Explain the role of businesses in regional integration.

Explain how governments can help regional integration.

Discuss ideas that you think could be used to help stop poverty in parts of your country.

Explain strategies that you think could be used to help stop poverty in your country.

Research what individuals in your country can do to reduce, reuse and recycle.

Unit 8: *Personal development*

Choosing a career: making the right choice

- Define relevant terms and concepts: employment, career, occupation, employer, employee, lifelong learning, entrepreneurship
- Reasons why people work
- Types of jobs that are available in the Caribbean
- Skills and knowledge needed to pursue specific careers
  - ○ knowledge and skills
  - ○ qualities needed for career
  - ○ qualifications
- Factors to consider when choosing a career
  - ○ health issues
  - ○ shift work
  - ○ opportunities for promotion
  - ○ qualifications and skills
  - ○ passion
- The importance of a résumé
- Issues employers and employees may face in the work place
  - ○ sexual harassment
  - ○ poor wages
  - ○ long hours
  - ○ unsafe working conditions
  - ○ unpunctuality/missed deadlines
- Evaluate ways of improving performance at the workplace
- Define relevant terms and concepts: appraisal, self-appraisal
- Examine expected work ethics at places of work
- Describe ways workers show dissatisfaction in the workplace
- Explore solutions to resolve issues in the workplace
- Define relevant terms and concepts: work ethic
- The role of the trade unions
  - ○ benefits of membership in a trade union

Choosing a career

We are learning to:

- define relevant terms and concepts: employment, career, occupation, employer, employee, lifelong learning, entrepreneurship.

Introduction to the world of work ❯❯

'What do you want to do when you grow up?' is a question many children hear. As you grow into a young adult, you may also be asking yourself: What are my passions and interests? How do I like spending my time? What are my talents and abilities? What would I like to achieve in my future?

Types of work ❯❯

The world of work has changed dramatically since the twentieth century. The types of **employment** available have changed. People have also changed how they work.

Construction worker carrying out an inspection.

You have already learned about **primary**, **secondary** and **tertiary** workers. Remember, primary workers extract or harvest resources, for example farmers, fishermen, miners. Secondary workers process or manufacture products, such as factory workers or builders. Tertiary workers provide services, like doctors, teachers or advertisers.

In the past, there were fewer **career** possibilities. The opportunity to study for a professional **occupation** did exist, for example as a doctor/nurse, lawyer, accountant, architect or teacher. Although these occupations are still available now, there is greater **choice** open to young people.

The development of technology has created many new **jobs** – from computer programmers, software developers and technicians, to people who run successful businesses using digital technology, social media and the internet.

Exercise

1. **a)** Look at the photos on these pages. Find other pictures in magazines of people doing different jobs.

   b) Describe what you can see in each picture and the jobs that these people do. Use the terms in the key vocabulary box.

2. In your own words, define career.

3. Which careers do you see as traditional occupations? Which would you describe as more modern ones?

Architects discussing a plan in the office.

How people work ▶▶▶

In the past, many people stayed in a single career for most of their lifetime. A person might get their first job with an **employer** and gradually work their way up in the company over many years. Today, this is very different.

Employment is the state of having paid work to do. The average **employee** stays in the same job for around three to five years. People have also started to value **lifelong learning**. They may continue education, training and acquiring new skills throughout their lives, which can lead to a change in career.

Some people are **self-employed** and they hire out their time in return for payment, for example in construction or retail, while some people become **entrepreneurs**.

Entrepreneurs are people who have started up their own business – a clothes shop or an internet business, perhaps – and have taken on the challenge of building a business.

Challenges ▶

The twenty-first-century workplace also brings its own challenges. In some industries, new technologies can replace particular job roles. This can cause **unemployment**.

People also live longer today than in the past, meaning that workers need to save more money for their retirement. A person who retires at age 65 may live for another 30 years or more, and will need to meet their needs when retired.

Exercise

4. What difference do you understand between the words occupation and career? If necessary, use a dictionary to help you come up with definitions.

5. In your own words, define the terms employer, employee, self-employed and entrepreneur.

6. What challenges exist for twenty-first-century workers?

7. What do you understand by the term lifelong learning?

8. Study the employment listings in your local newspaper. What does this tell you about the jobs that are available in your local area? Write a paragraph explaining which of these jobs you would like to do, and why.

Key vocabulary

employment

primary industry

secondary industry

tertiary industry

career

occupation

choice

job

employer

employee

lifelong learning

self-employed

entrepreneur

unemployment

Why people work

We are learning to:

- state reasons why people work.

Reasons why people work

Why do people spend so much time working? Why do we spend so much time thinking and talking about what work we will do after we have left school?

People work for four basic reasons:

- To obtain an income – working in a job allows people to earn an income. This in turn allows them to buy goods and services that will help themselves and provide for their family's needs. Needs are those things that are essential for everyday living, such as food, water, shelter and clothing.

- To provide for peoples' wants – income from work also supports peoples' wants – items that a person would like to have, but are not essential for everyday life or basic survival needs, such as a cell phone or fashionable shoes.

- To attain a better standard of living – income that helps to provide for our needs and wants also helps to improve our standard of living. The more income someone has, the more opportunities they have to improve their own and their family's lives.

- To use our **skills** and **qualifications** – being a productive part of the wider economy provides **self-esteem** for the individual, as well as a sense of feeling fulfilled and reaching their potential by using their skills, **knowledge** and creativity.

One other very important reason why people work is to contribute to the overall economy. They are contributing to society by applying their skills and knowledge to their job; and by paying tax they contribute money, which helps to provide goods and services the whole community needs.

Exercise

1. Write 150 words on the topic 'Why do people work?'

2. Explain the difference between a need and a want.

3. Why does earning more income help to improve someone's standard of living?

Discussion

In groups, discuss the four reasons why people work. Can you think of any others? Of the reasons given, which do you think are the most important?

Project

In groups, create a questionnaire asking people why they work. Choose five questions for your questionnaire, for example:

- What is your job?
- Why did you choose your job?
- Did you need qualifications to get your job?

When you have agreed on your questions, ask your parents, neighbours and teachers. See if you can find common reasons or a pattern to their answers. Write a paragraph outlining your findings, then share with the class.

Look at the diagram below, and read some of the reasons that people give to explain why they work. Then answer the questions.

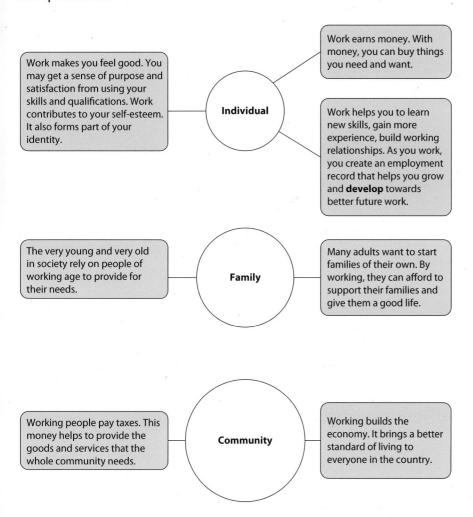

Work makes you feel good. You may get a sense of purpose and satisfaction from using your skills and qualifications. Work contributes to your self-esteem. It also forms part of your identity.

Individual

Work earns money. With money, you can buy things you need and want.

Work helps you to learn new skills, gain more experience, build working relationships. As you work, you create an employment record that helps you grow and **develop** towards better future work.

The very young and very old in society rely on people of working age to provide for their needs.

Family

Many adults want to start families of their own. By working, they can afford to support their families and give them a good life.

Working people pay taxes. This money helps to provide the goods and services that the whole community needs.

Community

Working builds the economy. It brings a better standard of living to everyone in the country.

Exercise

4. Name the three sectors of society that benefit from people working.

5. Why does working make a person feel good?

6. Why do you think working contributes to a person's self-esteem?

7. Which age groups in a family rely on other members of the family for income?

8. How does paying taxes contribute to the wider society?

Key vocabulary

....

needs

wants

skill

qualification

self-esteem

knowledge

Types of jobs

We are learning to:

* explore the types of jobs that are available in the Caribbean.

Career options ▶▶

We have looked at our personality skills and some factors that can influence our career choices. These pages look at some job options in the Caribbean.

Job profile

Accountant

Job description: An **accountant** keeps track of and records the flow of money in an organisation or business.

Work may include: Working on payrolls, completing audits; explaining billing and invoicing to staff and clients; budgeting; writing reports; understanding and implementing accounting procedures; keeping databases and records in order.

Qualifications: Business degree; specialised accounting certificate.

Interests: Finances, business, working with numbers.

Skills needed: Computer skills, working with spreadsheets, mathematical skills, logic, attention to detail.

Values and attitudes: Honesty, **persistence**, responsibility.

Accountancy is one of the job options available in the Caribbean.

Job profile

Insurance agent

Job description: An **insurance agent** sells **insurance policies** for an insurance company.

Work may include: Understanding and explaining policies; identifying and contacting new clients; helping clients choose policies that suit them; analysing clients' existing policies in order to advise about possible changes; keeping records and handling renewals of policies; helping clients settle claims.

Qualifications: High school diploma; additional qualifications such as business courses are optional. Agents may have to take courses to keep up to date with tax laws and regulations.

Skills needed: Communication skills; interest in others.

Values and attitudes: Planning ahead; honesty; **empathy**; good service skills.

Job profile

Teacher

Job description: A teacher works with students, presenting classes, lectures and assignments, and helping students to develop skills and knowledge.

Work may include: Preparing and presenting lessons, lectures and assignments; grading tests; preparing assessments; keeping records; counselling students and parents; enforcing rules; accompanying classes on outings or trips.

Qualifications: Teaching degree or diploma.

Skills needed: Communication skills, listening skills, ability to work with people; sensitivity to feelings; interest in specific subjects and flexibility.

Values and attitudes: Lifelong learning, reflection, patience, appreciation, service, responsibility, curiosity and empathy.

A teacher works with students, just like yourself.

Exercise

Work in groups. Choose one of the occupations shown on these pages.

1. Read through the information with your group.

2. Read through the values and attitudes under each career. Explain what you understand by each term and why it might be important for that job.

   a) Discuss the job description. Does it sound accurate to you? What else might you include in this job description?

   b) What hours does this occupation involve: ordinary office hours, or does it involve after-hours work? Are there any advantages or disadvantages to the hours?

   c) Brainstorm any other skills or interests that might draw someone to this occupation.

   d) Would this job appeal to you? Why, or why not?

3. Choose another job that interests you. Write up a similar fact file, giving a brief job description, a list of what the work may include, and necessary qualifications and skills. You may do research on the internet or interview adults in your community to find the information you need.

Key vocabulary

accountant

persistence

insurance agent

insurance policy

empathy

The hotel industry

We are learning to:

- explore the types of jobs that are available in the Caribbean.

One of the biggest industries in the Caribbean is the hotel industry. There are a wide range of career opportunities in this industry:

- A hotelier (or hotel manager) supervises and manages the running of a hotel.

- In bigger hotels, there are department **managers** in charge of different divisions, such as front desk, reservations, sales and marketing, conventions, restaurants, human resources, entertainment and accounts.

- An **events planner** organises events such as weddings, conferences, parties and other functions.

- **Marketing staff** find ways to advertise and promote the business.

- The housekeeping staff keep all areas of the hotel clean, tidy and fresh, and may also be responsible for providing services such as washing, sourcing equipment that guests need and maintenance.

- The reception staff welcome new guests, give advice and information and assist with requests and enquiries.

- The kitchen staff may include chefs, bar staff, sommeliers, waiters and cleaning staff.

- Tour guides arrange tours to places of interest.

The hotel industry is one of the biggest industries in the Caribbean.

Activity

As a class, make a list of the careers or jobs held by your parents or relatives. Organise a 'work-shadow day', when you can spend a day at a parent's or relative's workplace. Report back on your work-shadow day with a short oral presentation to the class.

Exercise

1. The first members of staff you meet at the front desk of a hotel are the:

   a) reception staff

   b) marketing staff

   c) housekeeping staff.

2. The number of staff in a large hotel resort is likely to be:

   a) about 10 people

   b) about 20 people

   c) more than 100 people.

Case study

Caterer

Read this interview with Philip, whose job is as a caterer. Then answer the questions below.

Q: What does a caterer do?

A: I meet with clients to work out what they need for their event. We work out a menu and a budget, then arrange to prepare, cook and deliver the food for the event.

Q: How did you start out?

A: I did a full-time course at the Barbados Hospitality Institute. As a student, I had some part-time work helping in restaurant kitchens. After my diploma, I worked as a chef at a hotel for two years.

Q: Why did you become a caterer?

A: I wanted to run my own business, and I enjoy working with people. I also like the challenge of making different menus for different clients.

Q: What is the hardest part of the work?

A: Each event has its own challenges. You have to transport the food to the venue. Sometimes we are preparing and presenting food in outdoor places that don't even have running water or electricity. You have to plan ahead carefully for each event!

Questions

1. How is catering different from working as a chef? Explain at least three differences.

2. Which college did Philip attend? Suggest some other careers that might be open to someone who studied at the same college as Philip. Then check their website to see if you were correct.

3. Suggest three kinds of events that a caterer might work at.

4. How could someone interested in the hotel or catering business gain experience and earn extra money while they are still at school? Come up with at least three suggestions.

As a caterer, you can be your own boss.

Project

Create a directory of job vacancies that are advertised in newspapers and magazines in your country. Create an A–Z list of the job types, listing the job title, role, wages/salary, qualifications/experience needed and where it is located. When you have finished your directory, choose three of the jobs you would like to do and explain why.

Discussion

As a class, discuss some different careers you are interested to hear more about. Arrange a guest speaker to come to your class to talk to you about their career.

Key vocabulary

manager

events planner

marketing staff

Personal development

We are learning to:

- recognise the skills and knowledge needed to pursue specific careers
- define relevant terms and concepts: résumé.

Knowledge and skills »

Although computers and machines can do many different kinds of work, we still need people to process resources into products, and to provide services. People bring their skills, knowledge, ideas, creativity and experience into their work.

- Knowledge is what we know and learn about a particular subject, and often we are able to pass it on to someone else. For example, you might know the rules of cricket and you pass that knowledge on to someone who is just learning the game.
- A skill is an area of expertise or the ability to carry out activities or job functions involving ideas, things and/or people. Skills are abilities (or talents) we have acquired through learning. They help us to do things well, and we develop our skills through new experiences and by practising them.

In order for a country to prosper, its people need to develop their skills and knowledge so that they can carry out the work that uses their talents in the best way.

Qualities needed for careers »»

We can each evaluate our own qualities, academic capabilities and potential to help work out our career paths.

Personal qualities: your personality, what you enjoy and what you are interested in.	**Academic capabilities:** your ability to study, read and understand, and do well in examinations and courses.	**Potential:** what you might be able to become in the future; even if you are not a strong student now, perhaps you could become one if you followed a course of study that really interested you.

Exercise

1. In your own words, define knowledge and skills.

2. What three things we should we evaluate when thinking about our career?

Qualifications >>>

Education is the main way that a country develops its human resources. Education takes place at many levels: in the home, at school, at institutions such as colleges and universities, and in the workplace.

At school, children learn the subjects set out in the national **curriculum**. Schools also teach skills that prepare children for life as a part of society, including communication, listening, problem solving, cooperation and fitting in with expectations. School may also teach values and attitudes, such as respect for rules and for their peers and elders.

Institutions >>

Once students have graduated from secondary school, they may further their training at institutions such as:

- teacher training colleges – such as Erdiston Teachers' Training College, Barbados
- technical institutes and colleges – for example, the Sir Arthur Lewis Community College and National Skills Development Centre, St Lucia; St Vincent Technical College, St Vincent and the Grenadines.
- universities – including the University of the West Indies and American University of Antigua – or overseas colleges
- nursing schools – for example, the School of Nursing at the University College of the Cayman Islands.

Governments spend hundreds of millions of dollars each year on **tertiary education**, for example National Development Scholarships, Student Revolving Loan Schemes and Scholarships for attending the University of the West Indies. Governments also run On-the-Job Training Programmes, which provide opportunities for nationals between the ages of 16 and 35 to gain practical experience in companies.

Research

From the directory of jobs you created in Unit 8.4, take five of those jobs and research which qualifications and skills are needed for each. You should also research which institutions offer these qualifications in the Eastern Caribbean.

Activity

Write a reflective journal entry about the kind of work you would like to do in the future, and how you see your work fitting in with your personal values.

Exercise

3. What is the main way a country can develop its human resources?
4. What skills do we learn in school to prepare us for work?
5. Name three types of further training institutes we can go to after mainstream schooling.
6. Name two government programmes that offer tertiary education funding or training.

Key vocabulary
....

curriculum

tertiary education

Choosing a career

We are learning to:

- describe the factors one must consider when choosing a career.

Factors to consider when choosing a career »

There are a number of factors to consider when thinking about your chosen career. Some of these are outlined below.

Health issues: people between the ages of 15 and 49 make up the most **productive** working group in any country. The same age group is the most at risk of lifestyle diseases such as heart disease and cancer, and sexually transmitted diseases such as HIV. Do companies support healthy choices for their employees, for example, by paying for medical insurance, providing paid maternity leave or even setting up exercise facilities?

Shift work: we have seen that there is primary, secondary and tertiary work. You should also consider if your chosen career can offer a **full-time**, **part-time** or **permanent** position or if it is **contract work**. Do you want to be **employed** or self-employed? Maybe you would prefer to be an entrepreneur.

QUESTIONS TO CONSIDER

Passion: do you have a passion about your chosen career? If you do not have a strong interest in the career you are thinking about, then it may not be the best career for you to follow.

Opportunities for promotion: does the career that you are thinking about offer opportunities for promotion?

Qualifications and skills: what are the academic qualifications and practical skills that you need for your career? Do you already have them or do you need to do some training to gain them?

Exercise

1. Which of the factors above do you consider to be the most important when thinking about a career?

2. Which of the factors would you consider to be least important?

3. Why do you think it is important to think about issues such as these before you choose your career?

Some of the other things to think about when choosing a career include:

- Needs and wants – Can the career you would like to follow provide the income you need for yourself and your family? How much are you likely to earn? Will your chosen career allow you to earn more money in the future?

- Values and attitudes – What is important to you? For example, do you want to earn a lot of money, help others, look after the environment, work with animals, be creative? Would you like to be self-employed, employed, work for a large multinational company or work as a volunteer?

- Interests – What do you enjoy doing? For example, do you like doing creative projects, helping others, teaching, working alone, solving problems, designing things, fixing things and so on? Are you able to turn your interests into your career? For example, if you like to make things would you like to be a carpenter? If you are interested in music, would you like a career as a musician?

- Potential – What do you want to do or achieve in your life? Who would you like to become? What are your dreams?

- Talents – What are you good at? What are your special talents? For example, are you good at working with numbers, do you have good communication or writing skills or are you a good problem solver?

- Social factors – What influences you? For example, what do your parents, friends, teachers or peers think you should do?

Other practical things to consider include:

- Will you be able to earn more as your skills and training develop?
- What type of environment is it to work in? Is it safe?
- How far would you have to travel every day? If your chosen career is not close to you, would you be willing to move closer to the workplace?

Activity

Go back to your job directory from Unit 8.4. Look at the jobs you have listed and identify which ones offer full-time and part-time work. Which job type would you prefer? Give reasons for your answers.

Some people like to work in a busy and noisy atmosphere.

Project

Identify a career that you would like to follow. In about 100 words, discuss three factors that have influenced your choice of career. Share with the rest of the class.

Key vocabulary

....

productive

full-time

part-time

permanent

contract work

employed

passion

Exercise

4. Look at the questions listed. Which one is most important to you? Which one is least important?

5. Why do you think your personal interests are important when thinking about a career?

How to write a résumé

We are learning to:

- justify the importance of a résumé.

Résumé writing >>

A **résumé** (or **curriculum vitae,** CV) is a document that summarises your skills, experience and education, and which you present when you apply for a job or for a course of study. Your résumé creates an impression of you that can determine your career opportunities.

Elements of a résumé >>>

A résumé should include key information, including:

- a summary outlining what you can offer the employer
- contact information – include your name, address, email, phone number
- experience – in reverse order, list your job title, name of employer, dates of employment and positions held
- education – school name, location, qualifications
- training and qualifications – related information
- skills and abilities – for example, computer skills
- interests and hobbies – for example, clubs you belong to, sporting activities, community activities
- references – two people who can vouch for your skills, character and qualifications.

A résumé, or CV, is an important document that is used by employers when they are interviewing candidates for jobs in their company.

Presentation of a résumé >>>>

Your résumé should be neatly presented and printed out on clean A4 paper. Never crumple or fold it – instead, present it in a folder or envelope. Employers receive many résumés, so they prefer the document to be short and easy to read. Don't go over two A4 sides. Carefully check your résumé to make sure that there are no errors in the language and spelling.

Ethics associated with résumé writing >>

When writing a résumé, you may be tempted to over-state things to improve your chances of getting the job. Ensure you avoid this, as you may get asked to back up the facts you present in your résumé. Avoid exaggerating things such as:

- more qualifications than you actually have
- changing job titles so they look more impressive
- claiming that you have done something at your present employer, when in fact someone else did it.

> **Did you know...?**
>
> It is important when writing your résumé that you write information that is true and honest. If an employer finds out that you have included false information, they will not offer you the job. Word may get around that you are dishonest. Therefore, always write the truth.

Case study

Look at the résumé below, which is for someone applying for a new teaching positon.

PATRICK **BARROW**

3 Lodge Road, St Michael, Barbados; tel. no.: 0111 222 3333; email: **pbarrow@email.com**.

SUMMARY

It is my mission to inspire students to pursue academic and personal excellence whilst striving to create a challenging and engaging learning environment in which students become lifelong scholars and learners. I use innovative teaching methods as well as effective use of multimedia teaching tools.

EXPERIENCE

1. St Stephen's Primary School in 2002. This was a temporary appointment for two months (September and October) due to the assigned teacher being ill.
2. St Winifred's School for the period November 2002 to July 2005.
3. Lester Vaughan Secondary School for the period September 2005 to present. I am currently teaching Economics, Principles of Business and Social Studies.

EDUCATION

Bachelor: BSc Economics from the University of the West Indies, Cave Hill for the period 2005 to 2008.

TRAINING AND QUALIFICATIONS

Skills: Teaching, Microsoft Office

Interests and hobbies: Cricket, reading, volunteer work

References: Available on request

Discussion

Discuss what kinds of achievements you would like to list on your résumé at the end of secondary school:

- What will your educational qualification say?
- Which interests do you currently have, and how are you following them?
- What activities would you be able to list on your résumé?
- What qualities would you use to describe yourself? Are there any adults you could list for references?

Activity

Draw up your own résumé. You can use the example on this page as a guide.

Exercise

1. What is the writer of the résumé passionate about?
2. Look at the list of key information that a résumé should contain and then at the résumé above. What is missing from the résumé? Why would this be a problem?
3. Do you think his key skills will enable him to be a teacher?
4. What are the two likely places you would submit a résumé?
5. Why is it important to have a well-presented résumé?
6. Explain why you should not give false information on a résumé.

Key vocabulary

résumé/curriculum vitae

Issues in the workplace

We are learning to:

- identify issues employers and employees may face in the workplace.

Issues in the workplace ⟫

Most forms of work require us to work and interact with other people, in **workplace relationships**.

Many jobs require that we work with other people. Our workplace relationships are **formal** and **involuntary**. They have clearly described roles and functions, and we usually can't choose who we work with. Workplace relationships vary according to **hierarchy**:

- **senior** roles – employer, boss, manager, mentor and so on
- **junior** roles – for example, new employees, who have less experience and less responsibility
- **equals** – teammates.

However, in a workplace with many different positions you cannot always judge people based on office hierarchy. It is a good idea to treat everyone with politeness and respect.

Friendships may grow as people work together, get to know each other and do things together outside the workplace. As they trust each other and feel a sense of connection to one another, they may share their personal or work problems more openly than in an ordinary work relationship.

Some work friendships develop further, into **intimate relationships**. Most employers discourage romantic or sexual relationships at work, as it can have damaging effects on the rest of the company.

Some workers get into conflicts with colleagues, and may even develop **enemies**. Having enemies at work can badly damage the cohesion of the group, and can reduce the job satisfaction of the people involved.

Workplace relationships differ from other personal relationships.

Exercise

1. What do you understand by office hierarchy?

2. Describe three kinds of personal relationships that can arise at work.

3. What are the main differences between work relationships and personal relationships?

Building positive relationships at work

Read this case study, which outlines how to behave at work. Then answer the questions below.

COMMUNICATE! – communication includes all the ways you speak to co-workers, from talking as you walk into the office, to discussions in meetings, to emails and telephone calls. Colleagues aren't mind-readers! Give clear information. Ask questions if you need to. Listen without interrupting.

BE FRIENDLY – a positive, friendly attitude will help you work well with co-workers. Be friendly and encouraging to others.

NOT TOO FRIENDLY – your co-workers, especially your seniors, are not your friends. Stay polite. Remember to keep your communication and behaviour appropriate for the workplace.

NOT NASTY, EITHER – you can't always choose who you work with, and you may find that you don't always like all your co-workers. You don't have to be friends with everyone at work. However, you can be professional, respectful and friendly. You can also avoid co-workers that you find difficult or disruptive.

TAKE RESPONSIBILITY – always do the things you say you will do. If you cannot complete a task, communicate this to your co-workers as soon as possible.

Be considerate to others and be mindful in your speech – do not take part in office gossip. Have a positive attitude. Don't complain.

CONSIDER YOUR VALUES AND ATTITUDES – the following values and attitudes can help to ensure you maintain positive relationships with co-workers: understanding, reflection, empathy, cooperation, tolerance, discipline.

You should be professional, respectful and friendly at work.

Questions

1. In your own words define communication in the workplace.

2. Why is it important to be friendly with co-workers?

3. What attitudes should you always show to co-workers, even if you don't get on with them?

4. Consider the values and attitudes listed on this page. In pairs or groups, choose one or more of these. Create a role play showing how to demonstrate this value/attitude in the workplace.

Key vocabulary

workplace relationships

formal

involuntary

hierarchy

senior

junior

equals

friendships

intimate relationship

enemy

Problems in the workplace

We are learning to:

- identify what constitutes sexual harassment
- how employees and employers should handle workplace problems.

Sexual harassment ››

Sexual harassment is any type of unwanted gesture or communication that has a sexual content. It may be:

- a sexual advance, such as trying to kiss, hug or touch a co-worker in a sexual way
- **obscene** or **suggestive** comments
- unwanted touching, such as brushing past someone too closely
- **inappropriate** emails, texts or phone calls
- **unsolicited** flirting
- unwanted comments such as general sexual remarks or **innuendoes**.

Although sexual harassment mostly affects women, it is not limited to men harassing women or bosses harassing their subordinates. An employer, employee, supervisor or client can harass a colleague, maybe making jokes and gestures that harass other workers. The harassment may be male to female, female to male, male to male or female to female.

Sexual harassment can be a big problem in the workplace.

What can you do about sexual harassment? ›››

- Speak up – point out clearly that you are uncomfortable. Request that the harasser stops.
- Keep a record – if you notice harassment continuing, keep records of what happened. Note the date and time, what happened and what you said or did.
- Tell someone – a boss, manager or the police.
- Consider leaving the job – if you do not feel safe at work, you may feel that you need to leave the job.

Discussion

Look at Units 8.8 and 8.9. Brainstorm a mind map of issues in the workplace (and any others you can think of). Consider ways to deal with these issues – add them to the mind map.

Exercise

1. Define the terms sexual harassment and harassment.

2. If someone is being harassed, what type of behaviour could this be?

3. In your own words, explain why it is wrong for sexual harassment to happen in the workplace.

4. In your own words, explain the consequences of sexual harassment in the workplace.

Activity

Use newspapers or the internet. Find an example of a sexual harassment case reported in the news. Write a short news report or create a short radio report about the story.

Case study

Sexual harassment in the workplace

Sexual harassment has many damaging effects.
According to an article in *Trinidad and Tobago Newsday*:

Not only does sexual harassment compromise safety and equality in the workplace, it can also affect a company's profitability. Sexual harassment leads to a stressful work environment. It increases illness and time taken off work. It reduces productivity and can even lead to increased employee turnover. Employers must therefore be made to create and uphold policies that allow us all to feel safe at work.

Other workplace issues

There are many other issues that affect workers in the workplace. Some of them are listed below.

- Poor wages – workers can be exploited by big companies by being paid a lower wage.
- Long hours – workers can also be exploited by having to work more hours in the knowledge that the worker can be easily replaced if they do not comply.
- Unsafe working conditions – this can involve working in dangerous or unsafe places, having to use unguarded machinery, exposure to chemical hazards (dust, fumes, gases), noise, bad lighting, high temperatures, badly designed facilities, having to use poorly maintained equipment, lack of training to use equipment and long work hours (which can cause loss of concentration and increase the likelihood of accidents).
- Unpunctuality of colleagues – this shows a lack of commitment to the job, lack of interest, and inability to do the job. It can lead to resentment by colleagues who do not consider someone a team player.
- Missed deadlines – this can lead to resentment by colleagues who are always on time; missing a delivery date for a job or client is not good business practice.

Exercise

5. Name three other workplace issues.

6. Name some of the health and safety issues that can occur in the workplace.

7. Why are punctuality and meeting deadlines important?

Research

In groups, look at Units 8.8 and 8.9. You would like to use a questionnaire to ask a company's employers and employees about some of the issues they have faced at work. Compile a list of 10 questions. For example:

- Is there good communication in your company?
- Are people often late for work?
- Is there a sexual harassment policy at your workplace?

Present the findings from your questionnaire to the rest of the class.

Key vocabulary

sexual harassment

obscene

suggestive

inappropriate

unsolicited

innuendoes

Appraisal of performance

We are learning to:

- evaluate ways of improving performance in the workplace
- define relevant terms and concepts: appraisal, self-appraisal.

Examining self and employer appraisal of performance

Today most employers conduct **appraisals** of an employee's performance at work. This is usually done on an annual basis (once a year) and reviews how the worker has performed over the last year, if they are happy in their role and if they met the standards required by the employer. It also includes a discussion of future training needs and aspirations.

Employees can also do self-assessment, or **self-appraisals**, for their employer. This involves a questionnaire and is used as part of the annual appraisal. The self-appraisal helps the employer to understand how the employee views their own performance and support over the last year.

Companies conduct appraisals of their employers at regular intervals, such as once a year, to find out how employees are getting on in their job.

Why are appraisals necessary?

There are a number of reasons why appraisals and self-appraisals are necessary. They:

- allow the employee to take an active part in an appraisal, rather than just get feedback
- help to give managers an insight into the employee's own view about their performance
- give the employee a chance to give their side of things
- help the employer to understand an employee's weaknesses and strengths
- help to decide what further training or help the employee would like, along with career development opportunities
- allow the employee to discuss proudly the things that they have accomplished in the last year.

Activity

Using the information on these pages, create role plays in groups of four to demonstrate how to improve performance in the workplace.

Exercise

1. In your own words define the terms appraisal and self-appraisal.
2. Draw a mind map to show why appraisals are necessary.

Alternative ways of getting the job done >>>

The appraisal process is a good tool to find ways to improve performance at work. There are a number of simple ways in which performance can be improved at work, no matter what type of job (or career) you may have.

Be organised – make sure that you know what you have to do on the day you go into work, that you have everything you need to do the job (information, materials, contacts and so on). Write things down in a calendar or diary.

Emails and messages – people in office jobs can get lots of emails, and it takes time to look at them and reply, as well as interrupting other work. People often reply to emails straight after they have received them, thinking that an answer is needed immediately. One strategy is to set regular intervals during the day to check email.

Become a lifelong learner – this is gaining new skills and knowledge throughout life and not just while you are at school or university. The University of the West Indies Open Campus offers Continuing and Professional Education programmes which encourage lifelong learning. These programmes are designed to focus on pre-university knowledge and skill-sets and career-specific skill-sets so all can benefit.

Time management – a lot of people have problems with their time management skills, such as missing deadlines or being late for work or meetings. This can have a negative impact on people you work with and the company you work for. Set off for work earlier, set alerts to remind you about deadlines, and do a little bit every day, so that you are more likely to meet deadlines.

Work as a team – people often work on their own, when it would be more efficient to work as a team with someone or get someone to help them. Sometimes it is because they think they can do the job better on their own, they prefer to do the job on their own or they don't like their colleagues. By working as a team and being cooperative, both the worker's and the company's performance will improve.

Exercise

3. In about 100 words, explain how performance can be improved at work.

4. Do you think some of the ways we have discussed are easy to implement in the work place? Why, or why not?

5. Name one regional institution that promotes lifelong learning.

Key vocabulary
....
appraisal

self-appraisal

Work ethics

We are learning to:

- examine expected work ethics at places of work
- describe ways workers show dissatisfaction in the workplace
- explore solutions to resolve issues in the workplace
- define relevant terms and concepts: work ethic.

Work ethics ❯❯

In Form 1, we examined what our ethical self is. This is your set of beliefs and principles about what is right and wrong. It also includes how you treat others and the choices you make when facing a moral dilemma.

Your **work ethic** is the same set of moral principles, but in the workplace.

An employer looks for good work ethics in their employees, such as:

- being **honest** in what you do and say at work
- showing **integrity**, or being **trustworthy**, for example being honest about meeting deadlines and not blaming other people for your mistakes
- being reliable and **responsible** enough and relied upon to do a particular job
- demonstrating **knowledge** about your work and being prepared to help others, who perhaps are just starting out
- being **self-motivated** – the ability to get on with your job or task without being supervised and to be trusted to finish the task
- being part of a team – working with your work colleagues to help solve problems and complete work quickly and efficiently, rather than doing it all on your own.

It is important to work as part of a team in whatever work you choose to do.

Exercise

1. In your own words, define work ethic.

2. Why do you think an employer looks for good work ethics in their employees?

3. Define these terms: integrity, self-motivated, honest.

4. Create your own mind map that shows the work ethics required in the workplace.

5. Use newspapers, magazines and the internet to find reports of poor and/or unacceptable work ethics. Write your own short news report about the stories.

Discussion

In groups, discuss whether it is acceptable for workers to take industrial action. Then create a role play showing a dispute in the workplace. Split the group into two, where one half are the workers and the other half are the employers. Make sure that your dispute is resolved.

- **Go slow** – this is when employees in an **industrial dispute** with their employer deliberately slow down their work rate. Soon, productivity drops, which causes profits to fall and results in losses for the company.

- **Work-to-rule** – there can be certain situations in the workplace where the employee works 'to rule'. This is where employees are in a dispute with their employer (usually about wages, safe working conditions or hours) and they do just enough at work so that they are within the terms of their job role or contract, and not so little that the employer can dismiss them.

- Protest/stay away from work – other ways workers can show dissatisfaction are to organise protests or simply to stay away from work (known as 'striking').

Workers showing their unhappiness with their employer.

Conflict resolution in the workplace

There are a number of ways in which work conflicts can be resolved:

- Have an informal discussion between the two parties to resolve their differences.

- If an employee has made a formal grievance against someone, usually a company has internal procedures to follow. If a grievance is found to be true, the person who has created the conflict will have to **resign** from their job.

- Get someone to mediate the conflict – they can listen to both sides impartially and come to an independent decision or suggest a solution.

If a dispute between an employer and employees cannot be settled and the employees are members of a trade union, an independent court **mediates** the case. The **Eastern Caribbean Supreme Court** is an appeal court which also functions to mediate industrial disputes in countries which are under its mandate.

Exercise

6. Define these terms: work-to-rule, dispute, go slow.

7. What are the possible consequences of going slow?

8. Describe how workplace conflicts can be resolved.

Key vocabulary

work ethic

honest

integrity

trustworthy

responsible

knowledge

self-motivated

go slow

industrial dispute

work-to-rule

resign

mediate

Eastern Caribbean Supreme Court

Role of the trade unions

We are learning to:

• examine the role of the trade unions in the Eastern Caribbean.

Role of the trade unions in the Eastern Caribbean

Trade unions started to become a feature of the **labour movement** in the Eastern Caribbean at the end of the nineteenth century, long before the formation of political parties. Trade unions have played an important role in raising the standard of living amongst working people.

The main function of trade unions is to look after the interests of their members. This can involve strike action, or interaction and negotiation with employers on behalf of members, to bring about changes in conditions. Some important regional trade unions are:

The National Workers Union, St Lucia, represents a multisectoral membership of over 5 000 workers. The aims of the National Workers Union include:

• creating unity among workers
• to plan and participate in joint trade union action where necessary
• protecting and defending the economic, social, educational, cultural and political interest of workers.

The Guyana Agricultural and General Workers Union (GAWU) represents 19 000 workers in sugar, fishing, rice, forestry, transport and other important sectors in Guyana.

The GAWU provides services which complement its main function as a trade union. For example:

• The GAWU operates a credit union for its members. In this way members can benefit from the collective bargaining power of the union as well as its collective economic power. Another benefit for members is that a single trusted organisation handles both their labour and monetary affairs.
• Labour education is also promoted by the GAWU, with plans for a labour college to be set up aimed at educating members about labour laws.
• The GAWU maintains links with international unions such as the World Federation of Trade Unions (WFTU) and the International Union of Food, Agricultural, Hotel, Restaurant, Catering, Tobacco and Allied Workers' Associations (IUF).

The Guyana Agricultural and General Workers Union is the largest union in Guyana

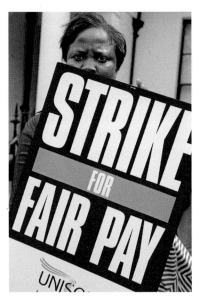

Trade unions help to organise workers to speak up with one voice.

Discussion

With your teacher, discuss the role of trade unions in the Eastern Caribbean, and why they are important.

The Barbados Union of Teachers (BUT) represents about 2000 members. In 1974, the government recognised the Union as the sole bargaining agency for teachers in the Public Service. The aims of the BUT include to:

- agitate for the rights of teachers
- agitate for correct conditions and terms of service for teachers
- raise concerns regarding health and safety of teachers and students in the various schools
- organise professional development workshops for its members.

The Barbados Union of Teachers represents about 2000 members.

Benefits of membership in a trade union »»

The main benefit of belonging to a trade union is **collective bargaining**. This is where the trade union will negotiate on behalf of the workers for more favourable working conditions and benefits, such as higher wages and better hours and working conditions. Collective bargaining by a union is for all its members, not just one. Trade unions can also help with:

- support, enabling the worker's voice to be heard
- equity and fairness in the workplace
- job security
- better training and promotion opportunities
- fair wages, housing assistance, death benefits
- legal advice/assistance when needed in connection with employment
- financial relief in sickness, accident, distress, unemployment, victimisation.

Exercise

1. Explain, in your own words, the main function of a trade union.
2. When were trade unions first officially recognised in the Eastern Caribbean?
3. Which trade union represents: forestry workers, teachers?
4. Outline the benefits of belonging to a trade union.

Research

Working in groups, identify a trade union in your country that interests you and has not been discussed so far. Find out:

- which industry they represent
- what their mission is
- the number of members registered
- their structure and activities.

Did you know...?

The first workers' association to be formed in Trinidad and Tobago was the Working Men's Reform Club, which was formed by 21-year-old Charles Phillip in 1897.

Key vocabulary

trade union

labour movement

collective bargaining

Questions

See how well you have understood the topics in this unit.

1. Match the key vocabulary word (i–vii) with its definition (a–g).

   i) employment
   ii) occupation
   iii) job
   iv) employer
   v) employee
   vi) lifelong learning
   vii) entrepreneur

   a) type of job or the work a person does
   b) education that continues over a whole lifetime
   c) the state of having paid work
   d) someone who has a job with a specific company or employer
   e) a specific set of employment tasks at a particular workplace
   f) someone who runs their own business
   g) someone who offers employment

2. Name the four basic reasons why people work.

3. Fill in the gap to name these types of job:

   a) An _____ keeps track of and records the flow of money in an organisation or business.
   b) An _____ agent sells policies for a company.
   c) A _____ works with students, presenting classes, lectures and assignments, and helping students to develop skills and knowledge.

4. Name the three qualities that you need to evaluate to help decide the career path you should take.

5. Complete the sentences:

   a) A _____ industry is an industry that harvests raw materials.
   b) A _____ industry is an industry that is mostly involved in processing and manufacturing.
   c) A _____ industry is an industry that provides services.

6. Name five factors that you should consider when choosing a career.

7. Name five ways to behave and communicate while at work.

8. Name five issues that employers and employees may face in the workplace.

9. Write a short report discussing some of the ways performance can be improved on at work. Use around 150 words.

10. Fill in the gaps to show the type of information that you should show in a résumé.

_____: PATRICK **BARROW**

_____: 3 Lodge Road, St Michael, Barbados; tel. no.: 0111 222 3333; email: **pbarrow@email.com**.

_____: It is my mission to inspire students to pursue academic and personal excellence whilst striving to create a challenging and engaging learning environment in which students become lifelong scholars and learners. I use innovative teaching methods as well as effective use of multimedia teaching tools.

_____:

1. St Stephen's Primary School in 2002. This was a temporary appointment for two months (September and October) due to the assigned teacher being ill.
2. St Winifred's School for the period November 2002 to July 2005.
3. Lester Vaughan Secondary School for the period September 2005 to present. I am currently teaching Economics, Principles of Business and Social Studies.

_____: Bachelor: BSc Economics from the University of the West Indies, Cave Hill for the period 2005 to 2008.

_____:

Skills: Teaching, Microsoft Office

Interests and hobbies: Cricket, reading, volunteer work

References: Available on request

11. Match these work ethics (i–v) with their descriptions (a–e):

i) honest
ii) integrity
iii) trustworthy
iv) responsible
v) self-motivated

a) can be relied upon
b) gets things done without having to be told to do so
c) always tells the truth
d) honest in one's principles
e) behaves in a sensible manner

12. Which court in the Eastern Caribbean helps to solve workplace disputes?

Checking your progress

To make good progress in understanding different aspects of your personal development, check to make sure you understand these ideas.

Identify the reasons why people work.

Examine the types of jobs that are available in the Caribbean.

Create a directory of job vacancies that are advertised in newspapers and magazines.

Explore the skills and knowledge needed to pursue specific careers.

Identify the factors to consider when choosing a career.

Understand the importance of a résumé. Draw up your own résumé.

Examine the issues employers and employees may face in the workplace.

Evaluate ways of improving performance at the workplace.

Role-play scenarios on how to improve performance in the workplace.

Examine expected work ethics at places of work.

Explore the role of the trade unions.

Outline the benefits of belonging to a trade union.

Unit 9: History of the Eastern Caribbean

In this unit you will find out ▶▶

Indigenous people and the Europeans

- The indigenous people of the Caribbean
  - migratory patterns, pre-European contact before 1492, location
- Treatment of the Amerindians in the Caribbean
- The early European presence on Caribbean development
- Economic, political and religious experiences of the Caribbean: 1700s–1900s
  - slavery, emancipation, apprenticeship, metayage, peasantry
  - rise and fall of sugar

Challenges to the social order: trade unionism and social activism

- Adult suffrage
- Key figures in trade unionism
  - Tubal Uriah 'Buzz' Butler, Vere Cornwall Bird, Robert L. Bradshaw
- Trade unions in the Caribbean
  - Antigua Trades and Labour Union, Grenada Manual and Mental Workers' Union, Oilfield Workers' Trade Union (OWTU)
- Social workers
  - Audrey Jeffers, Gertrude Protain
- Water riots, Trinidad, 1903; Protests of 1930s

Challenges to the social order: the Black Power Movement, 1970

- The causes and consequences, motivation and struggles, individuals and groups of the Black Power Movement

The West Indian Federation

- The factors which led to the establishment of the Federation, its achievements and what contributed to its failure

Independence

- Key figures in the independence movement
  - Dr Eric Eustace Williams, Errol Barrow, John Compton, Albert Gomes
- Grenada Revolution 1979–83
  - The factors that led to the revolution, its merits and demerits

Indigenous peoples and the Europeans

We are learning to:

- outline the presence of the indigenous people of the Caribbean: migratory patterns.

The first indigenous people of the Caribbean »

The **first people** of the Caribbean were the **Amerindians**, who settled on the islands roughly 18 000 years ago. First people are the first known population of a place, usually indigenous people.

The Amerindians were the first people who settled in the Caribbean.

About 18 000 years ago, the Amerindians began to migrate from their original settlements in Siberia, crossed over the Bering Straits and moved into Alaska and then south through North, Central and South America. During their movement southwards, some of the Amerindians established settlements and formed indigenous tribes, while the others moved further south.

The Kalinago and Taino »»

Between 2 000 and 2 500 years ago a new group of Amerindians travelled to the Caribbean from Venezuela. These were the **Kalinago** (or Carib tribe) and **Taino** (or the Arawak tribe).

The Kalinago settled mainly in the Lesser Antilles on islands like Grenada, St Vincent and the Grenadines, and Dominica, as well as in the north and west of Trinidad. The Taino settled mainly in the Greater Antilles on islands like Cuba, Jamaica, Haiti and the Dominican Republic, as well as Tobago. Both established their settlements along the coast, near rivers and at the top of hills.

The Caribbean at the time of Columbus' arrival »»»

By the time Columbus arrived in the Caribbean in 1492, the islands had a population of around 500 000 **indigenous** Amerindians. They had developed their own economic, political, social and religious systems.

Exercise

1. What do you understand by the word indigenous?

2. Name the two tribes that came to the Caribbean from Venezuela.

3. Where did the new tribes settle?

Did you know...?

The Taino tribe played a ceremonial ball game between two teams of 10 to 30 players per team, played with a rubber ball. Winning this game was thought to bring a good harvest and strong, healthy children.

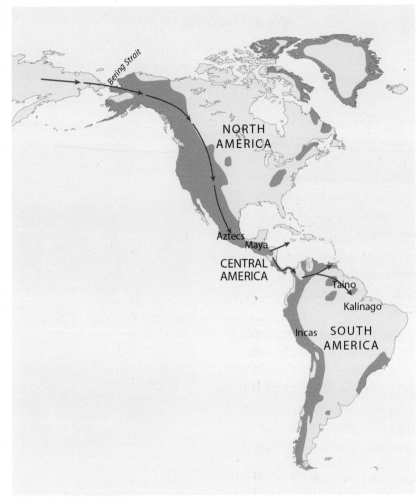

The migratory route of the Amerindians.

The indigenous Amerindians' food came from crops such as cassava, maize, sweet potatoes, peppers, beans and fruits. They also fished and hunted animals.

Cotton was grown to make clothes and bedding, as well as tobacco, which they smoked or chewed.

Project

Trace the map shown on this page and add the route our ancestors took to get to the Caribbean and the dates they did it. Then, create a map of the Caribbean and add where the Kalinagos and the Tainos settled.

Key vocabulary

first people

Amerindians

Kalinago

Taino

indigenous

Exercise

4. Explain in your own words the route our ancestors took to get to the Caribbean.

5. What crops did the new settlers grow?

6. How do we get the term Amerindian?

Pre-European contact

We are learning to:

- identify the evidence of pre-European contact before 1492
- identify the location of indigenous people's settlement in the Caribbean.

. . . .

Evidence of pre-European contact before 1492 》》

Even though the Amerindians settled in the Caribbean a long time ago, there are still many ways we can discover how they lived using the evidence they left behind.

There are very few documentary sources of what life was like for the Amerindians. Documents about the Amerindians were written by priests, colonial administrators, explorers, fortune hunters, sailors and merchants.

Evidence of what life was like for the Amerindians pre-1492 can be found at archaeological sites across the Caribbean, for example:

- **Artefacts** such as bowls, pots and clay jugs. Reddish-brown, fine-ware pottery bowls have been found at Pearls and Calivigny in Grenada and the Pitons and Troumasse in St Lucia. Bowls such as these were used for storing and presenting beer or food during meals, or festive communal and inter-village gatherings.
- Ceramic figurines, which were used in religious rituals, have been found at Canelles and Pointe de Caille in St Lucia.
- Clay anvils, stone axes and shell axes have been found at Calivigny in Grenada, and Soufrière and Morne Lezard in St Lucia. There is a collection of these artefacts from St Lucia in the Barbados Museum.

Pottery artefacts can help us learn about how our ancestors lived.

Exercise

1. What evidence can be found for what life was like for the Amerindians before 1492?

2. What type of artefacts have been found at Canelles in St Lucia?

3. Your teacher can organise a field trip to your local museum. Before you go on the field trip, work in groups and make a list of questions to which you think you will be able to find answers at the museum. Record your answers, then write a reflective piece of about 200 words about your ancestors.

Research

Trace a map of your country, research and then add the names of places that were named by your ancestors. Use your field trip to help you.

The Black Caribs of St Vincent ›››

Some of the Kalinago (or Caribs) in St Vincent mixed with runaway and shipwrecked African slaves to form a group known as the Black Caribs.

This group adopted the habits from both the original Kalinago and the European colonists, the French. For example, cassava formed an extensive part of their diet and some established small farms where they grew cotton, indigo and tobacco, like the French.

Skirmishes between the Black Caribs and the French were common. However, in times of peace, the Black Caribs traded food crops with the French settlers for ammunition.

The Treaty of Paris of 1763 granted the British control of St Vincent. They demanded that the Black Caribs swear allegiance to the British King. The Black Caribs refused and several battles were waged. Notable Black Carib leaders like Duvalle and Chief Chatoyer emerged and fought bravely against the British.

By 1796, the British had reduced most of the Black Carib strongholds to ashes. As many as 5 080 Black Caribs surrendered and were transported to Honduras. Some managed to escape to the hills, thus there are descendants of Black Caribs in St Vincent today.

CHATOYER the CHIEF of the BLACK CHARAIBES in S.? VINCENT with his five WIVES

Chatoyer, the chief of the Black Caribs.

Activity

Watch this video about the Arawaks:

www.youtube.com/watch?v=g_CzfvBM5A8

Make notes while you watch the video and add it to your notes for your field trips.

Exercise

4. In what ways did the Black Caribs adopt the ways of the Kalinago and the French?

5. What crops did the Black Caribs grow on their farms?

6. Why do you think the British destroyed the homes of the Black Caribs and transported them to Honduras?

Key vocabulary

artefact

Indigenous people: 1492–1800

We are learning to:

- value the contribution of the indigenous people of the Caribbean.

· ·

Treatment of the Amerindians in the Caribbean »

The Spanish were the first European settlers to arrive in the Caribbean. They were followed by the British, French and Dutch. Each European power established settlements and denied the Amerindians their rights as free persons. In turn the Amerindians resisted European occupation.

Christopher Columbus arrived in the Caribbean in 1498.

Case study

Carib's Leap, St Patrick, Grenada

The French settled in Grenada in 1649. They met the Kalinago already settled on the island.

Tensions emerged between the two groups as the Kalinago became quite weary of the increased number of French settlers establishing themselves on the island.

Matters came to a head in May 1650. The French attacked the Kalinago with the rallying cry 'There is no quarter, they must die'. The Kalinago fought **valiantly** but they were little match for the superior weaponry of the French. Approximately 50 Kalinago found themselves hard-pressed between the advancing French and the sea. Rather than surrender to the French, they jumped off the precipice into the rocks and sea below. The area is known as Le Morne des Sauteurs, or Leaper's Hill.

A **monument** has been placed at the site. It serves as a symbol of resistance by the Kalinago towards European colonisation.

In 1686, Spanish **missionaries** were sent to Trinidad, to convert the Amerindians to **Roman Catholicism**. The missionaries set up a mission near San Rafael, in central northern Trinidad.

In 1699, the missionaries began to build a new church at Arena, near San Rafael. The Amerindians objected to the Roman Catholic faith and to being used as labour to build the church. The Amerindians worked slowly on the church and the missionaries threatened to report them to the Governor.

The Amerindians attacked the priests and killed them, before ambushing the Governor and killing him and all his party except one, who reported back to the Spanish authorities. Soldiers killed hundreds of Amerindians, and captured a further 22, who were put on trial and sentenced to death.

Today the event is seen as an act of atrocious retaliation by the Spanish, who killed hundreds of people and then tortured those that they captured before sentencing them to death.

The story of the encounter between the Europeans and the Amerindians is a sad one. Europeans in possession of more sophisticated fire power – guns and muskets – often waged war on Amerindians armed only with weapons of stone and bone. The result was that thousands of Amerindians perished. Although the Amerindians were not classed as slaves – as the Africans brought to the islands would be later on – the Amerindians were not treated well in the Caribbean:

- Thousands died from diseases brought to the islands by the Europeans, such as influenza, measles and smallpox.
- Others died from overwork on European tobacco, cocoa and cotton estates.
- Some Amerindians were transported from islands such as Trinidad to work in other Spanish colonies.
- Some Amerindians fled from islands such as Trinidad and Tobago to Venezuela or Guyana.

Soon, the numbers of Amerindians in the Caribbean declined quite dramatically, and by 1800 they were almost extinct on islands such as Trinidad or Tobago, and numbered very few elsewhere in the Caribbean.

Contribution of the Amerindians

Descendants of the Amerindians can still be found in the Caribbean, for example in Dominica and St Vincent and the Grenadines. Evidence of their presence can also be found in:

- names of places, for example Arima, Paria, the Aripo mountains, Chaguanas, Guayaguayare and Mayaro in Trinidad, Mabouya, Canaries and Hewanorra in St Lucia
- plant and animal names such as carat and timite palms, tobacco, cacao, maize and manicou
- today's towns and villages are built on Amerindian settlements, such as Arima in Trinidad.

Exercise

1. List the European powers that colonised the Caribbean.
2. Outline the events of 1650 in Grenada and 1699 in Trinidad, and explain in both cases why they happened.
3. Why do you think the Kalinago in Grenada jumped rather than surrendering to the French?
4. Why did the numbers of Amerindians decline in the Caribbean up to 1800?
5. What evidence is there of Amerindian presence in the Caribbean today?
6. Explain briefly why the Amerindian population declined in the Caribbean.

Project

Your teacher will show you *The Amerindians* by filmmaker Tracey Assing. This film traces Trinidad's indigenous history and looks at the Santa Rosa Carib community. As you watch it, make notes about anything that interests you. Discuss these afterwards with your teacher.

Key vocabulary

valiantly

monument

missionaries

Roman Catholicism

The European presence in the Caribbean

We are learning to:

- analyse the impact of the early European presence on the development of the Caribbean
- identify present-day features which indicate the European presence in the Caribbean.

'Changing hands' 〉〉

The Spanish were the first Europeans to arrive in the Caribbean in 1492. They settled mainly in the Greater Antilles (Haiti, Dominican Republic, Cuba) and also in Trinidad.

Columbus sighted the islands of the Lesser Antilles (Grenada, St Lucia, Dominica) on his second and third voyages (1493 and 1498). He named Trinidad 'La Trinidad'.

The Lesser Antilles were settled mainly by the British and the French. The islands 'changed hands' as the fortunes of war changed in Europe. For example, at the end of the Seven Years' War in 1763, the British returned the islands of St Lucia, Martinique and Guadeloupe to the French. The French in turn handed over the islands of Grenada, St Vincent and the Grenadines, Dominica and Tobago to Britain.

Impact of the early European presence colonialism 〉〉

As we have seen, the British, French and Dutch followed the Spanish into the Caribbean. Each of these European powers claimed islands for themselves, though some islands changed hands between the European powers several times. For example, various European powers laid claim to Tobago at different times (see the timeline opposite).

In 1793, Tobago was captured by the British. The running of the island was given over to the British Crown. All male inhabitants had to take an **oath of allegiance** to the British Crown, and those who did not were regarded as prisoners of war. In 1802, Tobago was given back to the French, only to be recaptured by the British the following year. In 1833, Tobago became part of the Windward Islands.

Tobago was a prosperous island as a result of the tobacco plantations and later the sugar and cotton plantations. Slaves were brought from Africa to work on the plantations. Tobago traded with Guyana and Barbados more than with Trinidad.

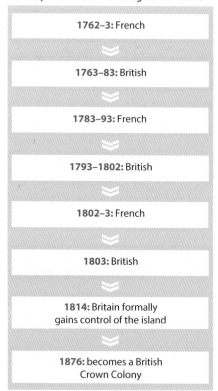

European control of Tobago 1763–1876

1762–3: French
1763–83: British
1783–93: French
1793–1802: British
1802–3: French
1803: British
1814: Britain formally gains control of the island
1876: becomes a British Crown Colony

When Tobago became a British Crown Colony in 1876, it was ruled by a Governor appointed by the British Crown and a council appointed by the Governor. The island was divided into parishes for the purposes of administration. Tobago remained part of this British colony until 1876, when it became a Crown Colony on its own. This lasted until 1899, when – after a series of economic and political problems – it was decided that Tobago could no longer be a separate colony. It then became a **ward** (a division) of Trinidad.

Since then, Tobago and Trinidad have been one nation, becoming an independent state in 1962 and the Republic of Trinidad and Tobago in 1976.

River Antoine Waterwheel, Grenada.

Present-day features 》》》

One legacy of the European presence in the history of the Caribbean is the number of place names with Dutch, Spanish, French and British origin:

- Dutch: Courland Bay, Luggarts Bay in Tobago.
- Spanish: Cape Gracias-a-Dios, Pedro Point in Tobago.
- French: Bocage and Vieux Fort in St Lucia; Beaulieu in Grenada; Bagatelle in Dominica.
- British: St Andrew and St John in Grenada; St Michael and St Thomas in Barbados.

Historical landmarks include:

- The River Antoine Water Wheel in Grenada was built in 1785 and is the only one of its kind in the Caribbean that is still operational. It produces the famous alcoholic drink Rivers Rum.
- Forts and fortifications – most of the forts built were by the French and the British. For example, Fort Frederick in Grenada; Fort Shirley in Dominica; Brimstone Hill Fortress in St Kitts.
- Other landmarks include the Barbados Museum Barbados, Romney Manor in St Kitts, Nelson's Dockyard Antigua and churches like the Cathedral Basilica of the Immaculate Conception (built in 1897) in St Lucia and St Matthew's Anglican Church (built in 1829) in Barbados.

> **Did you know...?**
>
> Tobago changed hands between European powers at least five times.

Research

Using the internet, research European place names in the Caribbean. Find pictures of each settlement as they look today, and add them to your research.

Exercise

1. Which European countries settled mainly in the Lesser Antilles?
2. Name the European countries that claimed Tobago.
3. What was the meaning of the name that Columbus gave Trinidad?
4. Which islands did Britain gain at the end of the Seven Years' War?
5. List three present-day features in which the European legacy is still seen in the Caribbean.

Key vocabulary

oath of allegiance

ward

Politics and religion in the Caribbean: 1800s

We are learning to:

- present using various media our understanding of the political and religious development of the Caribbean.

Representative and Crown Colony Government

In the establishment of its colonies in the Caribbean, the British implemented the **representative system** of government. Through this system the colonies were ruled by a Governor, Legislative Council and an Assembly.

The Governor was the representative of the Crown (the British), the Council was nominated by the Governor from prominent land owners and planters, and they advised the Governor and sometimes would sit as a Court of Appeal or second chamber for legislation. The Assembly was made up of landowners voted into office.

A person's ability to vote was dependent on ownership of property. As such, only wealthy planters and merchants were voted onto the Assemblies. This meant that the majority of the population who were enslaved had no voting rights and thus did not have a say in the running of the colony.

By the mid 1860s the system was changed to **Crown Colony** Government. This was a system of direct British rule through appointed officials rather than elected representatives. This system removed the Assembly and the planters' opportunity to vote. Neither were the recently freed slaves given the right to vote. The British therefore had greater control over the running of the colonies. Barbados was the only colony that maintained the representative system of government. Neither the representative system nor the Crown Colony system of government were truly representative of all the people in the colonies.

THE RIGHT HON. GEORGE MACARTNEY, EARL OF MACARTNEY, K.B.

Lord George Macartney, Governor of Grenada, 1776–9.

Key vocabulary

representative system

Crown Colony

Protestantism

Anglicanism

Methodism

Presbyterianism

Moravian

Hinduism

Islam

denomination

Exercise

1. Explain in your own words the representative and Crown Colony systems of government.

2. In groups, discuss the two forms of government used by the British in the Caribbean. Which form of government do you think best met the needs of the people of the region?

Each of the various groups of inhabitants and immigrants to the Caribbean have contributed to our wide variety of religious practices – from the original Amerindians, to the Spanish, French, Dutch and British. For example:

- Roman Catholicism – introduced to the Caribbean region by the Spanish and French. The French influence in islands like Grenada and St Lucia led to the prominence of Roman Catholicism.
- **Protestant** denominations, such as **Anglicanism**, **Methodism** and **Presbyterianism** – introduced by the British, for example in Barbados.
- **Moravian** Protestantism – introduced by German missionaries in the eighteenth century to the Eastern West Indies, including Trinidad and Tobago.
- **Hinduism** and **Islam** – introduced by the indentured Indians.

The Immaculate Conception Catholic School, St Kitts, built in 1893.

By the end of the 1800s most of the main **denominations** had set up schools in the Caribbean. For example, the Roman Catholic Sisters of Cluny set up St Joseph's Convent Secondary School in 1876 in Grenada.

Case study

Religion in Trinidad and Tobago

By the 1800s, Tobago was an almost entirely Protestant island, made up of Anglican, Methodist and Moravian churches. These churches also provided schooling for the island.

Because of the influence of the French and Spanish in Trinidad, Roman Catholicism was the most prominent religion. There were some Protestant churches in Trinidad, mainly as a result of the British estate owners and government officials, who were Anglicans. By the end of the 1800s in Trinidad, almost all the main denominations had set up schools – Catholic, Anglican, Methodist and Moravian.

Exercise

3. Which religion dominated Tobago in the 1800s?

4. Draw a mind map of the religions in the Caribbean in the 1800s, also showing which country those religions came from.

5. Who introduced Hinduism and Islam to the Caribbean in the second part of the nineteenth century?

6. Explain the growth in the number of schools by the end of the nineteenth century.

Did you know...?

Crown Colony government started in:

- Trinidad in 1802
- St Lucia in 1814
- Jamaica in 1865
- St Kitts, Antigua, Nevis and St Vincent in 1869
- Tobago in 1876

Economic systems in the Caribbean: 1700s–1900s

We are learning to:

- discuss the rise and decline of the sugar industry, slavery, emancipation, apprenticeship, metayage, peasantry.

Sugar and our heritage

The early colonists planted tobacco. However, with the rising demand for sugar in Europe and the failure of tobacco to compete with their North American neighbours, the colonists turned to sugar cane production.

Sugar was the most prominent crop grown in the Caribbean. It was often referred to as King Sugar. It was a very **lucrative** business.

Slaves forcibly taken from Africa provided the labour on the sugar plantations. **Slavery** was abolished in 1834. The plantation owners then introduced an **apprenticeship** system.

Slave woman hoeing sugar plants.

Apprenticeships and peasant farming

Apprenticeships were for ex-slaves who had to serve their former owners free of charge for 40.5 hours a week for four to six years. They were paid for any extra hours that they worked. The system caused a lot of conflict, and finally – on 1 August 1838 – all slaves in the British West Indies were given full **emancipation**.

After the abolition of slavery (between 1845 and 1917), the British brought indentured labourers from China, India, Malta and Madeira.

Slaves who had been set free started up their own small businesses and small farms in order to feed themselves and support their families. This was the beginning of **peasant farming** in the Caribbean. Peasant farmers grew crops such as yams, cassava, corn, coconuts, bananas, peas, sugar, cocoa, nutmeg, arrowroot and coffee, and reared livestock such as poultry.

Exercise

1. Why did the colonists change from tobacco to sugar production?

2. Why do you think sugar was referred to as King Sugar?

3. Define the terms apprenticeship and peasant farming.

Case study

The metayage system

With the advent of emancipation in 1838 some islands, for example, Grenada, St Vincent, St Lucia and Tobago opted for a new system of labour relations.

In order to keep sugar estates going, the **metayage system**, which was a form of sharecropping, developed. Under the system, the metayer (sharecropper) occupied a piece of land on which he or she planted cane.

At harvest time, the estate owner supplied carts which drew cut canes to the mill, where they were processed into rum and sugar of which the metayer received a percentage. In addition, the metayer was often allowed permission to build a cottage on the estate and provision grounds.

Due to the economic depression of this time, the estate owners could not afford to pay metayage workers. If the workers were not compensated by other means (food, shelter) then the sugar estates would have gone out of cultivation.

Research

Using the internet, and working in groups, research what life was like for people under the metayage system. See if you can find any evidence of it being used in your community or area. Discuss whether you think it was a good or bad system for those who farmed this way.

The rise and fall of sugar)))

Sugar reigned as king from the mid 1700s to the mid 1800s. The colonists thrived on sugar production. However, by the 1860s the process of decline set in. Sugar coming from the British and French Caribbean found it difficult to compete with European beet sugar and sugar coming from Cuba.

For example, in 1975 the government of Trinidad bought out Caroni, a sugar company that brought together many smaller sugar companies. The new company **diversified** into other products including citrus fruits, prawns and rice. By the end of the twentieth century, oil had become the country's most important resource, and the sugar industry gradually declined. It was just too expensive to produce sugar in Trinidad and Tobago compared to other places.

In other Caribbean countries, crops such as cocoa, nutmeg and bananas rose to prominence.

Diversification also came in the form of a movement away from agriculture into other industries such as tourism.

Exercise

4. Explain in your own words the term metayage.

5. What do you think were the main reasons for the decline of the sugar industry?

6. What other industries replaced the sugar industry in Caribbean countries?

Key vocabulary

lucrative

slavery

apprenticeship

emancipation

peasant farming

metayage system

diversified

Challenges to the social order

We are learning to:

- define and apply relevant terms and concepts: adult suffrage, democracy
- explain the contribution of key figures and groups in the fields of trade unionism and social activism in the Caribbean 1900–70.

Adult suffrage

The 1920s and 1930s saw a big change in the expectations of working people all over the Caribbean and other parts of the world. Workers wanted better working conditions, respect and the freedom to protest if necessary.

Workers forced the government to take notice of them and to recognise them. This was the beginnings of **social activism** and **social justice**, which led to the development of trade unions and political parties.

Workers digging and transporting natural deposits of asphalt at Pitch Lake, La Brea, Trinidad, c. 1935.

Constitutional reform began in 1924, when the Wood Commission allowed people in Dominica, Grenada, St Vincent, St Lucia and Trinidad and Tobago the vote. However, this was a limited franchise, because to be able to vote men had to be over the age of 21 and women over 31, and they had to own property over a certain value or have a high income. This small start was the beginning of representative government and **democracy** in the state.

After further social unrest in the 1930s, in 1939 the Moyne Commission recommended the lowering of voting qualifications. These recommendations took effect in the different islands at varying times. For example, in 1945 in Trinidad all citizens over the age of 21 were given the right to vote. Adult suffrage had been achieved, which was another step on the road to self-government for the people of the Caribbean.

Discussion

At present you have to be 18 years old to vote in the Caribbean. Do you think the present voting age is appropriate? Give reasons for your answer.

Exercise

1. Who was eligible to vote for the Legislative Council in 1924?

2. Do you think this was a fair system? Give a reason for your answer.

3. What did the Moyne Commission recommend?

4. Why do you think adult suffrage was an important step towards self-government?

Political parties

Throughout the British Caribbean, political parties started to form in the 1940s and '50s.

The political parties usually had the support of trade unions. For example, the Barbados Labour Party, formed in 1943, had the support of the Barbados Workers' Union, and the Grenada United Labour Party formed in 1951 had the support of the Grenada Manual and Mental Workers' Union.

Barbados attained **universal adult suffrage** in 1950, Grenada followed in 1951. The Barbados Labour Party and the Grenada United Labour Party contested and won the 1951 elections. Both parties were able to carry out legislation on behalf of workers. For example, the introduction of holidays with pay.

The first political party in Trinidad and Tobago was registered in 1934. This was the Trinidad Labour Party (TLP), and was led by A.A. Cipriani.

In 1936, the Trinidad Citizens' League under the leadership of Adrian 'Cola' Rienzi and T.U.B. Butler was registered.

As adults achieved full suffrage, more and more political parties were established to represent all the different interests in Trinidad and Tobago.

There was a Socialist Party and a West Indian National Party, as well as a United Front party. In 1950, the People's National Movement (PNM) was formed. The PNM was to dominate politics in Trinidad and Tobago in the years leading up to independence. This party was led by Dr Eric Williams.

However, islands such as Trinidad and Tobago were still not yet self-governing. The Governor was still appointed by the British government and some of the Council members were still appointed by the Governor. But political stability gave leaders from different parties the confidence to cooperate and to push ahead with plans for independence.

Supporters of the People's National Movement (PNM).

Research

Work in pairs and do your own research about one of the political parties that emerged in the 1940s and '50s Find out:

- who led the party
- what the party stood for
- how well they did in elections
- whether the party still exists.

Exercise

5. Name the party that was formed in 1950 in Trinidad and give the name of its leader.

6. Name two political parties that were formed in the Caribbean by the 1950s.

7. Define the terms social activism, social justice and adult suffrage.

8. Create a timeline to summarise the process to achieve adult suffrage and the emergence of political parties in the Caribbean in the twentieth century.

Key vocabulary

social activism

social justice

democracy

universal adult suffrage

Key figures in trade unionism

We are learning to:

- explain the contribution of key figures and groups in the fields of trade unionism and social activism in the Caribbean 1900–70
- use primary and secondary sources to research the origins of the early trade unions in the early twentieth century.

Tubal Uriah 'Buzz' Butler 〉〉

T.U.B. Butler was one of the most well-known political figures in the Caribbean in general and Trinidad in particular. From an early age, Butler had strong principles to fight for democracy and to end injustice. He fought in World War I and in the early 1920s worked in the Trinidad oilfields. In response to the social unrest of the 1930s, he founded the Trinidad Labour Party (TLP) with A.A. Cipriani in 1934.

In 1935, Butler organised a 'hunger march' from the Apex oilfields in Fyzabad to the Governor's residence in Port of Spain. Butler gave a speech on the march, which directly addressed the problems faced by oilfield workers, including: inadequate labour contracts, job insecurity, poor wages and incentives, and lack of transport for the workers to and from the work sites.

T.U.B. Butler worked in the oilfields in Trinidad.

Cipriani disagreed with Butler's more aggressive methods of bringing these issues to people's attention. Therefore, in 1936 Butler left the TLP and formed his own party – the Trinidad Citizens' League (TCL). In 1937, he called a strike at Trinidad Leaseholds Limited oilfields. The strike spread to other oilfields. At one rally, there were riots. Two police officers were killed and oil wells were set on fire. Butler was imprisoned for causing a riot.

When he was released in 1945, he formed the Butler Party, whose aim was to unite people of East Indian and African descent in Trinidad and Tobago. His party won seats in the 1951 election and he continued to take an active part in the politics of Trinidad and Tobago until his death in 1977.

Activity

Your teacher will organise a field trip to one of the trade union headquarters in your island. Write a short report about your visit. Use any pictures that the class may have taken.

Exercise

1. What contribution did T.U.B. Butler make to Trinidad and Tobago?

2. What were the reasons that Butler organised the 'hunger march' in 1935?

3. In your own words, explain what happened in 1937, and the consequences.

Vere Cornwall Bird (1908–86), **Antigua**

- Trade unionist and politician.
- Became president of the Antigua Trades and Labour Union in 1943.
- Formed the Antigua Labour Party.
- Became Chief Minister 1960–67. He later became the first Prime Minister of Antigua, 1981–94.
- Achievements included: better wages for workers in the sugar industry and the attainment of annual holidays with pay.

The airport in Antigua was named after Vere Cornwall Bird.

Robert L. Bradshaw (1916–78), **St Kitts**

- Trade unionist and politician.
- In 1945 he became president of the St Kitts and Nevis Trades and Labour Union.
- Served as the first Premier of St Kitts, 1967–78.
- Achievements included: became Minister of Trade and Production for St Kitts-Nevis-Anguilla in 1956; held the post of Minister of Finance for the West Indian **Federation**, 1958–62; was part of the delegation who travelled to London in 1977 to discuss independence; was awarded the title of First National Hero of St Kitts and Nevis in 1996.

Other important activists in this period include Phyllis Allfrey (1908–86), Dominica, who was the co-founder of the Dominica Labour Party. She was the only female to serve as a minister in the West Indian Federation. She served as the Minister of Labour and Social Affairs. Elma Francois (1897–1944), was a trade unionist who co-founded the Negro Welfare Cultural and Social Association (NWCSA) in Trinidad, whose aim was to unite workers to fight for better conditions. Together with T.U.B. Butler and others, she led the historic general strike in 1937. She was the first woman in Trinidad to be arrested in 1938 and tried for sedition. The jury found her not guilty.

Research

Work in groups. Using the internet, research the route of the 'hunger march' in 1935 in Trinidad.

Did you know…?

Labour Day is celebrated on 19 June every year in Trinidad and Tobago. This holiday commemorates the anniversary of the 1937 Butler labour riots.

Exercise

4. What contributions did Vere Bird make to Antigua and Robert Bradshaw to St Kitts?

5. What political party did Phyllis Allfrey co-found?

Key vocabulary

federation

Origins of trade unions

We are learning to:

- use primary and secondary sources to research the origins of the trade unions in the early twentieth century
- explain the contribution of key figures and groups in the fields of trade unionism and social activism in the Caribbean 1900–70.

Trade unions in the Caribbean

Trade unions were formed throughout the region as activists sought to improve wages and working conditions, reduce working hours, have paid holidays and sick leave, and compensation for injuries occurring at work. Examples of early unions formed include:

- In 1939, Antigua's first trade union, the Antigua Trades and Labour Union, was formed. Vere Bird was president of the union for many years.
- The Kitts and Nevis Trades and Labour Union was founded in 1940. Robert L. Bradshaw was one of its founders. Bradshaw later became the island's Chief Minister.
- In 1939 the St Lucia Workers' Co-operative Union was founded in St Lucia. George Charles (1916–90) was appointed General Secretary of the union in 1948. The union was a source of the emergence of the St Lucia Labour Party from which it was formed in 1949. George Charles served as president of both the union and the party.
- Eric Gairy (1922–97) formed the Grenada Manual and Mental Workers' Union in 1950. It was the first union to include all of the working class. Gairy formed the Grenada United Labour Party and won the majority seats in the Legislative Council under Universal Adult Suffrage in 1951.
- The Working Men's Association (WMA) was formed in Trinidad in 1894. It represented skilled workers of African descent who were masons, carpenters, railway workers and store clerks.

Eric Gairy formed the Grenada Manual and Mental Workers' Union.

Exercise

1. What was the name of the first union formed in Antigua?
2. How did George Charles and Robert Bradshaw serve their respective islands?
3. How was Eric Gairy able to win the majority seats in the Legislative Council in 1951?

The Oilfield Workers' Trade Union (OWTU) was founded in 1937, when T.U.B. Butler called a strike at Trinidad Leaseholds Limited oilfields to protest about working conditions. The strike spread to other oilfields and then to other workers in the industry, such as dock workers, sugar workers and railway workers.

When the strike was over on 2 July, the OWTU was formed. Its first meeting took place on 15 July 1937 and it was formally registered as a union on 15 September that year.

The aim of the OWTU was to protect the rights of its members (the oil workers), as well the wider working class and the nation of Trinidad and Tobago.

Adrian 'Cola' Rienzi was the OWTU's first president general. Rienzi's approach was to adopt 'an organised means of **collective bargaining** through which the claims or grievances of the workpeople could have found ample means of expression' according to the 1937 Report by the Forster Commission on Trinidad and Tobago.

Today, the OWTU is one of the largest and most powerful trade unions in Trinidad and Tobago and represents more than 11 000 oilfield workers.

The labour movements of the 1920s and 1930s are all expressions of our people's struggle for social justice and equality. As we have seen, examples in this period include:

- constitutional reform and adult suffrage
- the emergence of political parties and trade unions.

The head office of the Dominica Trade Union, founded in 1945.

Activity

Using a graphic organiser – such as a mind map or timeline – compile key events in the history of the OWTU in the period 1894–1937.

Activity

Research the history of any of the trade unions mentioned or a trade union from your country. Then, in your own words, write a short report on the history of the union. Include key events and milestones, the people involved and the aims of the union when it was founded. Add any photos that you can find.

Exercise

4. In what year was the OWTU founded?

5. What was the aim of the OWTU?

6. Who became the president of the OWTU?

7. Why do you think the OWTU was formed after the general strike in 1937 and not beforehand?

8. In your own words, explain the term collective bargaining.

Key vocabulary

collective bargaining

Challenges to the social order

We are learning to:

- explain the contribution of key figures and groups in the fields of trade unionism and social activism in the Caribbean 1900–70
- value the ideals of social justice, volunteerism.

Social workers »

As well as the struggles for workers' rights by the trade unions, and the emerging political parties, there were also a number of individuals in the Caribbean who cared about those less fortunate in society.

Audrey Jeffers (1898–1968) was a social worker who did a lot of work in Trinidad to help the underprivileged and homeless. In the early 1920s, the economy was in steady decline, resulting in high unemployment, low wages, widespread poverty and slum living.

In 1920, Jeffers started a junior school in her home and in 1921 formed the Coterie of Social Workers (CSW), which provided free lunches for poor school children in Port of Spain. This was known as the 'breakfast shed'. Soon, breakfast sheds also opened in San Fernando, Arima and Siparia. The CSW went on to establish homes for the elderly and the blind, hostels for young women and day nurseries.

Audrey Jeffers

In 1936, Jeffers became the first woman to be elected to the Port of Spain City Council. Today, the legacy of her breakfast shed initiative can be seen in school meals provided by the government.

Gertrude Protain (1914–2005) was the first woman to be nominated to the Legislative Council in Grenada in 1957. She championed the cause for higher education for girls by seeking an annual scholarship to be awarded to girls only. Unfortunately, it was rejected by the Legislative Council.

Exercise

1. Explain Audrey Jeffers' contribution to Trinidad.

2. Why do you think the Legislative Council rejected Gertrude Protain's motion for an annual scholarship for girls only?

Water riots, Trinidad, 1903 〉〉〉

An early example of the population standing up for social justice occurred in 1903 with the so-called 'water riots' in Trinidad. The riots occurred when the government failed to consult the public with proposals about installing water meters in Port of Spain. The protests outside the Red House (the seat of parliament in the Republic of Trinidad and Tobago) resulted in 16 people being killed.

A Commission of Enquiry found that:

- the government had acted in an unjust manner by not consulting the public about the proposals
- the lack of black representation on the Legislative Council was one of the causes of the riot.

Following these findings, a black member of the RPA was appointed to the Legislative Council.

Protests of the 1930s 〉〉〉

Throughout the Caribbean region in this period people used riot action as a means of protest against inadequate working conditions, poor wages and the right to agitate as one voice in the form of trade unions. Later examples include:

- In St Kitts, January 1935, the sugar workers took strike action and demanded better wages. The workers marched to garner support. The police were sent in to quell the disturbance, three workers were killed and eight injured.

- In St Vincent, October 1935, the government announced an increase in customs duties. This additional tax would have made it extremely difficult for people who were already struggling to feed and clothe their families. Demonstrations against the new tax were met with violence by the police. Three demonstrators were shot.

- In Barbados, July 1937, trade union activist Clement Payne encouraged workers to form trade unions and to take strike action to seek improved wages and working conditions. The government responded by having Payne deported. Riots broke out in protest at his deportation. The police brutally **suppressed** the riots, 13 people were killed and 47 were wounded.

The burning of the Red House, Water Riots, 1903.

Project

Look back on 9.8–9.10. Imagine you are a mason, carpenter, agricultural labourer, store clerk or oil worker working in the Caribbean in the 1920s and 1930s. In groups, role-play why you may be unhappy about your work. Create some slogans that could be used as protest banners about your work.

Key vocabulary

suppressed

Exercise

3. In about 50 words, explain the background that led to the protests of the 1930s.

4. Why do you think the colonial government responded so harshly to the protesters?

The Black Power Movement

We are learning to:

- explain the causes and consequences of the Black Power Movement in the Caribbean
- list the individuals and groups involved in the Black Power Movement
- appreciate the motivation and struggles of the persons and groups involved in the event
- present, using various media, issues connected to the movement.

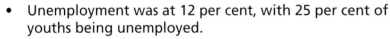

Causes of the Black Power Movement in Trinidad

At the start of the 1970s **Black Power** ideology swept across America and the Caribbean. The Black Power movement had developed in Jamaica in the 1960s. Major figures in the movement include Walter Rodney and the Abeng group. In 1970, it took hold in Trinidad and Tobago. Although Trinidad and Tobago had been independent of British rule since 1962, the social and economic development of the nation had not progressed in the way that many had hoped:

The Black Power protests in the 1970s.

- Unemployment was at 12 per cent, with 25 per cent of youths being unemployed.
- Institutional racism remained in the workplace. In 1970, 53 per cent of senior roles in companies employing over 100 people were held by white people.
- The 1965 Industrial Stabilisation Act restricted workers' rights to protest and settle work grievances.
- Despite gaining independence and having a government headed by Eric Williams, there were still inequalities in society.
- Too many businesses in Trinidad and Tobago were not owned by local people, so their profits did not stay in the country.

In addition to this, Trinidadians were influenced by the American **Civil Rights Movement**, whose plan was to end discrimination against African Americans. They were also affected by the **Black Panther Party**, founded in America in 1966, whose aim was to secure better rights for the American black community.

Exercise

1. Explain briefly the origins of the Black Power Movement in Trinidad.

Activity

Role-play the following scenario in pairs. It is 1970 and one of you is an activist preparing to go to a Black Power demonstration. Using the information on these two pages, decide why you are going to the protest. Your partner will be a television presenter, who will ask you why you think going to a demonstration will help the cause.

Consequences of the Black Power Movement in Trinidad

The Black Power Movement in Trinidad and Tobago was headed by Geddes Granger and Dave Darbeau of the National Joint Action Committee (NJAC) political party. George Weekes, President of the OGTU, supported them. The Black Power Movement in Trinidad and Tobago aimed to:

- end all injustice faced by people of colour in society
- ensure equal employment rights
- end foreign influence in the country
- improve the status of African culture in society.

Black Power leader Geddes Granger addresses a huge crowd during a demonstration early in March 1970, Trinidad.

Marches and demonstrations

In 1970, there were demonstrations against the government in several towns, attracting up to 50 000 people. Woodford Square in Port of Spain, renamed the People's Parliament, was packed with people at nightly meetings. When one demonstration turned violent the army was called in, but two of its officers rebelled when they were told they might have to shoot protesters. On 21 April 1970 Eric Williams declared a **state of emergency** and the mutineers were arrested, tried in military courts and put in jail.

The consequences of the 1970 protests

The consequences of the protests of 1970 were:

- the emergence of black pride and consciousness
- new government economic policies to develop the economy and create jobs – the government had money to do this due to the increase in the price of oil in 1973; for example, the government bought companies such as Caroni (1975) Limited and invested in iron, steel and chemical industries, as well as improving infrastructure
- the slow end to discrimination against black people in the workplace and an increased awareness of injustice in Trinidadian society.

Activity

Using the internet, or newspaper articles given to you by your teacher, research the events of the Black Power Movement and act out its story.

Exercise

2. Why do you think people were attracted to the Black Power Movement?

3. What were the aims of the Black Power Movement in Trinidad and Tobago?

4. In your own words, explain what happened in 1970, and the consequences.

Key vocabulary

Black Power

Civil Rights Movement

Black Panther Party

state of emergency

The West Indian Federation

We are learning to:

- outline the factors which led to the establishment of the Federation, its achievements and what contributed to its failure
- demonstrate an understanding of the values: loyalty, cooperation.

The formation of the West Indian Federation 》》

The West Indian Federation was formed by 10 British colonies who wanted to put forward the idea of existing as a Federation, or separate entity, from the United Kingdom. Federation is the act of forming a political unity under a federal government. The idea was first put forward at a regional conference held in 1947 at Montego Bay, Jamaica, and the West Indian Federation came into being in 1958.

The motto of the West Indian Federation was 'To dwell together in unity'. This motto signified the Federation's aim of establishing an **integrated** community that would work together, cooperatively and loyally, as a single unit.

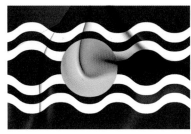

The flag of the West Indian Federation.

Discussion

In groups, discuss whether it was a good or bad idea to disband the West Indian Federation.

The aims of the Federation 》》

The West Indian Federation had a number of aims.

- **Independence** – members wanted to achieve independence from Britain and they saw **regional unity** as a way to do this. They also hoped this would prevent the United States from interfering in the Caribbean.
- Economic independence – much of the land and many of the businesses were owned by foreign companies.
- Free movement of people and goods – free movement around the islands of the West Indies. A new airline, British West Indies Airways, came into service, as well as two ships donated by Canada to improve transport between the islands.
- Goods prices – to get cheaper prices for imports and better prices for exports.
- Central planning – to allow economic development across the member states.

Although the Federation had failed, the idea of a unified body remained and organisations such as CARIFTA (1965) and CARICOM (1973) were later formed.

Did you know...?

The members of the West Indian Federation were:

Antigua and Barbuda

Barbados

Dominica

Grenada

Jamaica

Montserrat

St Kitts-Nevis-Anguilla

St Vincent and the Grenadines

St Lucia

Trinidad and Tobago.

Collapse of the West Indian Federation　

The West Indian Federation lasted until 1962. It was disbanded when Jamaica and Trinidad and Tobago decided to leave the Federation. However, a number of reasons contributed to the collapse of the Federation.

- The Federation was weak – financially, it was not possible for the Federation to function together, as each state had its own economy.
- The aim of freedom of movement had not been achieved.
- Trinidad and Tobago and Jamaica were the biggest countries in the Federation and they were expected to bear most of the costs of the Federation. They thought this was unfair.
- The smaller countries feared that the more powerful countries would dominate the Federation.
- There was disagreement as to where the capital of the Federation should be.
- Jamaica objected to the colonial status of the Federation and felt that it was holding back true independence from Britain.
- The most respected leaders of the time preferred to remain as leaders in their own countries, rather than lead the Federation.

In September 1961, Jamaica held a referendum in which the people of Jamaica elected to pull out of the Federation.

Jamaica and Trinidad and Tobago became independent countries in 1962. The other countries in the Federation achieved independence later on.

Mary, Princess Royal, and Governor Sir Solomon Hochoy were among the officials who attended the flag-raising ceremony at the Red House, to mark the independence of Trinidad and Tobago from the British Empire, August 1962.

Activity

Role-play a meeting of the West Indian Federation. There need to be 10 in the group to represent the countries, and another person to chair the meeting. In your mock meeting, you could discuss how to make sure that people and goods can move freely between the countries, for example.

Exercise

1. In your own words, describe the aims of the West Indian Federation.

2. When was the Federation founded?

3. Name some of the achievements of the Federation.

4. In what year did the Federation disband?

5. Why did Jamaica and Trinidad and Tobago feel that their involvement disadvantaged them?

6. Why was it difficult for the Federation to function in financial terms?

7. True or false? The aim of freedom of movement had been achieved by the Federation.

8. What were the consequences of withdrawing from the Federation for Jamaica and Trinidad and Tobago?

Key vocabulary
....
integrated

independence

regional unity

Independence

We are learning to:

- define the following concepts: independence, patriotism, pride, national consciousness.

The road to independence ❯❯

With the collapse of the West Indian Federation, and the independence of Trinidad and Tobago and Jamaica, the remaining islands (Antigua and Barbuda; Barbados; Dominica; Grenada; Montserrat; St Kitts, Nevis and Anguilla; St Lucia; St Vincent) formed a smaller union called the 'Little Eight'.

This union was short-lived as it faced similar problems and fears to the larger federation, in particular the lack of financial help from Jamaica and Trinidad and Tobago. In November 1966, Barbados gained independence. The remaining islands, with the exception of Montserrat and Anguilla, became associated states of Britain. This meant each colony had an elected government with a cabinet and premier. Britain retained responsibility for defence and foreign affairs.

By the 1970s each island had experienced an increase in **national consciousness, patriotism** and **pride**. As such, the demands for independence mounted. Grenada was the first of this group to attain independence on 7 February 1974. Dominica followed in November 1978, and St Lucia and St Vincent in October 1979. Antigua and Barbuda attained independence in November 1981, and St Kitts and Nevis followed on 19 September 1983.

Following independence, important changes took place in how countries governed themselves. For example, in Trinidad and Tobago:

- A **bicameral** legislature was set up, which consisted of a senate and an elected House of Representatives.
- The Governor-General still represented the English Crown, but this person was a citizen of Trinidad and Tobago.
- A new **constitution** was drawn up.
- The government had full control of all national and international matters and was allowed to make its own policies.

Exercise

1. What organisation was formed after the collapse of the West Indian Federation?

2. Read 9.12 and 9.13 and create a timeline to summarise when countries in the Eastern Caribbean gained independence.

Statue of Vere Bird, first Prime Minister of Antigua and Barbuda.

Project

Choose one of the islands which gained independence as described (or your own country) and using the internet, research how they celebrated independence.
Write a newspaper article describing the celebrations and add any pictures that you may have found.

Did you know...?

The Grenada national flag is red, green and gold. The red represents courage, the green represents the fertility of the land, the gold represents the wisdom and warmth of the people. The nutmeg is a symbol of the island's most famous crop.

Case study

Study these extracts from speeches made by Errol Barrow, Prime Minister of Barbados.

The first speech was made to the United Nations in December 1966. The speech took place nine days after Barbados had gained independence.

'We shall not involve ourselves in sterile ideological wranglings because we are exponents not of the diplomacy of power, but of the diplomacy of peace and prosperity.

We will not regard any great power as necessarily right in a given dispute unless we are convinced of this, yet at the same time we will not view the great powers with perennial suspicion merely on account of their size, wealth, or nuclear potential.

We will be friends of all, satellites of none.'

The second speech was made by Mr Barrow to a political rally on 13 May, 1986 in Barbados.

'What kind of mirror image do you have of yourself? Let me tell you what kind of mirror image I have of you, or what the Democratic Labour Party has of you. The Democratic Labour Party has an image that the people of Barbados would be able to run their own affairs, to pay for the cost of running their own country, to have an education system which is as good as what can be obtained in any industrialised country, anywhere in the world.'

Read this extract from a speech made on 31 August 1962 by the first Prime Minister of Trinidad and Tobago after gaining independence, Dr Eric Williams.

'You are on your own in a big world, in which you are one of many nations, some small, some medium size, some large. You are nobody's boss and nobody is your boss.'

Questions

1. When did Barbados attain independence?

2. What world organisation was Errol Barrow addressing in the first speech?

3. What do you think Errol Barrow meant when he said 'we will be friends of all, satellites of none'?

4. What kind of mirror image did the Democratic Labour Party have for the people of Barbados?

5. What do you think Dr Williams meant by, 'You are nobody's boss and nobody is your boss'?

Statue of Errol Barrow.

Activity

Your teacher will play you some calypsos about the period, such as 'Independence Calypso' by Lord Brynner.

Key vocabulary

national consciousness

patriotism

pride

bicameral

constitution

Figures of the independence movement

We are learning to:

- explain the contribution of key figures to the independence movement
- appreciate the values of leadership, perseverance, self-discipline.

> **Significant personalities of the independence period**

There were a number of people who made a significant contribution to the independence movement in the Caribbean.

Profile

Dr Eric Williams (left) arrives for the Commonwealth Conference, 1962.

Dr Eric Eustace Williams (1911–81)

Dr Eric Williams played the most significant role in the process of independence for Trinidad and Tobago. Williams was educated at Queen's Royal College in Port of Spain. He won a scholarship and went to read history at Oxford University in the UK, where he graduated with a First in History in 1935. He returned to Trinidad in 1948.

In 1956, he founded the People's National Movement (PNM) and in the general election that year the PNM won 13 of the 24 available seats. The PNM was the first party government in Trinidad and Tobago, and Williams was appointed its first leader.

Williams recognised the need for a political party that stood for self-government, economic development, unity between races and the political education of the people. He also attacked racial inequality, the plantation system and political backwardness. He was a firm believer in democracy.

In 1962, Williams became the first Prime Minister of Trinidad and Tobago. He served from 1962 until he died in 1981. It was only through Williams's **perseverance, leadership** and **discipline** that he succeeded in his quest for independence.

Exercise

1. What contributions did Dr Eric Williams make to Trinidad and Tobago?
2. In which year did Dr Williams found the PNM?
3. What were the policies that the PNM stood for?
4. In which year did the PNM form their first government?

Profile

Errol Barrow 1920–87

Errol W. Barrow served in World War II in the British Royal Air Force. He attained undergraduate degrees in Law and Economics.

In 1951 he was elected to the Barbados parliament as a member of the Barbados Labour Party (BLP). He felt there was a greater need for change in Barbados than the BLP could offer so he formed his own party – the Democratic Labour Party – in 1955.

With the support of the Barbados Workers' Union he was able to win the 1961 elections. He sought to improve the island's public works by building roads and dams, cutting canals, improving sanitation and planting forests.

In 1965, with the dissolution of the 'Little Eight', Barrow petitioned the British government for independence. He won the election held after that and became the first Prime Minister of Barbados on 30 November 1966.

Profile

John Compton (1925–2007)

John Comption joined the St Lucia Labour Party in 1956 and rose to the post of Deputy Leader under George Charles. In 1961 he formed a new party, the National Labour Movement. He served as premier in 1967. He became first Prime Minister of St Lucia on 22 February 1979.

Profile

Albert Gomes (1911–78)

Gomes was the founder of the Federated Workers Trade Union in 1937, and held a number of public offices, including on Port of Spain city council (1938–47) and as a Member of Parliament (1958–61). He was known for campaigning to end the censorship of calypso – achieved in 1951 – and for championing workers' rights and challenging authority.

Project

Your teacher will ask you to complete a class exhibition about your island's independence. Include the following: the key people involved, a timeline of events, photographs and drawings.

John Compton, the first Prime Minister of St Lucia.

Exercise

5. What contribution did Errol Barrow make to Barbados?
6. When did John Compton become the first Prime Minister of St Lucia?
7. Outline Albert Gomes' contribution to Trinidad and Tobago.

Key vocabulary

perseverance

leadership

discipline

The Grenada Revolution 1979–83

We are learning to:

- explain the factors that led to the Grenada Revolution 1979–83
- outline its achievements and what contributed to its demise.

The Grenada Revolution 1979–83 〉〉

On 13 March 1979 a **coup d'état** led by the New Jewel Movement (NJM) ousted Eric Gairy from government in Grenada and established the first **socialist** revolution in the English-speaking Caribbean.

The New Jewel Movement felt that Gairy had committed a number of atrocities against the Grenadian people, including the squandering of government funds, seizure of cooperatives (banana and nutmeg) and **victimisation** and violence against opponents.

Some leaders of the New Jewel Movement, including Maurice Bishop, had suffered beatings from Gairy's infamous Mongoose Gang. Having lost the 1976 election, the NJM turned to a military coup d'état in 1979 to forcibly remove Gairy from power.

This revolutionary socialist government was called the People's Revolutionary Government (PRG). Maurice Bishop was Prime Minister, chairman of the Central Committee and commander in chief of the armed forces.

In four and a half years a number of achievements were attained including:

- free secondary education
- advances in health care
- national insurance scheme
- housing for low-income families
- the construction of an international airport
- the building of feeder roads, particularly in rural areas
- the building of community centres
- extension of electricity services
- the establishment of a national transportation service
- a fishing processing plant and fisheries school and an agro-industries plant.

Maurice Bishop, one of the leaders of the New Jewel Movement.

Research

Using the internet and books from your library and working in groups, discuss whether the merits of the Grenada Revolution outweighed its demerits. Make a presentation to the class.

Activity

Create a timeline and use pictures that tell the story of the Grenada Revolution. Make a collage and share it with the class.

The end of the Grenada Revolution »»

The People's Revolutionary Government was accused of excesses that led to opposition in Grenada, the rest of the region and abroad. These included imprisonment of opponents without trial, torture, restrictions on freedom of the press and militarisation of the state.

US Marines with prisoners in Grenada, 1983.

The United States was not pleased with the new socialist state and advised its citizens not to travel to Grenada. This had a negative impact on the tourism industry. By September 1983 the PRG was in crisis. The Central Committee felt that its socialist agenda was not being fulfilled effectively.

The Committee decided that joint leadership was the way to achieve this goal. Maurice Bishop, as Prime Minister, was asked to equally share power with the Deputy Prime Minister Bernard Coard. Initially, Bishop saw the idea as a vote of no confidence against him, but he agreed to implement it.

In early October 1983, Bishop **reneged** on his decision and was placed under house arrest by the Central Committee. On 19 October he was freed by a mob of hundreds of people to shouts of 'No Bishop, No Revolution' and was taken to Fort George (then called Fort Rupert). At the Fort, Bishop and a number of his colleagues and civilians were killed.

Bishop's death heralded the end of the revolutionary process and the **invasion** of the island by the United States of America and Caribbean forces on 25 October 1983. Bernard Coard and 16 other members of the Central Committee and New Jewel Movement spent 26 years in prison for the killings at the Fort.

In May 2009, the Point Salines International Airport was renamed the Maurice Bishop International Airport in Bishop's memory.

Exercise

1. Why did the New Jewel Movement oppose the Gairy regime?

2. What were some of the achievements or merits of the Grenada Revolution?

3. Why do you think the revolution came to such a catastrophic end?

Key vocabulary

coup d'état

socialist/socialism

victimisation

renege

invasion

Questions

See how well you have understood the topics in this unit.

1. Match the key vocabulary word (i–vii) with its definition (a–g).

   i) first peoples

   ii) indigenous

   iii) integrated

   iv) diversified

   v) constitutional reform

   a) joined together or working cooperatively as a single unit

   b) the first known population of a place, usually indigenous people

   c) changing the laws and policies by which a state is governed

   d) originally present in a place; living there naturally; not imported from another place

   e) enlarge or expand a range of products, operations or industries

2. What is an artefact? State a number of places in the region where artefacts have been discovered.

3. Consider two perspectives on the fate of the Black Caribs of St Vincent, and create them as a reflective diary entry.

4. Why do you think the Amerindians resisted the Europeans in the Caribbean?

5. Why did the islands of the Caribbean 'change hands' between different European powers?

6. Name the religions introduced to the Caribbean islands by **a)** the Spanish and French, **b)** the British, **c)** the Germans and **d)** indentured Indians.

7. Write a reflective diary entry of a European travelling to the Caribbean in the early 1600s. Note down the relations between the indigenous people and the Europeans.

8. What did Audrey Jeffers achieve in 1936?

9. Who was Gertrude Protain and what was her contribution to Grenada?

10. Who was the first Prime Minister of:

    a) Trinidad?

    b) St Lucia?

    c) Barbados?

11. Use the internet to research the biography of one of the people involved in the Grenada Revolution 1979–83; Maurice Bishop or Bernard Coard. Write about 150 words, and include any photos you can find.

12. Name the party that Errol Barrow founded and the year in which he did so.

Checking your progress

To make good progress in understanding different aspects of the history of your country, check to make sure you understand these ideas.

Explain the presence of the indigenous people of the Caribbean.

Understand the colonial economic, political and religious systems in the Caribbean.

Use primary and secondary sources to research aspects of the history of the Caribbean.

Explain the contribution of key figures and groups in trade unionism and social activism.

Explain the origins of the trade union movement in the Caribbean in the early twentieth century.

Use a graphic organiser to compile the key events in the history of the OWTU.

Explain the causes and consequences of the Black Power Movement in the Caribbean.

Explore the formation and collapse of the West Indian Federation.

Role-play a meeting of the West Indian Federation.

Explain the road to independence for the islands of the Eastern Caribbean and the contribution of key figures to the independence movement.

Explain the factors that led to the Grenada Revolution 1979–83.

Write about what the independence of your Caribbean island means to you.

End-of-term questions

See how well you have understood the ideas in Unit 7.

1. Create a fact file that outlines the objectives of the following institutions:

   • West Indian Federation

   • Caribbean Free Trade Association (CARIFTA)

   • Caribbean Community (CARICOM)

   • CARICOM Single Market and Economy (CSME)

   • Organisation of Eastern Caribbean States (OECS)

   • Association of Caribbean States (ACS)

2. Read Units 7.1–7.6 and compile a timeline of the key events in the history of the Institutions that contributed to the integration process of the Caribbean region. Include the West Indian Federation, Caribbean Free Trade Association, CARICOM, CSME, OECS and ACS.

3. Write a short essay to express your opinions about the benefits of CARIFESTA and its contribution to regional unity. Use 150 words.

4. Write a newspaper report explaining the causes of poverty in the Caribbean and some of the strategies being implemented to combat poverty.

See how well you have understood the ideas in Unit 8.

5. Match the key vocabulary word (i–iii) with its definition (a–c).

   i) primary industry

   ii) secondary industry

   iii) tertiary industry

   a) industry that processes or produces resources, e.g. building, manufacturing
   b) industry that provides a service, e.g. teaching, advertising
   c) industry that harvests or extracts resources, e.g. farming, fishing

6. Match each job title from the word box with its job description:

| teacher   accountant   events planner   insurance agent   tour guide   hotel manager |

a) An _____ keeps track of and records the flow of money in an organisation or business.

b) An _____ sells insurance policies for an insurance company.

c) A _____ works with students, presenting classes, lectures and assignments, and helping students to develop skills and knowledge.

d) A _____ supervises and manages the running of a hotel.

e) An _____ organises events such as weddings, conferences, parties and other functions.

f) A _____ arranges tours to places of interest.

7. Write an article for a magazine in which you offer advice about the factors to consider when choosing a career. Write about 200 words.

8. Write a paragraph to explain why it is important to have work ethics.

Questions 9–14 >>>

See how well you have understood the ideas in Unit 9.

9. With the map you created in 9.1 of the route our ancestors took to get to the Caribbean, write a report detailing who the first people of the Caribbean were, where they came from, the tribes, where they settled and how they lived.

10. You have been asked to give a talk to a local history society about the treatment of the Amerindians in the Caribbean. Write a short report of what you will talk about.

11. Write a report outlining the arguments for and against the West Indian Federation. Write about 150 words.

12. Explain the origins of peasant farming and how the metayage system evolved. Write about 150 words.

13. Read 9.8 and 9.9. Create a timeline to summarise the contribution of key figures and groups in the fields of trade unionism and social activism in the Caribbean 1900–70.

14. Explain the role of Audrey Jeffers, Phyllis Allfrey and Gertrude Protain in the history of the Caribbean.

15. Write a reflective piece expressing what the independence of your island/country means to you. Use around 100 words.

Glossary

accountant someone who keeps track of and records the flow of money in an organisation or business.

active a volcano which could erupt at any time.

adult suffrage the right of adults to vote in an election.

advertising the promotion of goods or services for sale through impersonal media, such as radio or television.

aftershock a smaller earthquake that follows the main one.

AIDS Acquired Immune Deficiency Syndrome – a disease.

air pollution substances found in the atmosphere that are harmful or dangerous.

air pressure the weight of the air.

Amerindians the first people of the Caribbean.

amnesty official pardon.

Anglicanism a Protestant denomination; Anglicans believe they follow a 'middle way' between Catholicism and Protestantism.

animal hide animal skin.

anonymous without giving one's name; keeping one's identity secret.

apartheid a system in South Africa where people were kept apart on racial grounds.

appraisal the official or formal assessment of the strengths and weaknesses of someone or something. Appraisal often involves observation or some kind of testing.

apprenticeship someone who works for someone else, learning a skill.

apps a computer programme used on mobile phones.

arson deliberately setting fire to a building, a car, etc; arson is a crime.

artefact an object that is historically or culturally interesting.

associate member a member state which does not have all the benefits of full membership.

autonomous able to make their own decisions rather than being influenced by someone else; an autonomous country, organisation, or group governs or controls itself rather than being controlled by anyone else.

balance of trade the difference in value between imports and exports in a given year.

ballot a vote.

ballot box a box in which ballot papers are collected.

ballot paper a piece of paper on which a voter records his or her vote.

bicameral two houses or chambers in a government.

bilateral agreement agreements between two countries.

biotechnology using living organisms such as cells or bacteria in industry and technology.

Black Panther Party a civil rights movement founded in the USA in 1966, whose aim was to secure better rights for the American black community.

Black Power a name used by African Americans in the USA to describe a movement that aimed to achieve self-determination for people of African/black descent.

bullying when an individual or group tries to intimidate others through physical or verbal abuse.

bureaucracy an administrative system operated by a large number of officials.

Cabinet part of the executive, consisting of the Prime Minister and Ministers.

calypso a song about current issues sung in a West Indian form.

campaign series of events which are organised to help a candidate get elected.

candidate a person who seeks election.

capital money; anything that an economy needs in order to produce goods and services.

career long-term path in a job or occupation.

Caribbean Court of Justice (CCJ) a court which serves CARICOM member states and settles disputes between them.

CARICOM the Caribbean Community.

Carifesta Caribbean Festival of Arts.

CARIFTA Caribbean Free Trade Association.

CDEMA Caribbean Disaster Emergency Management Agency.

cellular phone a mobile phone.

cementation a process by which crystals help to glue sediment together, forming a rock.

chantwell a female singer who sings lyrics to big drum music.

chatrooms a place on the internet where people swap messages.

choice someone or something that a person chooses from a range of things.

Christianity a religion that follows the teachings of Jesus Christ.

civil offence an act relating to relationships between members of a society, such as trespassing on someone else's property.

Civil Rights Movement a mass protest movement that started in the USA in the 1960s, which was against racial discrimination.

climate pattern of weather conditions in a place, usually taken as an average over 30 years or more.

climate change the change in the Earth's temperature and weather patterns as a result of increased carbon dioxide in the air.

climate graphs information about the temperature and rainfall in one place over a particular period of time.

climate zones horizontal belts found at different latitudes with varying average weather conditions.

cloned animals an animal that has been produced artificially from the cells of another animal and is exactly the same as the original.

collective bargaining negotiation between one or more trade unions and one or more employers.

communicable diseases a disease that is passed from one person to another, e.g. hepatitis, influenza and HIV/AIDS.

communication the transfer of information between a sender and receiver.

communication technology the transfer of information between a sender and receiver using technology.

compaction the weight of the sediment squeezes down on the previous layer and squeezes out the water.

competition similar goods or services available in the same marketplace.

competitiveness producing goods that are as good or better or cheaper than goods produced by others.

composite volcano a cone-shaped volcano made up of alternating bands of lava and ash.

condenses the process where water vapour cools and turns back to a liquid.

conflict resolution the process of ending a conflict by finding a peaceful way to do it.

conflict a serious disagreement which can often become violent or involve fighting between groups of people.

Glossary

conservation preserving, protecting and restoring something.

constituency an area in a country where voters elect a representative to a local or national government body.

constituent a person who lives in a constituency.

constitution the principles and laws by which a country is governed.

constitutional reform the process where changes are made to the constitution.

consumer a person who uses goods and services.

consumer society when consumers buy more new goods than they really need, due to having more disposable income.

consumerism the excessive buying of goods and services.

continental crust the part of the crust where the continents are situated.

contract work short-term work, based on a temporary contract; contract workers are also sometimes called freelancers.

convection current movement within the mantle caused by heat.

cooperation the act of working together to a shared outcome.

core centre of the Earth.

coup d'état the overthrow of a government by the use of force.

courage the quality of mind that enables one to encounter difficulties and danger with firmness and bravery or without fear.

crime an activity or offence that is against the law.

criminal offence an act relating to a crime, such as robbery or murder.

Crown Colony a country ruled by the monarch of another country.

crust the outside layer of the Earth.

CSME the Caribbean Single Market and Economy.

cultural bonds cultural ties that bring people together.

cultural festivals festivals that promote cultural activities like dance and story-telling.

cultural transmission the way a group of people pass a society's culture from one generation to the next.

curriculum the courses or subjects that are taught in schools, colleges and universities.

cyber abuse abuse via computer applications, usually over the internet.

cyberbullying bullying that takes place through internet chat rooms or social media.

deforestation the removal of trees and vegetation to create open spaces for human activities.

demand the amount of goods and services consumers are willing to purchase at a particular price and point in time.

democracy a system of government in which a country's citizens choose their rulers by voting for them in elections.

democratic government a government that is elected by the citizens of a country.

denomination a group having a distinctive interpretation of Christianity.

dense something that is dense contains a lot of things or people in a small area.

dependence relying on someone or something.

deposited laid down.

depression an area of low pressure with cloudy, wet and windy weather.

diaspora the dispersion of people who originally came from a particular nation, but now live in many different parts of the world.

dictator a ruler who has complete power in a country, especially power which was obtained by force and is used unfairly or cruelly.

dignity the need and right to honour and respect.

disbanded broken up.

discipline when someone is able to behave in a controlled way.

distribution the process of getting goods from producers to consumers.

distribution chain the series of intermediaries who help to get goods from producers to customers.

diversify to enlarge or expand a range of products, operations or industries.

dormant has not erupted in 10 000 years but could do again.

drones a small type of aircraft that is controlled by someone from the ground.

drugs legal medicines or illegal substances that people take because of the effect that they provide.

earthquake a sudden shaking of the Earth's crust.

Eastern Caribbean Supreme Court an appeal court which also functions to mediate industrial disputes in countries which are under its mandate.

ebooks electronic book.

eco-friendly not damaging to the environment; sustainable.

e-commerce businesses that provide goods and services over the internet.

economic development improving a country's standard of living.

economic integration cooperation in business e.g. trading, finance.

economy the system of how industry, trade and finance is organised in a country, region or worldwide to manage wealth.

ecotourism tourism that does not damage or destroy the natural environment or local culture.

efficient achieving something with the least amount of effort and expense.

election a process during which voters choose candidates by voting for them.

Election Day the day on which voting takes place in an election.

elector a voter or person who has the right to vote in an election.

electorate people who are entitled to vote in an election.

elements of weather elements such as temperature, precipitation, humidity, air pressure and other elements that make up the weather conditions.

eligible to qualify for.

emailing electronic messages sent from one computer to another computer.

emails electronic messages sent from one computer to another computer.

emancipation being freed from slavery.

empathy the ability to share another person's feelings and emotions as if they were your own.

employed someone who is paid to do a job by someone else.

employee someone who has a job with a specific company or employer.

employer someone who offers employment.

employment the state of having paid work.

empower to give someone the means to achieve something, e.g. to become stronger or more successful.

endangered in danger of extinction in the foreseeable future in a significant portion of its range.

enemies people who are hostile towards each other.

entrepreneur someone who runs their own business.

environmentalist someone who is concerned with protecting the natural environment.

epicentre the point directly above the focus on the Earth's surface.

equals people in positions of equivalent power or responsibility.

ethics rules for living in society and what are considered to be the right and wrong things to do.

ethnicity features relating to the culture of a society that have an historical importance to that society.

evaporation the process where water surfaces are heated (usually by the sun) and water turns to water vapour.

events planner someone who plans and organises events e.g. parties and weddings.

exports goods that are sold in other countries.

extinct (species) a species that no longer exists on Earth.

extinct (volcano) a volcano that has not erupted in the last 10 000 years and will not erupt again.

extrusive rock forms above the surface.

eye the centre of a hurricane.

family planning the practice of controlling the number and frequency of children a family has.

faults cracks in the Earth's crust.

fauna indigenous animals.

federation a group of states that has one central government but independent local governments.

federation a group of societies or other organisations which have joined together, usually because they share a common interest.

femininity the qualities that are considered to be typical of women.

fertile soils that are rich in nutrients.

fertilisers chemicals that promote fast plant growth.

first people the first known population of a place, usually indigenous people.

first-past-the-post system (FPPS) a type of electoral system in which the candidate with the most votes wins.

floating voters voters who have not decided for whom they will vote.

flooding the submerging of land under water, especially due to hurricanes.

flora indigenous flowers or plants.

focus the point, underground, at which an earthquake happens.

fold mountains mountains formed when two continental plates move towards each other.

foreign exchange the foreign currency that is obtained from a system known as the foreign exchange system.

foreign exchange system a system involved with changing one currency into another.

formal having fixed definitions and roles.

foundations the layer of bricks or concrete below the ground that buildings or other structures are built on.

franchise the right to vote.

free and fair an election where the parties taking part do not try to persuade citizens to cast votes in their favour by using force or intimidation.

free trade trading between countries without tariffs and restrictions.

friendships personal relationships where people trust and confide in one another and spend time together on a voluntary basis.

frostbite when skin is exposed to very cold temperatures and freezes.

full-time working or studying for the whole of each normal working week rather than for part of it.

fusion creating something new by joining two or more forms together.

gang an organised group of criminals.

genetically modified (GM) crops where scientific techniques have been used to change the DNA of crops, allowing them to grow in more difficult climates or environments.

genocide the deliberate killing of a large number of people, often in an attempt to get rid of a particular ethnic group.

geothermal energy energy stored in the form of heat beneath the Earth's surface.

global worldwide; relating to the whole world.

global positioning systems (GPS) a navigation system that provides data about time and location.

global village the way in which people all over the world have become connected through technology.

globalisation a process of making the world more connected, with goods and services being traded globally and people moving around freely.

go slow when employees deliberately work slowly.

goods things that are grown or manufactured.

griot a storyteller.

hierarchy a power structure.

high viscosity thick, gloopy and slow flowing lava.

Hinduism one of the world's oldest religions, Hinduism comes originally from India. Hindus believe that there is a universal soul called Brahman; this universal soul can take the form of many gods and goddesses.

HIV Human Immunodeficiency Virus, which causes AIDS.

honest the quality of always telling the truth.

House of Assembly the body which is responsible for local government and legislation.

House of Representatives the lower house of parliament.

house-to-house canvassing when people who work for political parties knock on the doors of citizens in the constituency to try and persuade them to vote for their party.

humanitarian aid help for people who are suffering e.g. medical care, food, and water.

humid moist; damp.

humidity how much water is in the air.

hung parliament when no party has gained the overall majority of seats in parliament to take control and to form a government.

hurricane shelter a purpose-built shelter to protect people from hurricanes.

hurricane, cyclone, typhoon, willy-willy the four names given to tropical storms around the world.

identity the characteristics a person or place has that distinguish them from others.

igneous rocks rocks formed from the cooling of hardening of magma.

imports goods bought from other countries.

inaccessible somewhere not easy to get to.

inappropriate not suitable for a given context; not acceptable to a person or place.

independence being able to do things without assistance or direction.

independent candidate a candidate who does not belong to any political party.

indigenous people or things that originally belong to the country in which they are found, rather than coming there or being brought there from another country.

industrial dispute a disagreement between workers and their employer.

industrialise when a country is able to grow due to its many industries.

information and communication technology (ICT) technologies for transmitting and storing information electronically.

information overload the experience of receiving too much information and being unable to process all of it.

infrastructure structures like bridges, roads and water ways.

infusion where one thing (or more) is added to another, to make something else.

inner/outer core sections of the Earth's core.

innuendoes hints or underlying messages.

instant messaging (IM) a typed message sent and received via the internet through messaging software.

insurance agent someone who sells insurance policies for an insurance company.

insurance policy a document that gives details of the agreement between an insurer and the person who is insured.

integrate to bring together ideas and people so that they work together or become part of the same group.

integrated involving people from all groups and cultures.

integrity to be honest in your principles.

interdependent/interdependence the state of relying on each other.

inter-governmental cooperation between multiple governments.

intermediaries those who are part of the distribution chain, e.g. wholesalers and transport agents.

International Criminal Court an international court which prosecutes people for crimes against humanity.

international tribunal an international court of justice.

internet café a place where people can go and pay to access the internet.

intimate relationship a close personal relationship, often a romantic or sexual relationship.

intimidate to make another person feel powerless and afraid.

intrusive rock forms inside the Earth.

invasion the forced entry of a foreign army.

investment putting money into the development of a company with the expectation of gaining a profit.

involuntary something that you do not choose.

irrigation a man-made system of supplying land with water.

Islam the religion of Muslims; based on the Qur'an, it teaches that there is only one God and that Mohammed is his prophet.

isohyet maps maps that are used to show rainfall figures.

job a specific set of employment tasks at a particular workplace.

Judaism the religion of the Jews; based on the Old Testament and the Talmud, its central point is a belief in God as the transcendent creator of all things and the source of all righteousness.

Judiciary the branch of government that consists of judges and magistrates who apply the laws of the country.

junior younger or having less power and responsibility.

justice administering the law in a fair way.

Kalinago a group of Amerindians who travelled to the Caribbean from Venezuela and settled mainly in the Lesser Antilles.

knowledge the understanding someone has about a particular subject.

labour the work that people do to provide goods and services.

labour movement organisations of working people who campaigned for better working conditions.

lahar mixture of water and volcanic ash and debris that flows down a volcano.

landslide the sudden movement of rock, earth or debris down a slope.

latitudes horizontal lines circling the Earth, showing distance from the equator.

leadership when a leader (or leaders) influences a group to achieve a common objective.

liberalised a system which is designed to allow easier trading conditions.

lifelong learning education that continues over a whole lifetime.

limited franchise a system of voting where not all the population are allowed to take part.

livestock animals used in farming.

low viscosity thin, runny and fast flowing lava.

lucrative producing a profit.

macho a term which describes men who play up their masculinity in an overly aggressive way.

magma liquid rock found inside the mantle.

magnitude the size of an earthquake.

majority the largest number of votes or the greatest number of seats won by a party in an election.

manager someone who manages other employees, works out schedules and responsibilities and ensures that a department is running properly.

manifesto the views and proposed policies of candidates and political parties in an election.

mantle the middle layer of the Earth.

market any structure that allows people to buy and sell goods and services.

market goods to create demand for goods in order to sell them.

marketing the process through which demand for a product is created, e.g. advertising.

marketing staff a team that promotes and sells a product or brand; this may be through advertising, promotional events and offers, and through social media, e.g. Facebook and Twitter.

masculinity the qualities traditionally associated with being a man.

mass media media that can reach thousands of people at the same time.

mediate to intervene (between parties or in a dispute) in order to bring about agreement.

mediation a person who is not involved in a conflict and can help guide the two sides towards an understanding.

mentor someone who gives advice and help to another person over a period of time.

metamorphic rocks formed under extreme pressure or heat.

metayage system a form of sharecropping in which the metayer (sharecropper) occupied a piece of land on which they planted cane.

Methodism a Protestant denomination; based on the teachings of a Christian teacher called John Wesley and emphasises helping the poor and working to serve the community.

migrate to move from one place to another.

mitigation strategy a plan to reduce the loss of life and property during evacuation by lessening the impact of disasters.

mobility when transport networks enable the movement of people and goods from one place to another.

moksha the Hindu goal of becoming one with Brahma and being released from the cycle of reincarnation.

monument a structure built to remind people of a historical event or famous person.

Moravian one of the oldest Protestant denominations from Germany; it has a long tradition of missionary work in the Caribbean.

mudslide when wet soil or sand moves suddenly downhill.

multilateral agreement an agreement between more than one country or international organisation.

multinational corporation an organisation that has business interests in more than one country.

national consciousness a shared sense of national identity.

national hero/icon individuals (or groups and community activists) who are recognised for their significant contributions to their national heritage or the development of their country.

National Identification Card an official document (card) that states who you are.

natural disasters disasters that occur in nature, e.g. floods, storms, earthquakes and volcanoes.

needs things that are essential for everyday living, e.g. food, water, shelter and clothing.

nominated proposed as a candidate.

nomination procedures that candidates have to follow in order to be able to stand for election.

Nomination Day the day on which candidates register their intention to stand for election.

oath of allegiance to swear loyalty or commitment to someone or something.

obesity/obese someone who is overweight.

obscene offensively sexual or vulgar.

observer status allowed to attend meetings but not take part in the decisions made at the meetings.

occupation a type of job or the work a person does.

oceanic crust the part of the crust where the oceans are situated.

online being connected to the internet.

online gaming sites a place on the internet where people play online games with each other.

online shopping buying goods over the internet.

opinion polls ask people for their views about how they intend to vote; this information is used to try to predict the outcome of the election.

overpopulated where there are too many people, animals, or things in a particular area.

ozone layer a protective layer around the Earth's atmosphere that stops harmful ultraviolet rays from the sun reaching the Earth.

pan-Africanist views that advocate for political unity among African countries.

part-time when a person works for only part of each day or week.

passion a very strong feeling about or in something.

pathologist someone who studies diseases and illnesses.

patois a form of language spoken in a particular region that has developed from a mixture of other languages.

patriotism showing a deep love for and devotion to your country.

peacekeepers civilian people and military personnel who protect and help people in situations where there is or has been conflict or upheaval.

peasant farming the small-scale rearing of livestock, growing of vegetables and ground provisions.

peer pressure when your peers (people of the same age – your classmates) try to influence you to do something.

permanent going on for an indefinite or long period of time.

perseverance when someone continues to do something, even if it is difficult to achieve.

persistence continuing to do something even though it is difficult or other people are against it.

pesticides chemicals that kill insects, weeds and fungi that damage crops.

phone neck an injury to the neck caused by the overuse of electronic devices.

physical resources made by humans through their abilities and skills, e.g. buildings, technology.

plate boundary/margin where two plates meet.

poaching when animals or birds are caught illegally.

polling station where people go to vote on election day.

pollution when the air, land or sea is damaged by exposure to dangerous substances.

population density the average number of people living in one square kilometre.

port a harbour area where ships load and unload goods or passengers.

poverty being very poor; not having enough money or food.

precipitation any form of moisture that falls to the ground e.g. rain, snow, sleet.

prejudice an idea about someone or something that is not based on facts, but on pre-conceived ideas only.

Presbyterianism a Protestant denomination that follows a version of Christianity which originated in the 1500s from a teacher called John Calvin.

preservation the act of looking after something so that it lasts.

President ceremonial head of state (in Trinidad and Tobago).

pride a sense of respect you have for something.

primary industry an industry that harvests raw materials.

Prime Minister a political leader and head of government.

producer (manufacturer) the person or factory that makes or grows products (goods).

productive capable of producing goods and services that have monetary or exchange value.

products goods that are grown or manufactured.

proportional representation (PR) a system of voting in which each political party is represented in a parliament or legislature in proportion to the number of people who vote for it in an election.

Protestantism a branch of Christianity that moved away from some of the traditions of the Catholic Church; all later denominations of Christianity come from Protestantism.

pyroclastic flow a cloud of extremely hot gas and ash that erupts from a volcano, destroying everything in its path.

qualifications the qualities and skills that are needed to be able to do something.

quality of life the measure of happiness that a person has in their life.

Qur'an the Muslim holy book.

race groups into which human beings can be divided according to their physical features, e.g. the colour of their skin.

racial integration when people from different cultural groups live and work together on an equal basis.

racism when prejudice or discrimination is shown towards an individual or group of people based on their race or ethnicity.

range the difference between the maximum temperature and the minimum temperature.

recycling to process a material into a new material, e.g. recycling old broken glass to make fresh glass.

reducing to make or use less of something.

referendum when all the citizens of a country can vote on a specific issue.

refugee a person who has been forced to leave the place where they live because of conflict or natural catastrophe.

region an area of the world, e.g. the Caribbean.

regional integration the joining together or working together of countries that are nearby, in order to make them more economically and politically powerful.

regional unity cooperation and working together with people who live in a certain area.

religious pluralism the idea that many different religious belief systems can co-exist in the same society.

religious prejudice where prejudice or discrimination is shown against an individual or group of people who follow a particular religion.

renege not following through on a promise or agreement.

Representative system a system of government where the Caribbean colonies were ruled by a Governor, Legislative Council and an Assembly.

representative democracy a democracy in which elected officials represent the citizens of a country.

represents acts or speaks for someone else.

resign a formal announcement that someone is leaving a job or position.

responsible to behave in a sensible manner.

résumé/curriculum vitae document summarising skills, education and experience.

retailer the person or shop that buys goods in bulk from the wholesaler in order to sell the goods in smaller quantities to the consumer.

reunite to come together again after being separated.

reusing to use something again.

Richter scale the scale used to show the strength of an earthquake.

rural places which are located in the countryside, away from towns and cities.

sanitation the supply of clean water and efficient sewage system.

saturated filled to capacity; having absorbed all that can be taken up.

science systematic study of something in order to build knowledge and understanding with the aim of making life easier for humans.

screen time the time people spend looking at an electronic device or electronic devices such as computers, laptops, phone or tablets.

seasons how a year is divided, generally with specific weather patterns associated with each season.

secondary industry an industry mostly involved in processing and manufacturing.

secret ballot a method of voting which is not visible by other people.

secretariat a permanent administrative office.

sedentary not active, mostly sitting down.

sedimentary rocks formed under seas and oceans.

seismic waves shock waves that are sent out from the focus and travel through the crust.

seismic/seismic activity the movement of tectonic plates and the resultant activity, e.g. earthquakes or volcanic eruptions.

seismographs an instrument used to measure ground movement.

self-appraisal the evaluation of one's own strengths and weaknesses.

self-employed when you organise your own work and taxes and are paid by people for a service you provide, rather than being paid a regular salary by a person or a firm.

self-esteem how you feel about yourself.

self-motivated to get things done without having to be told to do so.

senator a government official who is a member of a Senate and is involved in making or passing laws.

senior older or holding greater power and responsibility.

services activities such as banking, hairdressing or tourism which are sold to consumers.

sexism when prejudice or discrimination is shown against an individual or group of people based on their gender.

sexual harassment any attention, touch or comment that has unwanted sexual content.

shantytown/slum an area of makeshift housing in urban areas for very poor people.

shield volcano a wide, low-lying volcano found at constructive plate boundaries.

skills to have the ability, creativity or knowledge to do something well.

slavery people who are the property of another person and have to work for that person without payment.

smartphone a mobile phone that can run applications like a small computer; it can send and receive email, browse the internet and take photos.

smog a mixture of fog and smoke which is often seen in large cities.

soca a mixture of funk, soul, reggae and calypso music.

social activism to campaign for better social conditions in society.

social integration when people of all cultural groups, sexes and ages live and work together in an area.

social justice fairness in society.

social media websites and applications that allow people to post and share content in order to connect with others.

social networking site a place on the internet which allows people to interact with each other.

socialist/socialism a person or political view aimed to create a system in which everyone has an equal opportunity to benefit from a country's wealth.

solidified when a liquid changes into a solid.

spa a place where water with minerals in it comes out of the ground.

standard of living the level of comfort and wealth that a person or family has.

state of emergency a time when the government suspends normal constitutional procedures because of a national danger or disaster.

stereotype having a one-sided thought or belief about how another person, or group of people, acts or behaves.

stilts long upright pieces of wood or metal on which some buildings are built, especially where the ground is wet or very soft.

storage space in which things are stored or kept until needed, e.g. a warehouse.

storm surge a rise in sea level that occurs during hurricanes.

subduction zone the downward movement of an oceanic plate pushed underneath a continental plate.

subsistence a method of farming where only enough food is produced for the farmer and their family.

suggestive suggesting sex or sexuality.

supporters people who approve of and vote for political parties.

suppressed prevented from continuing by means of force or authority.

survive to continue living; staying alive.

sustainable economic growth achieving economic growth while not harming our natural resources.

sustainable tourism allowing tourists to visit an area, or country, with little negative impact on natural resources and the environment.

sustainable able to continue at the same level without destroying the resources it relies on.

tablet an electronic device the size of a book, larger than a phone and smaller than a computer, with applications similar to a laptop or smartphone.

Taino a group of Amerindians who travelled to the Caribbean from Venezuela and settled mainly in the Greater Antilles.

technological something that is based in science and can be applied to everyday life to solve problems.

technology devices and systems which have been created for practical purposes.

tectonic plates a section of the Earth's crust.

temperature the measure of how hot or cold something is.

terrain the physical features of an area of land.

terrorism the use of violence, such as bombing, to achieve political aims or to force a government to do something.

terrorist someone who fights against a government using violent means and causes injuries to civilians in the process.

tertiary education education, following secondary education at a school, college or university.

tertiary industry an industry that provides services.

text thumb an injury to the thumb caused by overuse of electronic devices.

threatened likely to become endangered within the foreseeable future throughout all or a significant portion of its range.

tolerance ability or willingness to accept people, views and beliefs that are different to one's own.

trade the activity of buying, selling, or exchanging goods or services between people, firms, or countries.

trade agreements an agreement between two or more countries in relation to providing goods and services.

trade sanctions a trade penalty imposed by one nation onto one or more other nations.

trade union an association of workers that acts on behalf of a group of workers.

transnational company has branches or owns companies in many different countries.

transparent when a situation is seen to be open and honest.

transportation systems, such as roads, water (both inland and sea), air and rail, used for distributing goods from the places they are produced to the places where they can be sold.

transported carried.

treaty a formal agreement between countries.

trustworthy to be someone who can be relied upon.

underemployment the state of having work that does not fully use one's skills or abilities.

unemployed/unemployment when someone does not have a job.

unicameral a system of government that has a single legislative chamber.

unity being united or joined; working together.

universal adult suffrage the right of all adults to vote.

Universal Declaration of Human Rights (UDHR) declaration regarding human rights by countries that are members of the United Nations.

universal suffrage the right of all adults to vote.

unsolicited not invited or asked for.

urban belonging to a town or a city.

urbanisation increasing numbers of people living in cities.

valiantly doing something with determination, courage or bravery.

values what we believe is important in life.

vegetation plant life as a whole, especially the plant life of a particular region.

vendor a person or a business that sells things.

victimisation unfair treatment.

violate to break (the law).

volcanic eruption when volcanoes explode.

volcano a hill or mountain that allows lava, gas and ash to escape.

vote a choice made by someone in an election.

voters' list a list of all persons allowed to vote.

votes the ballot of voting papers on which you choose your candidate in an election.

wants items that a person would like to have, but are not essential for everyday life or basic survival.

ward a smaller division within a county, usually used for voting purposes.

warehouse a large building where raw materials or manufactured goods are stored until they are exported to other countries or distributed to shops to be sold.

weather conditions of the atmosphere, such as temperature, wind, air pressure and rainfall.

West Indian Federation a group of ten Caribbean states that formed a federation from 1958 to 1962.

wholesaler a business that buys goods in bulk from a producer and then sells the goods to retailers.

work ethic a set of moral principles that are followed in the workplace.

work-to-rule where workers do just enough to fulfil the requirements of their job roles, but no more.

workplace relationships relationships with people that we work with.

Index

Index

Acknowledgements

The publishers wish to thank the following for permission to reproduce photographs. Every effort has been made to trace copyright holders and to obtain their permission for the use of copyright materials. The publishers will gladly receive any information enabling them to rectify any error or omission at the first opportunity.

p:8 AA World Travel Library/Alamy Stock Photo, p:9 dpa picture alliance/Alamy Stock Photo, p:10 WENN Ltd/Alamy Stock Photo, p:11 Fernando Medina/Getty Images, p:13 Steve Speller/Alamy Stock Photo, p:14 WENN Ltd/Alamy Stock Photo, p:15 maramorosz/Shutterstock, p:16 Michael Fitzsimmons/Shutterstock, p:18 PHB.cz (Richard Semik)/Shutterstock, p:19 Larwin/Shutterstock, p:19 ziggysofi/Shutterstock, p:20 Sean Pavone/Shutterstock, p:21 Monkey Business Images/Shutterstock, p:22 Sirtravelalot/Shutterstock, p:28 Rawpixel.com/Shutterstock, p:29 JAY DIRECTO/AFP/Getty Images, p:30 GaudiLab/Shutterstock, p:31 Northfoto/Shutterstock, p:32 Decorwithme/Shutterstock, p:33 Rose Carson/Shutterstock, p:34 Twin Design/Shutterstock, p:36 Rj lerich/Shutterstock, p:38 Forewer/Shutterstock, p:42 George Brice/Alamy Stock Photo, p:44 Kaleidoscope/Alamy Stock Photo, p:45 Vacilando/Shutterstock, p:46 ValeStock/Shutterstock, p:52 Wavebreakmedia/Shutterstock, p:53 Sudowoodo/Shutterstock, p:54 Voyagerix/Shutterstock, p:55 Mario Tama/Getty Images, p:56 Mila Supinskaya Glashchenko/Shutterstock, p:57 Franz12/Shutterstock, p:58 GeorgiaCourt/Getty Images, p:66 John Gomez/Shutterstock, p:67 Sean Drakes/LatinContent/Getty Images, p:70 Niyazz/Shutterstock, p:71 Jeff gynane/Shutterstock, p:72 Jeff Morgan 09/Alamy Stock Photo, p:72 Paul Fleet/Shutterstock, p:73 Jeffrey Coolidge/Getty Images, p:74 SEAN DRAKES/Alamy Stock Photo, p:76 Niyazz/Shutterstock, p:77 Alexandru Nika/Shutterstock, p:78 PEDRO REY/AFP/Getty Images, p:80 photosounds/Shutterstock, p:81 a katz/Shutterstock, p:82 Eric Crama/Shutterstock, p:83 David R. Frazier Photolibrary, Inc./Alamy Stock Photo, p:84 yui/Shutterstock, p:85 Domenico Tondini/Alamy Stock Photo, p:86 Said Khatib/AFP/Getty Images, p:88 Jake Lyell/Alamy Stock Photo, p:89 Jason Stitt/Shutterstock, p:90 Jose Jimenez/Getty Images, p:91 Hector Retamal/AFP/Getty Images, p:92 ALEXANDER JOE/AFP/Getty Images, p:93 Jonathan Torgovnik/Getty Images, p:96 Lichfield/Getty Images, p:98 Evelyn Hockstein/MCT/MCT/Getty Images, p:99 Shirley Bahadur/AP Images, p:100 Caribbean Court of Justice, p:101 Maxstockphoto/Shutterstock, p:106 Image Source/Alamy Stock Photo, p:107 Damsea/Shutterstock, p:108 Trevor Mogg/Alamy Stock Photo, p:109 wavebreakmedia/Shutterstock, p:110 Bokic Bojan/Shutterstock, p:111 ImageBROKER/Alamy Stock, p:112 Veryan dale/Alamy Stock Photo, p:113 imageBROKER/Alamy Stock Photo, p:114 Evgeniia Ozerkina/Shutterstock, p:115 imageBROKER/Alamy Stock Photo, p:116 Ange/Alamy Stock Photo, p:117 Thanakorn Hongphan/Shutterstock, p:118 Philip Wolmuth/Alamy Stock Photo, p:119 National Geographic Creative/Alamy Stock Photo, p:124 Johan Swanepoel/Shutterstock, p:127 Designua/Shutterstock, p:128 luigi nifosi/Shutterstock, p:129 Science History Images/Alamy Stock Photo, p:130 Vvvoe/Shutterstock, p:131 Styve Reineck/Shutterstock, p:131 Tyler Boyes/Shutterstock, p:132 Ioat/Shutterstock, p:133 Trgrowth/Shutterstock, p:134 NigelSpiers/Shutterstock, p:135 Prometheus72/Shutterstock, p:136 Travel and Learn/Shutterstock, p:137 Barry Lewis/Alamy Stock Photo, p:140 Sean Pavone/Shutterstock, p:141 Designua/Shutterstock, p:142 Mmoodboard/Alamy Stock Photo, p:143 Arctic Images/Alamy Stock Photo, p:144

Stuart Hunter/Alamy Stock Photo, p:145 Ingólfur Bjargmundsson/ Getty Images, p:146 Suranga Weeratuna/Alamy Stock Photo, p:147 Steven gillis hd9 imaging/Alamy Stock Photo, p:147 Johann Helgason/ Shutterstock, p:148 Mike Hill/Alamy Stock Photo, p:149 Filip Fuxa/ Shutterstock, p:150 CkyBe/Shutterstock, p:152 Brian A Jackson/Shutterstock, p:153 biletskiy/Shutterstock, p:156 Harvepino/Shutterstock, p:159 FashionStock.com/ Shutterstock, p:160 NG Images/Alamy Stock Photo, p:161 Bill Bachmann/Alamy Stock Photo, p:162 POOL/AFP/Getty Images, p:163 Mark Pearson/Alamy Stock Photo, p:164 RHIMAGE/Shutterstock, p:165 Mechanik/Shutterstock, p:172 Rodney Legall/Alamy Stock Photo, p:173 MANDEL NGAN/AFP/Getty Images, p:174 Yyuiyui/Alamy Stock Photo, p:176 Robert Nickelsberg/Alamy Stock Photo, p:177 Philip Wolmuth/Alamy Stock Photo, p:178 506 collection/Alamy Stock Photo, p:179 Niyazz/Alamy Stock Photo, p:180 The Organisation of Eastern Caribbean States (OECS), p:181 The Organisation of Eastern Caribbean States (OECS), p:182 ORLANDO SIERRA/AFP/Getty Images, p:183 Ognjen Stevanovic/Alamy Stock Photo, p:184 Anfisa focusova/Shutterstock, p:185 Gareth Copley/Getty Images, p:186 Robert Fried/Alamy Stock Photo, p:187 Sean Sprague/ Alamy Stock Photo, p:190 mavo/Shutterstock, p:192 mangostock/Shutterstock, p:193 Massy Group, p:194 Janine Wiedel Photolibrary/Alamy Stock Photo, p:194 Roberto Herrett/Alamy Stock Photo, p:197 Michael Dwyer/Alamy Stock Photo, p:198 travpher/ Shutterstock, p:199 Sam Pollitt/Alamy Stock Photo, p:204 Bragi Thor Josefsson/Getty Images, p:204 Monkey Business Images/Shutterstock, p:208 GeraldConnell/Getty Images, p:209 MBI/Alamy Stock Photo, p:210 David Gilder/Shutterstock, p:211 Michaeljung/ Shutterstock, p:215 SpeedKingz/Shutterstock, p:216 ONOKY - Photononstop/Alamy Stock Photo, p:218 Moodboard/Alamy Stock Photo, p:219 Tony Tallec/Alamy Stock Photo, p:220 Amir Ridhwan/Shutterstock, p:222 laflor/Getty Images, p:224 Steve Dunwell/ Getty Images, p:225 Ian Townsley/Alamy Stock Photo , p:226 Janine Wiedel Photolibrary/ Alamy Stock Photo, p:226 satit_srihin/Shutterstock, p:226 Said M/Shutterstock, p:227 John James/Alamy Stock Photo, p:232 Universal History Archive/UIG/Getty Images, p:234 Carlos Mora/Alamy Stock Photo, p:234 Marekuliasz/Shutterstock, p:235 BLM Collection/ Alamy Stock Photo, p:236 Ann Ronan Pictures/Print Collector/Getty Images, p:239 Rolf Richardson/Alamy Stock Photo, p:240 Granger Historical Picture Archive/Alamy Stock Photo, p:241 Brian Gibbs/Alamy Stock Photo, p:242 North Wind Picture Archives/Alamy Stock Photo, p:243 Ian Brierley/LatitudeStock/Alamy Stock Photo, p:244 Hulton Archive/ Getty Images, p:245 Sean Drakes/Alamy Stock Photo, p:246 Hulton-Deutsch Collection/ CORBIS/Getty Images, p:247 Ian Hamilton/Alamy Stock Photo, p:248 Keystone-France/ Gamma-Keystone via Getty Images, p:249 Clive Tully/Alamy Stock Photo, p:250 University of the West Indies, p:251 Colonial Office/The National Archives UK, p:252 AP Image, p:253 Bettmann/Getty Images, p:254 yui/Shutterstock, p:255 Keystone/Hulton Archive/ Getty Images, p:256 Gordon Mills/Alamy Stock Photo, p:257 Rolf Richardson/Alamy Stock Photo, p:258 Popperfoto/Getty Images, p:259 Allstar Picture Library/Alamy Stock Photo, p:260 Keystone Pictures USA/Alamy Stock Photo, p:261 PJF Military Collection/Alamy Stock Photo.